Within the Shadows of Life

Written by:
Richard Tabler

Cadmus Publishing
www.cadmuspublishing.com

Copyright © 2021 Richard Tabler

Published by Cadmus Publishing
www.cadmuspublishing.com
Port Angeles, WA

ISBN: 978-1-63751-128-2

All rights reserved. Copyright under Berne Copyright Convention, Universal Copyright Convention, and Pan-American Copyright Convention. No part of this book may be reproduced, stored in a retrieval system, or transmitted in any form, or by any means, electronic, mechanical, photocopying, recording or otherwise, without prior permission of the author.

The character of our society, our commitment to the rule of Law, fairness and equality cannot be measured by how we treat the rich, the powerful, the privileged, and the respected among us. The true measure of our character is how we treat people, the disfavored, the accused, the incarcerated and people like myself… the condemned.

We are all implicated when we allow other people to be mistreated. An absence of compassion can corrupt the decency of a community, a state, a nation. Fear and anger can make us vindictive and abusive, unjust and unfair. Until we all suffer from the absence of mercy and we condemn ourselves as much as we victimize others. The closer we get to mass incarceration and extreme levels of punishment like it is today, the more I feel it's necessary to recognize that we all need mercy, we all need justice and most of all we all need a measure of grace.

Contents

Chapter One 1

Chapter Two 10

Chapter Three... 16

Chapter Four 23

Chapter Five.. 37

Chapter Six.. 47

Chapter Seven 55

Chapter Eight 59

Chapter Nine 69

Chapter Ten 83

Chapter Eleven 94

Chapter Twelve.. 101

Chapter Thirteen... 104

Chapter Fourteen 109

Chapter Fifteen.. 126

Chapter Sixteen 132

Chapter Seventeen 137

Chapter Eighteen 142

Chapter One

I was born on Monday February 5th, 1979, at 9:20am in the Visalia Community Hospital in Visalia, California. My parents are Lorraine C. Lee of Kingston, Jamaica and Robert W. Tabler of Glendale, California.

I have three older siblings named Greg, Sean and Kristina, throughout of my whole family I only know about my older sister Kristina and my mom. Robert and my two older brothers and I have nothing to do with each other nor do we really know anything about one another's life. I never felt any kind of love from Robert or my brothers. It just was never there nor the feeling of being accepted when I was younger. Around the age of 12 my parents got divorced in the superior court of Modesto, California on August, 6th, 1991. From that point on I would start to bounce back and forth between the two of them. When I was living in California, I would go to both Turlock JR. High and Turlock High School's, though I would never finish school there. Instead, I ended up getting mixed-up with the wrong crowd and doing drugs at a very young age. It's at this point in my life I would blame my parents for not giving me the love I needed nor the proper direction in life. Robert was always doing things for both Sean and Kristina while they were living under his roof. My oldest brother Greg, I didn't start to know about until years later because when he was born, he was placed for adoption, which would be luck on his part though he would never know it. It was always Sean and Kristina who had Robert's full love. Kristina was bought a little red car and Sean got, not one, but two motorcycles.

    Let's talk about that right there, so you can see what I'm talking about. Sean was given by his dad (I call Robert his dad because he never acted in any way shape or form like a father to me) a red and black with white 1989 Kawasaki Ninja 600R Motorcycle. I remember this one well because one night while staying over at my best friend's house way out in the country named Adam Enos. His mom had driven me home and when I went to go into my bedroom my brother Sean was asleep in my bed. I woke him up when I came in and took notice that he was wearing a sling around his left arm area. That's when I found out that he had tried to run from the police out in the country, and while going around a bend in the road had lost control and wrecked. He totaled his bike and when the cops caught up to him, they slowed down to ask him if he saw a guy on a motorcycle fly past this way. He told them it was him and that he was hurt. Did he go to jail? Nope. Went to the hospital then his dad came and got him and that's how he got to be in my bed. Two days later a tow truck showed up at our house to drop off what remained of the motorcycle. Sean totaled that bike and was lucky to walk away from the wreck. Not three months later though, his dad bought him another 1989 Ninja 600R this one white and black. Whenever my brother or his dad would ride this bike in and around town, they thought they were the shit. I just wanted to feel that same love some time in my life, that wantedness from others. It didn't really matter that I wasn't getting the material things because at the time that wasn't important to me. I was just a kid. When Robert got tired of having me stay with him and my siblings, he sent me to stay with my mom, who was living in Fort Myers, Florida. While I was there, I attended for a short time Fort Myers Middle School. Before she too would get tired of having me and send me back to Robert. This isn't how any child should feel while growing up, and it's sad to think about how many kids are still going through this same thing in their young lives even now. After being sent back to California, I started doing whatever the hell I wanted to do. I had no direction and nobody cared about me so why should I care about myself and what I was doing. There was only one time that Robert did anything for me that was something I really wanted. When I was 16 years old, he drove me to Sacramento, California so I could attend the motorcycle training course. This is something you have to do in order to get your motorcycle license, also known as your M1. Throughout the course they train you on Kawasaki's little bikes. You learn that 70% of your stopping power is done by the front brake and the rest by your back brake. A motorcycle is nothing like a bicycle. Where your brakes are up by the handle bars. There are so many parts to riding a motorcycle. Once you start the bike after placing it in neutral, you'll notice when your there when a green light shows by your gauges. Once there sitting on your bike, your left hand controls the clutch and your left foot controls you're shifting down by the left peg. Your right hand controls your front brake, your throttle and your right foot down by the peg can relax! Back brake is down by the right foot peg. Of course, you have turn signals and everything, but learning to ride a motorcycle right is one of the greatest things. Once I had learned these things and how to control my bike and ride safely and had passed the schooling, I was given my certificate and I took that back to Turlock and went to the local DMV to take my driving course for my car license. Passing both I now had my M1 and my driver's license at 16 years old. The one thing Robert never knew about me though, was that I had been racing dirt bikes with friends, so I knew how to ride long before that.

As for learning how to drive a car, I knew the basics, but it was my sister Kristina who took me out one day and taught me how to drive a stick shift. Who would know that her teaching would come in handy to her little brother and his life of crime as a driver? Not much longer after I had my M1 my older brother Sean and I got into a fight. I had been doing some things I knew I shouldn't be, like stealing from my brother and his dad (money) and using it for drugs and to buy things I wanted. Sean had come home and caught me and instead of telling his dad, he made me go outside on this rainy day and start digging a hole in the ground while getting rained on. At first, I was okay with it because I had got caught. But after he had made me dig it and fill it in over and over and over again. I thought he was just being a dick and told him to fuck off. Mistake. I saw my brother snap in front of me and he changed. See, Sean was bigger than his little brother, I was just this skinny kid and he was this football player and the guy screwing all the girls kind of dude. He didn't put his hands on me so much as he started choking me. I didn't fight back, I just let him do it cause one I didn't really want to live anyhow, and two what would be the point? Once he saw that I was about to lose consciousness though, he let me go. I got up and looked at my brother in a way that spoke volumes without having to say anything to him. He knew that that ended the two of us being called brothers. I vowed I would never love my brother after that nor would I ever do anything with him or for him. (Years later, that would change only one time).

The next day while Sean was at school CSUS (California State University Stanislaus) and his dad was at work. I left school from Turlock High early and went home. Stole money from both Sean's bedroom and his dad's, then walked out and into the garage. Took the key for Sean's Ninja off the hook, placed the bike on its center stand then placed it in neutral and started it up. Letting it warm up, I opened the garage door then went inside and put on my jacket and grabbed the tank bag for the bike. Went back out to the bike and placed the tank bag on it then took it off its center stand. While sitting on it, I put on my gloves and helmet, put it in first gear and left. My first stop was the local gas station to fill the tank. While at the gas station and getting gas I also bought myself something to drink and some snacks for my trip. Caught the freeway which is known as Highway 99 and went south down to around Bakersfield, California before catching and cutting over onto Highway 15 and into Mojave and through the desert of South Eastern part of California and into the end of the Sierra Nevada desert before going into Las Vegas, where I found out that my mom was now living. She had moved a few months before after getting an offer from a friend of hers to become a part owner of a restaurant called Flame and BBQ, located at 1770 S. Rainbow Blvd. While staying with my mom after showing up on her door step with a stolen motorcycle and nowhere to go as a runaway at 16 years old. My life got worse if that was even possible. My mom was dating this guy named Terry Brotherton, who was a rent-a-cop working at one of the casino's there in Las Vegas. He was a big dude that enjoyed drinking and cheating on my mom. My mom you need to understand is a tiny thing at only about 5'4. She has always had a great heart, but she knew deep in her heart and soul that she couldn't take care of me and that is why she left me early on to live with Robert and my older siblings. She too had a hard life growing up when she was younger and living back home in Kingston, Jamaica. I just didn't know this until I got older. Terry would soon come to introduce my mom into a new way of living that would take serious effect on her way of living and would have devastating effects on my own life. During my first two weeks in Las Vegas, I did nothing but ride the bike around and take in the sights of Las Vegas. I met a lot of guys and girls who would meet down on Las Vegas Blvd on Friday nights and talk shop about their bikes. They would also meet up at Red Rock and do their illegal races against other bikes and sometimes against cars, each of which were souped up just for racing. I started hanging out with this group of people, some who were cops and some that also worked and were stationed at Nellis Air Force Base and others that worked at the casinos. A couple of the cops and the fella's from Nellis taught me how to do standup wheelies on the Ninja. One of the girls that would be there all the time and racing the guys and sometimes their cars had a Kawasaki ZX10 and taught me how to race and shift properly. One day when she was to meet me and she knew I was a runaway, she gave me a leather jacket, pants and boots. She explained to me that if I was going to ride right, I should wear what would protect me should I crash. She said I owed her nothing but to remember her and she said that she too went through a rough life like I was going through before she joined the Air Force. Her name was Amber.

After a couple of weeks staying with my mom and her boyfriend, Terry. I was told that I would need to start going to school if I wanted to continue living with my mom and Terry. I ended up being enrolled at Sunset High School West over at 2832 E. Flamingo Road there in Las Vegas. What a lot of people didn't know was that Sunset High was a school for troubled assholes like myself. There were as many guns, knives and drugs at this school as any other. The thing is it didn't matter where I was going to school, it never took long for me to leave it. School just wasn't my thing. Next thing I knew I was doing illegal racing and then getting into trouble with the cops in Las Vegas. One night while riding with friends and on our way to downtown Las Vegas, we stopped at the local Honda Dealership. It was while we were all there that I got to talking with one of their mechanics in the back. As the two of us were talking he said that he had another bike that he was selling or was willing to take a trade for. He had been looking for a 1989 Ninja and I explained to him that I had one of these sitting out front. We walked to the front of the dealership and I showed him the Ninja. He asked what I wanted for it and I said let's take a look at the bike he was talking to me about. We walked back to the back where we were and he motioned me to the side. Around the corner was this bright yellow and chrome 1992 Suzuki Katana 600. Upon a closer look and talking with the mechanic I learned that he had just placed a 1989 GSXR 750 motor within the frame of this Katana 600. It bolted and lined up perfectly. Everything about this bike screamed racing. There were so many illegal parts that wouldn't pass a DMV testing for riding it on the streets. I told him that I would trade him if he wanted to do so right now. The only thing was that the bike was in my older brother's name back in California but I'm sure we could figure a way out to get this done. He said no problem and we walked inside and before leaving the dealership I was the proud owner of this new bike and he was the owner of the Ninja!

    Once we all got downtown, we decided to take a ride up to Red Rock in an evening race to the loop that comes out at Blue Diamond. As we were racing up the straight away towards Red Rock outlook, we were all running pretty much side by side up the street. Just as we were passing the last parts of the city and getting ready to start into the mountains and parts of Red Rock, I noticed that everyone was slowing down. That's when I looked over my shoulder and saw the cops! I started to slow down by down shifting, but then I got the great idea of trying to out run them up into the mountains. I had been in 4th gear and was slowing when this thought overcame me and I down-shifted once more into 3rd, before rolling the throttle and taking off. Shifting up through my gears and making it to 5th gear before having to down-shift for a slow sweeping left turn up into the mountains, coming out of the turn, shifting up into 4th then down to 3rd again before catching another straight that allowed me to reach 5th gear before a tight right had me dragging my right knee-puck on my leathers. Only to come screaming around that turn and have to apply my brakes while forcing myself into the upright position because the cops cheated. Right in front of me was the Las Vegas Police Department Helicopter sitting in the middle of the road. I pulled to the side of the road where when the cops behind me caught up decided to slam me against the hood of one of their cars and scream at me how stupid it was for me to try and run from them up through these mountains as just last week, they had another try the same thing only to run right into a jackass (donkey) crossing the road in front of him. They spent hours picking up parts of his body and his bike from the crash site, while the jackass got up and walked away!

Once the officers cooled down and they found out that I didn't mean any serious harm as everyone once in their life tries to run from the cops, they decided to let me go, but not before calling my mom at her work and explaining to her what had happened. Before they hung up from talking with her, they handed the phone to me and she went off on me, before calming down and explaining that the cops were going to give me the chance I had wanted by running; but if I lost my bike would be impounded and I would be taken to jail. When I asked her what she was talking about, she said the cops would explain it to me as it was their idea, then hung up on me. I gave the cop back his phone and asked what he and my mom had been talking about. I was told that since I wanted to race that they would escort me back down the road and at the straight away that they had first took notice of all of us coming up. We would stop. From the turn down into the city we would set up side by side and race to the first light where the rest of the cops would be sitting and waiting for us. The deal was if I beat him to the light, they would let me go, but if I lost, I would go to jail and my bike impounded. This was only because they had just gotten the new chevy Camaros in that they were using as their cop cars for chasing drivers/riders that ran from them and they haven't had the chance to test them out yet. I was thinking to myself yeah right, you guys are full of shit and I'm going to jail. Once we were all back down by the said straight away, the cop's pulled to the side of the road, and while looking way down towards the end I could see that they were serious. The road was free of all cars and bikes to the first light! That shit was crazy as I was only 17 years old now! There was one thing on my bike that I too had never tried out because there was never any real place to try it other than the drag strip. This was one of the reasons that the mechanic had also traded me and why he had a better motor placed into the Katana frame. Under my seat was a valve that was connected to a bright blue canister that was mounted on my right back swing-arm (under my seat, I mean that where I sit, yet on the outside not directly under). On this canister are the letters NOS. The mechanic had been building my bike before I came along, just so he too could race it (illegally). I couldn't run it on normal fuel and had to pay more for the higher/costly JP fuel that came in a blue can. Please note that while the cops had been explaining to me what would take place, they had never stopped to really look over my bike and were always on my left side, even when I was up in the mountains and pulled to the side. Thus, they never saw the NOS canister. As I'm sitting on my bike I had been debating if I should use the NOS or not. I decided to use it and set about reaching back and down to open the valve on the canister. Once this was done, I told myself to relax as best I could. Right next to my left hand by where I grab my clutch was another button that would give me my hit of NOS when the time was right. Placing my helmet back on and making sure it was snug, I waited for the cops and the one cop I would be racing down. Once he and I were both ready, another officer down the road flashed his lights, this was for us to get ready. I placed my bike into 1st gear and smoked my tire, while the cop did the same. Then we were both ready. The cop down the way flashed his lights again and we both took off. From 1st gear through to my 3rd gear the cop and I were neck and neck, as our speeds are hitting into high 90's. I start to pull away after hitting 4th and then 5th gears, just after shifting into 6th gear my speed is showing 140mph. It's now or never as the cop is about two and half lengths behind me. I hit my NOS button. To say that I smoked the cop would be an understatement. I won hands down no questions asked, but I lost more than I won. At the end of the road and at the light there's a gas station and it was there that my friends had been waiting for me. When I got off my bike and placed it on its center stand, I was shaking like a leaf and refused to get back on it to ride it home. My friends and I loaded it up into one of their trucks and we drove to a friend's. That thing scared the shit out of me! It would be weeks before I got back on it. While I wasn't riding or going to school, I had gotten a job at All Air which was this place that installed air conditioners on huge homes and at casinos. I was taught how to drive and work a crane and lift, but again for reasons back then I couldn't sit still or hold a job for long. I left and through a friend that worked at this one casino started working at New York, New York Hotel and Casino in the gamming room for the kids. It was around this time that my friends made the offer to me to go up to the State line and the casino there for some fun and maybe a race. So, I went with them. For reasons unknown to me at the time, once we got to the State Line and casino, I called my mom. At the time we were living at 1836 Winners Cup.

Chapter Two

Things Become Worse

We were having a blast on our way to the State Line and Casino, just fucking around and poppin' wheelies and goofing off with one another. When we were there, I made the telephone call home to my mom to check in with her, something I didn't do often. Instead of my mom answering her phone or her boyfriend Terry, her best friend Sheila answered, and the first thing out of her mouth was, "Richard, your mom is alright. " I had stepped away from my friends in the parking lot to make this call home, and now I could hear myself raise my voice as I asked Sheila what she meant my mom was alright. In fact, I remember telling her to put my mom on the phone, only for her to say that my mom couldn't come to the phone. What the fuck?! I hung up on Sheila and walked over to my friend's and told them that I needed to get home as fast as possible because something had happened at home with my mom but nobody would tell me what. I just knew that it was something bad and needed to get there. As I was walking away one of my friends that was stationed at Nellis Air Force Base ran to catch up with me and told me to take his bike. I asked him if he was sure and he said yes. We traded keys, and I told him to go ahead and race my bike if he wanted. It's got a full canister of NOS and the tank is almost full itself. His name was Chris and his bike was a 1992 Honda CBR 900RR that was red and black. Placing my helmet on tight and shifting into first gear I left my friends to get back on the freeway and ride as fast as I dared back into the city of Las Vegas. Hitting speeds of over 100+ mph I was able to make it back into Las Vegas and to my mom's house in time to see the cops leaving and some still standing around. It took me about 50 minutes. Getting off the bike and walking into the house I noticed two things right away. One, my mom wasn't in the living room nor kitchen like she always is, and two, Sheila met me when I was coming inside and she was stone cold sober. Thinking that she was in her bedroom with Terry I went that way only to find out that I was in for one of the biggest shocks of my young life. My mom was in her room but Terry wasn't with her nor was he anywhere in the house or anywhere around to be found. That's why the cops had been there and they too wanted to talk to Terry. My mom was laying in her bed with tears running down her face as soon as she saw me and I saw what had happened. While my mom was sleeping or taking a nap, Terry had come home drunk and thought to try and beat my mom and suffocate her while she was sleeping. Only he failed (thank God) and then he took off and my mom called the police and then her friend Sheila. To see my pride and gold beaten like that with both her eyes black and blue and hand marks around her throat, that shit broke something deep within my core as a youngster. My mom seeing that this was fucking me up, did the one thing she could but to her it meant everything. She begged me to not tell my older brothers and sister. I never told anyone in our family, but I did call my friends up at the State Line and Casino, because two of them were cops there at the Las Vegas Police Department and the other three were stationed at Nellis Air Force Base. I explained to them what had happened and they told me to meet them at Chris's place on Base. I told them okay and hung up then went and told my mom that I was going to a friend's on Nellis Air Force Base and would be back later, and if she was going to be okay with Sheila. She told me that she would be okay and to keep in touch. I gave her a lite hug and kiss on the cheek and then left. When I got to Nellis Air Force Base which is northeast of Vegas. One of Chris's friends were waiting for me in Chris's truck at the gate to escort me onto the base after I signed in as a visitor. I followed him way over to the other side of the Base and to the barracks that they were assigned to. Once there we didn't wait inside for very long before Chris showed up on my bike and with everyone else. I explained to everyone what had happened and that Terry Brotherton was missing (hiding). We agreed to leave all the bikes there at Chris's barracks and take his truck and two others, but first they wanted to make stop at the armory because as Chris said he wanted to sign out his guns (Chris worked as Nellis Military Police). Once this was done, we all drove around looking for Terry. We drove over to his daughter's house, where she was married to some fat dude; though she didn't know where her dad was. He was not inside because she let me go inside to have a look around. We drove over to his work at Circus Circus, Casino and Hotel, and nobody there had seen him since he left work six hours before. We drove to Danny's II over off of S. Rainbow Blvd. The parking lot was full but he wasn't there either. Chris and some of the other fellas along with Amber made some calls to their friends, asking that they please let them know if they see someone matching the description I had given them and that they had also given from seeing Terry before. As it turned out, and it was a good thing for Terry; we never found him nor caught up to him anywhere that night nor the following couple of days after.

After that night though and the following few days, my mom and I never spoke about what all had happened. I think she knew though and could see that something in her young son had been broken. About one month later Terry showed back up and was once again in my mom's life and they were back into their relationship as if nothing had happened. I couldn't understand how she could do this, and yet at the same time I thought to myself that if he beat her again it was her own fault. Would I do anything about it on her behalf without her ever knowing? Who knows, we may never know. Sure enough, not much later they got into it over Terry cheating on my mom. In her own way when she found out, she went into his closet and cut off one arm of each shirt and one pant leg of each of his pants. To me this was childish, but to each his/her own right? It was also my pushing point, because when I tried to stand up my mom even thought she was a fool for getting back into the relationship. My own flesh and blood went off on me and told me to mind my own business and to get out. I wasn't yet 18 years old and had just sold the Katana after scaring the shit out of myself trying out the can of NOS. I made up my mind earlier that night that since she wanted to get beat up on and stay with that asshole who would keep doing that until someone beat him up or put him in the ground, that I would steal her brand-new Chevy Camaro and drive back to Modesto, California. That's just what I did and though I wouldn't know it she would call the cops and report her car stolen. It was around one week later while I was in Modesto, that the cops would catch up to me and arrest me for GTA (Grand Theft Auto). When the cops searched the car, they also found drugs that I had been selling. After being placed into the cop car and transported to the juvenile hall because I wasn't yet an adult. The cop was relaxed as he was taking me out of the backseat, he failed to realize and understand that I had removed the cuffs and took off running. He gave chase, we ran for what seemed like forever and I had just made it to the highway (99) which sits just about half a mile from the juvenile hall center in Modesto, California. When another cop car and other officers showed up to give assistance to their partner. As the officers were trying to take me into their custody, I started fighting them. Thus, I was given more charges on top of my GTA and drugs. I was charged with obstructing/resisting and assault on a peace officer. I was sentenced to five and a half months in the juvenile hall center better known as CYA (California Youth Authority) being that it was my first time in trouble. The sentencing Judge was easy on me. What was worse was the only person to show any kind of support for me when I got into trouble wasn't either one of my parents. Nope. It was my one and only sister, Kristina.

When I finally got out of CYA, I was an adult as I had just turned 18 years old. I had nowhere to go and nobody that would take me in. I was to report to a parole office for probation but that never happened. I ended up going to the only place where I know people and that was to and into parts of Deep east Oakland, California and also San Francisco, California. While in both these cities I did what I could to survive because I had no family that wanted anything to do with me. I started out small and working for a dealer in the Bay Area's mostly in San Francisco. Selling crack, weed and cocaine. Before I knew it, I was shooting the shit up myself. It was the only way to escape all the pain I was feeling at a life I didn't understand. The rush of taking a hit for your first time is something that one cannot honestly explain, though I can tell you one drug I started selling when I got into doing sales deeper for my supplier. While I was a young homeless person was black tar heroin. This drug I can tell you scared me straight into getting the fuck out of the Bay. When I tried it, I thought I was going to die from the rush alone, while others around me were throwing their guts up after injecting it. It was around this time that I was making my way back to where I was staying while selling, that I passed my older brother Sean and his then girlfriend (who is now his wife). They were going to eat inside of a restaurant. My brother saw that I noticed him, notice me. But neither of us said anything to the other. I had a feeling deep inside that once he went inside, he would come back out and try to talk to me. So as soon as they were inside, I took off running up the street to hide behind a dumpster. Sure enough, when I looked back down the road, my brother was outside looking up and down the street for me. After that day I never saw my brother again, until years later, and it would be the first time we would speak face to face as well as being the last time. When I got back to where I was staying, I explained to the guy's that I had decided to leave and go back into the valley of Turlock and Modesto. One of them told me he was ready to go to and asked if he could skip out with me. I said yeah, let's go. We left the condo and walked down to market street where we boosted a car. Once we were through the hills and on our way down into the valley, we stopped off in the city of Tracy, California. Here we decided it would be best to get another car because we had been in this one long enough and someone would have by now reported it stolen. Stopping in an all-night shopping center, we got out and walked the lot before finding a black Infiniti. I busted the back window, reached around to the driver's door and popped the lock up and opened the door. No alarm went off so we did our thing and about 90 seconds later had the car started and were driving off catching the freeway. Stopping off in Modesto at first my friend Aaron's house and then his friend's house, where we both obtained a mixture of drugs and guns. My mind went into a hate level and I thought to drive us to Turlock where we ended up at Robert's place of business in the middle of the night. Going to his office, I went around to the back door and busted his glass door, thus leaving it open to anyone who wanted to enter his office in the middle of the night to steal everything. All throughout my young life I would have many run ins with the law along with some serious escapes from them too. I had even tried suicide by cop once and I did in fact get shot by them but not a killing shot. They shot me with their bean bag slug from their shotgun. That shit seriously hurt like a bitch!

Chapter Three

Going to Jail and Learning How to Fight

Around the end of 1999, I ended up in Florida again and as usual was running wild. My mom was also living back there in Cape Coral and dating this guy named Doug Reiter. Doug, for the most part, was good to my mom and not abusive physically but mentally he was to her. I was told flat out that I couldn't stay with them and honestly, I wasn't looking to stay with them. I ended up in Florida because I was mixed up with some bad shit. I was still doing my own wild thing and now I was stealing shit from buildings, houses and other places, but on a much bigger scale. I had even started taking guns and turning around and selling them. I wasn't breaking into places in or around Cape Coral, but in cities like Fort Myers and down south in Miami and the Keys. It was while breaking into a place in Key West that I met someone named Danny. You know you're in serious shit when you break into someone's house and find out they're still inside and that they've been watching you on their home security cameras that you failed to see or notice. The outside of this home looked like shit, and that's why I had decided to break into it, but the inside looked nothing like the outside did. It was while I was walking out of the master bedroom that I was met with a sawed-off shotgun in my face. There is no place to run from something like that without getting your ass handed to you. The rush of breaking into places is one thing, but the fear and adrenaline that is running through your body as your looking down the barrel of a shotgun in your face cannot be described. At the time, I didn't know his name was Danny, this would come after he and I spoke for a while. Before we got to this point though, he was asking or yelling at me why the fuck and what the fuck I was thinking breaking into his house!? I explained to him that I was just trying to make some money and that I was always on the run. I started to apologize, but he didn't want to hear any of that shit he said and told me to stop. I stopped. I mean what else was I to do with a shotgun in my face. Pointing with the gun he told me to walk into his living room and have a seat so that we could talk.

I did as I was told. Once he saw that I wasn't going to try and make a run for it, he placed the shotgun down and had a seat himself. He said that his name was Danny and that instead of taking me out back he would offer me a job running for him. I accepted. He started laughing and said that I shouldn't be in such a rush to accept his offer before understanding what I would be doing. Being young I thought that he was talking about running things around for him at an office, not so. What Danny meant as he explained to me was driving for him all over the place, mainly up and down the East Coast. This he said would place money into my pocket and give me a place to sleep without having to break into anyone's house nor sleep on the streets. He asked me what my name was and I told him it was "Blue". He said not my nickname, but my real name. I told him it was Richard. He said that I was to call him Danny at all times and he would call me Blue. He got up and asked me to follow to him into the kitchen, leaving the shotgun in the living room. Once we were in the kitchen, he made us both something to eat, and told me that I had some guts breaking into his house. Then he started laughing his ass off. After he got his laugh, he asked me if I knew how to drive and I stated that yes, I knew how to drive and ride a motorcycle. To show him that I could he had me once again get up and follow him into the garage where he tossed me the keys to his SUV. Inside he instructed me to drive him anywhere, to show him that I could handle an SUV of that size. After driving in the city and up to Fort Myers, he had me drive him back to Key West and to his house. Seems pretty simple right?

Wrong. What I didn't know at that time was that Danny would have me moving his narcotics and vehicles. Nobody in my family ever would know this, nor anything close about what kind of shit I was doing when I wasn't around them and acting like a bum. The only thing they ever knew was that I was always getting into trouble for stealing things and writing bad checks. I ended up driving from the Keys all the way up to places in Michigan and over to cities and places around Boston and New York; and places that had funny ass names out in the middle of nowhere like Parsippany and Egg Harbor Township, New Jersey. It was cool driving for Danny and I learned many things about the narcotic industry and of the vehicles being moved/chopped. Danny had ways about welding onto the underbody of a vehicle so that you could hide either a body or cocaine as well as bales of money. But as always, all good things must come to an end some time, and some of the people that Danny worked for and ran with were serious about the shit they did. One late night as I was returning to Danny's home in the Keys and walking in through the backdoor like I always did, I found Danny sitting next to his kitchen table doing his best to hold his intestines inside of himself. I froze up until he told me to take what I could find left from the safe in the bedroom behind his dresser, then to get out and don't tell nobody anything. Coming back into the kitchen I tried to get Danny to let me call him some help but he wasn't trying to hear any of that. He told me to go on and get out of there and to take his SUV as far as I needed. That was around I want to say April of 2000 down in Key West, Florida. Danny and I became friend's and he taught me tons of shit. Sure, it wasn't all good things to the way someone in society thinks, but to someone always on the run or doing illegal things in his/her life, it would be golden. He was one of the only people to give me such lessons about things. I ended up drifting back into Cape Coral and Fort Myers, Florida. Not for long though before I was stealing a struck from a dealership and fleeing in it to parts of Michigan. I made it all the way up to Detroit, Michigan. Here is where I dumped the truck and boosted another car and drove to Lansing, Michigan, where I met a young girl named Tonya S. Wilson. At the time, my life was nothing but always being on the run from the cops for something and for doing drugs. After leaving Danny behind at his house, which would never sit right with me even to this day. I still knew where to get a hold of some of his people and the drugs they delt with and cars that needed moving from point A to point B. Most of the people that Danny worked for and was a part of himself was a gang that wasn't heard of so much back then like it is now a days, MS 13.

Tonya and I hooked up. She was a good girl who had one older brother named Chester and her mom, though both of them drank and did their own share of drugs. Tonya wanted something better, thus when I told her that I was done freezing my ass off in Michigan, she said that she wanted to go with me. She knew that I didn't have a place to stay and that I was on the run from the cops, but she still wanted to go with me and even offered to use her car for our return trip together to Cape Coral, Florida. I don't know to this day how it happened but we ended up being allowed to stay and live with my mom and Doug. She didn't like Florida that much and decided to return to Michigan on her own. We parted ways, and not long after she left, I was picked up by the cops and being busted for an outstanding warrant for GTA (Grand Theft Auto) along with assault on a peace officer, forgery, terrorist threats, transporting narcotics and commercial burglary. I was taken downtown to the jail and booked and processed. My thumbprint and fingerprints were taken along with my mug shot. Then I was transported to the camp where inmates waiting to go to court are housed for the time being. This is still in parts of Lee County, Florida, though it's way out in the middle of swamp land. Aside from your initial processing upon being received at camp, you're on your own once you're placed into a dorm. In other words, if you didn't know how to fight, you were going to learn really fast how to do so. Camp is just what they called the place. It wasn't really a camp of sorts, but dorms that were all connected together through an electronic steel door between each one. The front of each dorm was entered through a steel door that was opened by a control booth and the officers about 50 yards from the dorms. There is a chain-link fence running all the way around the place. At each entry, the steel door would roll open and you would step inside to another small cage-like area. Once you stepped inside, the outer door behind you would close and the inner steel door would open into the eating area of the dorm you were being housed in. At that place there is usually six tables that seats four inmates, and above the tables are two TV's mounted high up on the walls. Beyond this area you'll see two rows of bunks (double beds) on each side of the main run down the center of it all. Following the walkway through the sleeping area all the way to the back and you'll find the showers and toilet areas. Each dorm holds between 25 and 30 inmates of all race and size. The inmates control their own dorm, not the law or the correctional staff. Meals are brought to us three times each day on a small cart that is placed into the entry area that you first enter through. Other than that, we're left to our own devices. My bunkmate was this guy named Anthony Q. He was this big ass black dude that was awaiting trial for murdering two cops. One of which he ran over with his truck and the other he shot in the head when they raided his home after fleeing there. Not everyone who is in jail or prison was always a criminal. Anthony Q was a law-abiding citizen of Florida who taught Jujitsu and Kempo Karate. He held a 3rd Dan Blackbelt in both. Mixed throughout our dorm was every kind of street gang you could think of. From Folk Nation and Latin Kings, to Damn's and Crips and KKK, BGF, Mexican Mafia and your blue-collar criminals and plan old white guys scared to death. For recreation we were allowed outside into the fenced in area for a couple of hours weather permitting. Usually, the weather was going full blast rain and thunder and would be knocking out the power which would allow the steel doors that separated the dorms to open. This is how all kinds of fights would break out between each of the dorms. Inmates would come in from another dorm and try to steal shit from us. This caused us all to stand together, though at other times and many at that we would be fighting amongst one another. I myself had numerous fights, along with many broken noses and ribs. Nobody taught me how to fight when I was growing up, but after getting my ass kicked by three of the KKK members after they tried to get me to side with them and some of the other whites in the dorm, and I in turn calling them the Ku Klux Klowns, instead of the Ku Klux Klan. They didn't think I was funny and went about showing me what they thought. I lasted about five minutes and was able to break at least one of their noses before getting knocked to the floor. Nobody stepped in to help me because I look like a white guy, though I'm not 100% white. I'm mixed. The thing that caught my bunky's attention though was that I had heart and didn't think about backing down (just stupid). This caused him to take me under his wing as he said. From that point forward he taught me what he could about fighting and how best to defend myself against an attack of any kind other than with someone holding a gun some distance from me. Throughout my lessons with Anthony, he would have me always call him Sensei Q. Everything that he taught me was hard to learn and understand. Anyone can throw a punch and kick someone, but doing so, so that you fuck somebody up is another thing all together. Everyone in the dorm would laugh at me when he was giving me these lessons because I was calling him Sensei Q. He would take both of our mattresses and roll them up and tie them to the end of the bunk, so we would be standing in the middle of the run that went down the center of the two rows. When the mattresses were rolled this way and wrapped with a sheet around them, they took on the shape and form of a heavy punchbag. I never saw anyone fight the way Q did. When he showed me how he went after this heavy punchbag, hitting and kicking it. The man's hands were a blur. I tried counting his punches but could never keep up. His demonstrations were so smooth and always looked practiced. After four months into my stay in this dorm and being taught by Sensei Q. He told me to take five minutes and show him what all I had learned from him, as he would be leaving for the start of his sentence. I remember it like yesterday… staring at the bag with a practiced intensity. My workout started long before I threw my first punch. I could feel the aggression levels build rapidly inside. In my mind, an attacker rushed towards me, intent on doing me serious harm. Just when I felt the moment was right, I exploded into the bag. I worked a series of punches first, my arms pumping like pistons, fists diving deep. My body snapped from side to side as I sent punch after punch into the mattresses. My feet moved in short crab-like steps. I then began to incorporate knees and elbows into my combinations, opening up with punches then crowding close to slam home short-range blows. When I finished, Q was laughing his ass off and telling me that I wouldn't win any prizes for my form, but would seriously fuck someone up because I did fight and move like a Pitbull. I ended up serving a little over one year in the dorms, and Q left about one week after my show to start serving his two life sentences for killing those cops. When I got released, I was to report to a parole officer in downtown Fort Myers, Florida. My parole officers name was Carol

Romer #11664. I had reported to her from around September of 2000, she worked in the downtown central part of Fort Myers, and was a real ball buster. When I reported to her, she was told that I was gang affiliated with Folk Nation, and that people had seen me with numerous guns and drugs, which would be a violation of my parole. I told her that none of this was true and that I wasn't gang affiliated with Folk Nation. She didn't care and said the first time I fuck up she was sending me back inside. That was the last and only time I saw that bitch before I absconded and was again on the run. I did a fast lick and stole a street bike from a local motorcycle shop. Stopping at my mom's place to let her know that I was leaving again, in my sprint to be gone I broke the speed limit and was pulled over by the police. Thank god for full faced helmets and it being night time and for fake ID's. I didn't have a driver's license for Florida, so I was using one under another name. I was written a ticket for speeding and then let go. The bike was stolen but I figured that it wasn't in the computer system yet; but either way it was time for me to find new wheels and to get out of Florida for a while. I went down to the Keys and hooked up with one of Danny's old friend's I knew he trusted. I was tasked with a Chevy Blazer along with five pounds of marijuana and two kilos of cocaine, that was to be dropped off in Egg Harbor Township of New Jersey. After that I was driving another stolen SUV back into California and it was there I was busted for my outstanding warrants.

Chapter Four

Gladiator School

It was just after the new year of 2001 and I was sentenced to almost four years in prison. I was picked up along with about thirty others from the jail in Modesto, California, and driven to Tracy, California, where I would get my first taste of prison. I was twenty-two years old and had been living a fast and highly illegal life style, and now I would be entering a place known as Gladiator School. The Duel Vocational Institution, better known to all who enter it as DVI. DVI is where you go once you've been sentenced and are entering the CDC system (California Department of Corrections). While here you're processed and asked numerous questions about your life and schooling along with work if any. You're asked your age and if any at the time gang affiliation, and ethnic. Once they have all this done, you're given a cell to live in until they decide where they're going to ship you to. This is somewhere up or down the coast of California and depending on the amount of time that you have and the nature of your crime, they decide whether or not to send you to a serious prison or a minor one with light security. While I was housed there awaiting to be transported to another prison, I would spend time in the following cells/dorms: HW-208, EH-340, WK-331, B-233 and K-123. Most of the prison is ran by nothing but racist shits who hate all blacks with a vengeance and most of the Mexicans. These are the white supremacist that can be found in all of society's prisons today. The first cell I was housed in had one around my own age, who had been awaiting transport to another prison as well. The windows of the cell were broken out and there was a single light bulb for us to see by during the night time. During the winter time we were freezing our asses off. Once each day we were allowed out of the cell to walk down the stairs from the third tier to tier one for a shower. The shower area is one of a giant open space with around thirty showers nozzle, just before entering this part of the showers though there is a place for you to remove your clothing, then you walk into this area butt naked, and shower with everyone else in a butt to nuts fashion. You get in and wash and then get out and walk back to your housing. The only other time we're allowed out of the cell is to walk to breakfast, at which time we're given a paper sack with a lunch inside and then we come back down for dinner. The individual I was housed with had the problem of always talking like a tough guy. He spoke about how he and his friends beat the shit out of this black kid and his girlfriend, and that when I got to whatever prison they decided to ship me off to, that I should go directly to the Wood-Pile (prison talk for where the whites hang out and group together). Once there I should show them my paperwork, etc... He just never shut the hell up. I was never one that spoke much in prison in California, but I do remember my first fight, if that's what you call beating the shit out of your celly. I was going on my third month being housed in that cell with him and hearing him talk about this and that and all this shit that didn't meant shit to anyone. Then one morning when he woke up, I was already up and had washed my face and drank a cup of coffee. The second his feet touched the cell floor, I threw a punch directly into his throat, which almost crushed his trachea. By not hitting him hard enough though it didn't do this. But it still choked him, causing him to grab at his throat while going to the floor. Once he was on the floor, without saying anything to him, I started to stomp on his face and body. Once he was unconscious the cell door was opened for us to go to breakfast and it was then I dragged his sorry ass out of the cell and down the metal stairs to tier one. Once there the officer's slammed me to the ground and placed handcuffs on me behind my back, before asking or screaming at me what the fuck was going on. I calmly explained that my celly fell down the stairs. They didn't think that was funny nor were they trying to buy that shit I was selling, because he had a boot print on his left cheek. I explained that he wouldn't shut the fuck up about beating up some black kid and his girlfriend, and that was when I got pissed and told them I WASN'T A FUCKING RACIST! I was written up for assault on an inmate with bodily injury and a note was stuck in my file that you couldn't house me with a white prisoner, even though I looked white myself.

One week later I was shipped off to CMC-West (California Men's Colony) in San Luis Obispo, where I would get written up for an article 115 for getting a tattoo and then I would be again shipped across the street to CMC-East because they received word that I was planning an escape. Snitches deserve stitches, and child molesters deserve ditches. Upon being received at CMC-East I was told to report to D-Quad for my housing. Once I reported to the officers of the building on D-Quad, I was given a key to 7 Building cell #D-7173. For the first 72 hours I would be locked down (unable to leave the cell). I could however see and talk with the inmates that were passing underneath my cell window as I was assigned a cell on the first floor, which was even with the yard. Once I was finally allowed out of the cell, I found myself walking the yard and getting a feel for everything and where everyone was. Over at the weight pile is where all the so-called peckerwoods/whites hung out and got together. The Mexicans were over by the handball courts and the tables along the back wall beneath tower #5. The Damn's hung out around the bleachers under tower #7 and the Crip's got together by the telephones under tower #8. The Black Panthers and the BGF (Black Gorilla Family) got together in the middle of the yard and around the horseshoe area. Your other odds and ends walked the yard. These were guys that didn't belong to any set of family, such as myself. While you're in CDC (California Department of Corrections) you're given a pair of blue jeans, a buttoned down blue long sleeve shirt, white socks, white boxers, a pair of black boots and a blue jacket. Throughout your stay within CDC, you can have 50-pound package sent to you from your loved ones or friends once every 60 to 90 days. This can have canned goods and clothing and CDs for your CD player, everything that you can think of along with tobacco products of any kind and lighters. (I don't know how it is today though.) You could also order a TV from an outside vendor along with once in a while they would allow you to order things like pizza when they were doing a run like that. The yard there consists of a yard with a soccer field, handball courts, basketball courts, horseshoe area, bleachers and tables. In the middle of the yard is a little store that they allow you to purchase all kinds of commissary items from foods to canned goods to ice cream with this paper money they would sell you. This was due to the number of prisoners that were not allowed to get away from work to purchase their own commissary. Plus, if you got the urge to eat an ice cream before the start of a movie that was coming on later that night, you could walk out to the yard before it was closed down for the night and get whatever you wanted while watching the movie or TV show that was coming on. On the far side away from both buildings there on D-Quad was the kitchen and medical area. All your meals from breakfast to dinner were taken in the chow hall (kitchen). The chow hall sat above the yard, so to get there you had to walk around the yard to and then climb a set of steps and show your ID to the officer at the door. Once you show your ID, you can grab a tray, which is this thin silver-metal thing that is supposed to be a plate for prisoners. After grabbing your tray, you go through the food serving line like you were back at school somewhere. Then you take a seat. Most of the tables are assigned to the ethnic you're a part of and running with while in prison. The cells themselves are either two-man or single-celled. The two-man cells have a very small living area to them. Once you enter a cell there is a bunkbed shoulder high on either your left or right side. On the opposite side is another bunkbed, but this one is on a chain that allows it to fold up and sit along with the wall and out of the way. Straight back to the back of the cells are a single window that is wired with mesh but does allow you to open to get fresh air inside your cell. Right beneath the window is your toilet/sink and a mirror. Right next to this is a single desk. Up along the wall from the front of your cell is a shelving area made from wood that hangs down from chains allowing you to store your commissary and clothing. The bunkbed that doesn't fold up along the wall has a shelf at the foot of it but out of the way so that you could set your TV. You and your cell mate would take turns each day cleaning the cell so that it was always clean. While using the restroom during the night, the rule was if you're doing the #2 you flushed every time you dropped one. You also wiped the rim of the toilet after using it, then washed your hands. Also, your celly would rotate with you on cooking for each other if neither of you were going to the chow hall for your meals. Only after 11:00pm did the yard close down and you had to be inside your cells. At this time, the officer assigned to that floor you were living on would come around for count time and when he or she got. to your cell door you would have to show your ID card and state your name and number. Like my name and number back then were: Richard L. Tabler, #T-07607. Once count was finished the officer would throw the bar which would lock down all cells preventing you from opening your cell from the inside like you were able to do throughout the whole day. When you were not inside your cell and you left it, you could lock it with the key you had. This was to make sure that neither you nor your celly lost anything, nor could anyone just enter your cell and steal whatever they wanted to. Prisoners also were allowed to hold jobs in CDC, unlike say the state of Texas. Where they still believe in slavery and not paying the prisoners. In CDC, you could work in food service, auto repair, metal shop, clothing, garbage, you could clerk for rank and there was maintenance and yard work as well. Also, if you were at a prison that allowed it, you also got paid as a firefighter. The pay started for jobs from anywhere at 0.50 to $1.80 an hour. Also, please note that back when I was telling you all about the cells, note that they are not big cells and that you could not stretch out your hands without hitting the walls. Only from front to back were they long around 11 feet. So, the cells are around 11 X 3 1/4 feet.

Your friends and family members could send money to your Inmate Account. The amount can range from $1.00 to $1,000.00 anytime they wanted. There was no set amount they could or could not send to you. Money just like in any prison in America helps the inmates survive, because the foods that we are served does nothing to fill a grown man, let alone a dog if he were locked within a prison of the American people.

Things within the prison system were anything but kosher. There were always fights breaking out between one or two inmates every day, and sometimes it was between officers and inmates, but these were very few of. Only when the fight was serious did the officers do any paperwork and file a written report. Most of the times everything was ran by the inmates, such as the whites. This, in turn, is what would cause the fights to break out amongst one another. Just like out there in society, there is nothing but racism. I had my fair share of fights and only one of them ever started out one-on-one. Most of the times when I was assaulted it was two or three on one to try and teach me a lesson and to click up with some set. When I was moved from 7 Building to that of 8 Building #8307, I was housed with a big black youngster named Poo Bear. He and I would also walk the yard together. He was doing time for GTA and DWI. When he got caught, it cost him his scholarship at UGLA. The fight that was my first major one took place about two months after I had gotten to the prison and was in the chow hall. I had gotten my tray and was sitting down at a table with my celly on my left and Mac across from me and Smurf on my right. Each of these men are black, and I'm the only looking white inmate sitting at their table. The rule of prison was that you sat at your own color table. If you were black you sat with the blacks, and if you were Mexican you sat with the Mexicans/Latinos and so on so on. You never mixed races with one another. Sitting there as I was, I was breaking every rule you could find within prison, but I didn't care. I was going to do my time how I wanted to do my time. I had just finished eating the main course on my tray and was taking a drink of milk, when my celly told me that one of the main peckerwoods was walking my way fixed on me. I kept eating and drinking, but took notice of how it became quiet within the chow hall. Not five seconds after Poo Bear said this to me, I felt a tap on my left shoulder, and these words, "Look out Wood! Come have a seat at the Wood table." I continued to eat as if I hadn't heard him say anything. Mac across the way from me and the other two at our table had stopped eating and were waiting to see what would happen. Again, the peckerwood tapped me on my left shoulder but a little harder this time and said, "Look out Wood, you're not to be sitting at this Nigger table! Come sit at the Wood table!" Instead of continuing to eat, I took another drink of my milk, but this time I was thinking about what to do as I was drinking. Once again, he tapped my left shoulder and went to say something but never got the chance to do so. I was in motion before anyone could understand it. I had picked up my metal tray and was coming around in a half circle and crashing the metal tray into and across his face, which in turn slit open his face from the jaw up to his ear. This also in turn caused everyone within the chow hall to break out into fighting, or I guess I should say rioting. All I can say is that it lasted for a while before it was broken up by the correctional officers and their riot teams. Once everything was said and done and we were all allowed to walk back to our cells. I did so with a busted lip and a black eye along with a large bump on the backside of my head. Nobody left that chow hall that day without shedding some of their own blood.

It was amazing that nobody was brought up on disciplinary charges that day. On the way back to our buildings all of us were laughing about what had happened, but most were shocked that I had did what I did without giving any kind of warning to anyone. It was good to be able to laugh with one another, but things aren't always able to be laughed at or about. Payback against me for what I did would be short in coming to find me. While walking the yard one evening, I found myself on the receiving end of a violent attack. Understand that the only reason the blacks backed me in the chow hall fight was because my celly was black and I was sitting at the blacks' table. Had none of these things been so, I would have ended up fighting on my own against who knows how many peckerwoods (whites). Coming from under Tower 6 one evening I was attacked by two skinheads with socks packed with batteries. This made for a rude weapon. Before I knew that they were behind me I was being struck down with one of these packed socks with the first hit striking me in the back of the head and neck area. While the first attacker was hitting me in the head and neck area the other one was hitting me in the stomach and legs. It was after that first blow to the back of my head that caused me to go to the ground stunned. That is the worse place you ever want to go in prison during a fight. You never want to be the fool on the ground because now they can stomp you and kick you and there is nothing that you can do other than curl into a ball and do your best to protect your head and face. They beat the shit out of me. In the end I took either a boot or a sock of batteries to my face which broke my nose. Right after it happened my celly and a few others showed up trying to take me to medical. I told them to take me back to our cell so I could clean up. With every step we took, it felt like my insides were on fire and I hurt all over. Once we were at the cell, I told Poo Bear to take a walk while I cleaned up. As I was washing the blood from my face in the sink and pulling off my shirt to wash, the building officer for floor 3 showed up at my cell door asking what happened. I told him that I fell down on the bleachers and was just cleaning up, and that all was good here. As I went back to washing my face, he said bullshit and told me to come out of my cell. Outside my cell there were four other officers already waiting for me to escort me down to the Quad Captain's Office. Once there I was again asked what happened and again, I said that I fell down the bleachers. They asked who attacked me and I said I fell. They stopped me and said that someone already told them I was attacked on the yard. At that point I stopped talking and had refused to identify my attackers, even though I knew who they were. I was escorted off the Quad to the Emergency Room over at medical. Once I was checked out and cleaned up, I was then taken over to the ASU (Administrative Segregation Unit) Building. At first, they charged me with being the victim of an attack, then they changed it to me being charged with an Article 115 for battery on an inmate. About one month or maybe two months later I was found not guilty and the charges were dropped, and I was released back onto the Quad. Once back on the Quad I was again assigned to 8 Building with Poo Bear. He brought me up to speed with everything that had taken place while I had been in the ASU Building. Soon as I had left a lot of the Brothers had gotten together and were talking about striking back and going all out into a race war on the yard, but that was shot down because I didn't belong to any set or family. I was a loner with a black celly and nothing else. While Poo Bear was bringing me up to speed on everything, there was a knock on our cell door, and then this HUGE black dude poked his head inside and said that I was wanted down on floor 2 to speak with someone. I told the big guy that I was good, and he said that it wasn't a request, that someone wanted to talk with me and if I didn't want to walk down there, he would take me down there. I looked at Poo Bear who raised his shoulders in a like what the fuck.

 I got up and went out and followed this dude down to floor 2, when Poo Bear tried to follow us down the run of floor 2, the big dude stopped him and said only I was to come down there, but not to worry because nothing was going to happen to me. Guess that was enough for Poo Bear, because he didn't follow us! So many things were running through my mind at that time. I was thinking that this was a trap and I was fixing to get into it again, but way worse. Before I could decide what was going on though, we were at a cell door at the end of the run, on floor 2. Knocking on the door, I was told to enter. Thinking this was it I went in fast ready to fight. Only to realize that it was legit and there was this bald black guy sitting right beneath the window facing the door. He was only about 5'4 and he was just sitting there watching me watch him. Within his hands he held a roll of paperwork that he unrolled as he was watching me. Letting me see that my name was printed at the top, he went on to tell me to relax that he only wanted to speak with me about some things.

He told me that he and some of his family had been watching me since I rolled up on CMC-East. When I took on a black celly, word went around that there was a white guy that could only be housed with blacks or Mexicans. That he couldn't be housed with any whites for any reason. When he heard this, he had all my paperwork pulled and then he had family outside of these prison walls do a search as well. He said that he thought I handled myself well in the chow hall the day of the riot behind that peckerwood coming at me the way he did. He also thought I had heart at the way I handled getting my ass beat by the two skinheads. But he wanted to know why I didn't say anything about who had attacked me when everyone knew that I knew. I said that I wanted to return the favor and fuck them up some time. Turning a page on the papers he held he said something that to this very day, still has me wondering how the fuck he found out. He asked me about the story or rumor of me and the abattoir. I looked at him like what was he talking about, but he could see that it was true. When I asked him what he really meant, he said that there is talk on the streets back in Florida about how a young kid named Blue who looked white but wasn't had pushed a pedophile through an industrial meat grinder. I said that if it was true then it must have been because he had just raped his daughter after torturing her with a lighter, and he just happened to be standing next to it laughing.

I asked him what all this was about and why he had asked me here today. He said that he thought I might like to join up with the family that he and many others had belonged to. It was a spinoff of BGF and its founder was another Brother who was killed in prison. This individual was named George Jackson, who everyone who is about anything and is willing to look further then what one is told will know that he was killed inside his prison cell by white officers who said he was trying to escape. How could that be when he was killed inside of his cell? George Jackson was killed by white men inside San Quentin State Prison back in the 70's after founding Kumi African Nations. He said that almost everyone inside prison was with someone or another and that if I kept going about doing my time as a loner, I would always be fighting with everyone. You had the KKK, Peckerwoods, Skinheads, Aryan Circle, Aryan Brotherhood, Bloods, Crips, Latin Kings, Folk Nation, Gangster Disciples, BGF and Black Panthers plus many other off the walls set that would take a run at me, not counting the officers themselves. However, most of the blacks would leave me alone, except for the Bloods and Crips, as they're always trying to make a name for themselves. By coming into our family, you don t have to worry about any of the bullshit. There's no jumping you into it, it's as simple as reciting an Oath spoke by each of the Family. You would have to start speaking fluent Swahili and reading and studying the Holy Qur'an. There are laws and byelaws for all Members of Kumi African Nations. I asked why me, or more importantly how can I be in this Family? I was told that they had all my paperwork and that they knew that I come from a mixed background. That my mom is full blooded Jamaican and my father is white trash (my words). That, because of this, I would be accepted as a member so long as I stayed sincere and was able to recite the full Oath. After which point, I would be offered either of the two tattoos, one of which is of a soldier holding a flag with 415 on it or the simpler one of Kumi. There was no fighting unless absolutely necessary, and then it would have to be okayed by the elders. I accepted his offer. He then told me that his name was Mac, but in the free he was known as Carl Skinner of Oakland, California. I would come to know Mac well and we would both become close friends and family. I learned to speak fluently in Swahili and also in Ibo, as well as my own language of English. I studied the Holy Qur'an and was given a tattoo on my right back arm... Kumi.

    Mac is currently serving two life sentences for Murder 1. About three months after my time in the ASU Building and being attacked the two inmates that attacked me were released back onto D-Quad. Once I was given the green light to do so, my chance at retaliation came in the worst place right in front of the building I was assigned to. Simply put, as I was coming out of the building, they were coming into it. I did the only thing I could and that was to grab hold of a shovel that one of the maintenance inmates had standing by the building. Grabbing it up and swinging all in one motion I caught inmate David Salerno #J-98438 upside his head with the edge of the shovel blade. Then while everyone was in shock, I turned on his buddy, inmate John Emmons #E-30529, and caught him in the lower back before beating them both over and over until I was tackled down by officers. I was taken straight to the ASU Building and later that night I was transported to Pelican Bay State Prison in Northern California. My stay there was short, but not short enough. Pelican Bay broke my mind in ways that would break any normal person. I refuse to even speak about what I went through at that place (it's bad). After doing my stint in Pelican Bay, I was shipped to CTF Soledad (Correctional Training Facility) Soledad. This was in the beginning of 2003, and just as I was getting into being settled, I was told to pack up because I was being shipped to CSP Corcoran (Corcoran State Prison). I would only be there for a little over one month before being sent back to CTF Soledad. As usual, it didn't take long for trouble to find me there either, but not before Mac was transported from CMC-East to CTF Soledad and we became cellies. Things were crazy at CTF Soledad. I had been working as a Captain's clerk for about three months before I got into it with an officer and bought myself a one-way ticket to Ad-Seg. While housed at CTF-Soledad, I was in two cells: D-242 and O-143. CTF was bad, but their Ad-Seg was way worse, if something broke out on the yard between you and someone else or a riot broke out, you didn't have to worry about getting a fast response from the officers. They walked around with their weapons hot and gave out only one warning. That was to lay down on the ground with your arms out away from your sides. If you failed to do this you were shot on the spot. If you ever ask an officer that works at a real badass prison, where they aim to shoot inmates, they'll tell you they aim to stop the threat. Meaning they're aiming to kill you not to just injure you. They're aiming for your head.

From CTF-Soledad, I was extradited back to Florida on an outstanding warrant and violation of parole. Here is where things get interesting.

When you're being extradited to another State from one State, there are numerous ways for them to transport you. If the State that wants you want you bad and fast, they'll have the US Marshals pick you up and fly you back on a plane. If they don't need you that fast, or you're not that important to them, they'll have a transportation company pick you up on the Blue Bird Bus with numerous other prisoners waiting to be transported to other States as well. From CTF-Soledad I was packed up in a van by a transportation company, along with three other inmates from parts of CTF-Soledad. Inside the van were others both of the male and female sexes chained together. From CTF-Soledad, we were transported to a point over in Palm Springs, California, at which point we all got onto a Blue Bird Bus for cross country travel. Once I was chained up to the inmate that would be chained to me throughout the trip, we were told to walk onto the bus. On the bus there is the driver and a front cage officer to watch over things from the front by said driver, and yet in between the cages that separate the women prisoners from the male prisoners. Then at the very back of the bus hidden in his/her own cage with a tinted window is another back gunner. Each of these officers is armed with his/her personal weapon on their side along with either an AR-15 or a shotgun. Each prisoner is chained to another, unless he/she is in a single cage for either further security or for their own safety. Prisoners have leg irons on, with a chain running from the leg irons to a belly chain where your hands are cuffed in the front of you. From the belly chain another chain runs to the other inmate that you are chained to. During this trip, I was chained to a loud mouth from CTF-Soledad who wouldn't shut up. If he wasn't talking to the female prisoners when he was told numerous times not to by the front-gunner (not the driver), he was talking shit to the gunner herself. She was pretty and had nice long legs, but who in their right mind wants to piss off a woman with a gun? Not I. From Palm Springs, California, we traveled across the country with stops in Arizona, New Mexico, Colorado, and many other States. Please note, that while we were traveling across the country, the Transportation Officers did stop every morning at a fast-food joint to purchase everyone on the bus breakfast and lunch. For dinner we were taken to the city jail where we were picking someone up or dropping off to spend the night. Somewhere along the way and around the city and

State of Kansas City, MO, or Nashville, TN, the idiot I was chained to and I got into it. I don't remember what caused it other than he wouldn't shut up and it was early in the morning as we were getting ready to stop for our daily breakfast. All I do remember was the bus was already slowing down when I turned to him and told him to just shut the fuck up. He looked at me like I had grown horns, before telling me to shut the fuck up or do something about it. When we had got onto the bus back in Palm Springs, I had taken a paperclip that I found on the van, and had been working it into shape every time that we stopped somewhere, before once again having to hide it. That morning I had been working at the padlock on my belly chain and handcuffs. Without him or anyone else knowing it, I had already picked the lock and my hands were separate from the belly chain. When he told me to do something about it I did just that. I snapped and had him in a choke hold, because there wasn't any room to fight on a bus and in those seats. The only thing one could really do was choke someone's ass out, and that is just what I set to do. The only thing I could hear was the screaming from everyone. That shit was loud as hell as all the prisoners were screaming for me to kill him, with the female gunner screaming for me to let him go. Talk about mixed signals! What seemed like forever was really only a few minutes, but I had somehow carried us into the walkway between the seats. I didn't have a good solid hold on him at first because he didn't just sit there. He tried his best to get away from me, only to fail to realize that he was chained to me. Fear does that to people. You forget things when you fear for your life and you panic. Once I got a good hold on him though, it didn't last long because I had failed to pay attention to my surroundings and where the front gunner was throughout this ordeal. One minute I was choking this bitch out from all my built-up anger at being stuck on this fucking bus for weeks, and for all the shit I would now miss, to being knocked smooth the fuck out after being hit with the stock of the shotgun. I can honestly tell you that is the only time that I have ever in my life been knocked out cold. When I came to, I was in a county jail and awaiting special transportation. My actions caused the transportation company to have to transport me the rest of the way on my own by van. This worked out great, because I ended up in Fort Myers, Florida, within the next three days.

Once there, I was processed and sent out to the camp. I only had to do a short amount of time before being released in April of 2004. The minute my feet touched ground outside of jail, I ran.

Chapter Five

Road Trip

The first place I went to when I got out after getting laid was to say goodbye to my mom. I had this feeling that I wouldn't be seeing her again but didn't want to tell her that. I just wanted her to know that I loved her and that I was leaving. From my mom's house I walked down the road to a friend's house there in Cape Coral, Florida. From this house I caught a ride with one of his sisters into downtown and to the first car dealership. After she had dropped me off, I walked inside and asked to test drive a dark blue Chevy Silverado quad cab that was a 2004. The car sales man took a copy of my ID card that I had stashed at my mom's house, then handed me the keys and told me to be back in thirty minutes or so. I drove out of the lot to another friend's shop, where I had another set of keys made. I also had him place the truck up on the lift to remove the speed chip that these newer cars and trucks have in them. It's a computer chip that prevents them from going over a set speed. I had plans on stealing this truck later on that night. After returning the truck back to the dealership, I explained to the salesman that it was a little steep for my liking, but would think it over the next couple of days. We shook hands and I left. Walking down the street to Taco Bell, I got something to eat. While eating inside, I thought about everything that I needed to do and wanted to do. While sitting there I got a call on my cell phone, and from Taco Bell went to one more friend's house that was three blocks from where I was. (I do not say names here because these people are involved with illegal shit.) At this friend's house, I smoked a little weed and popped some ecstasy, also known as X. As I was sitting there chillin', a group of people started showing up for a party my friend was throwing. Next thing I know as I'm sitting back on his couch just in front of his big screen TV, he places in my hands two triple stack of Buddha pills. Without missing a beat, I throw them into my mouth and chew them up before swallowing them and washing the nasty ass taste down with some chick's fuzzy navel flavored wine cooler. Almost spitting that shit out, I grab a bottle of Dos Equis that I had been drinking. After about thirty minutes I'm starting to feel the effects of the X. This girl I don't know climbs onto my lap and starts blowing into my face with a Vicks inhaler. The thing is she had reversed the insides of it so that she could blow into my face while also giving me a message on my upper body and neck area. The effect this had on me was one of a super high and rush that had me wanting to fuck, and that's what this chick and I were doing right then and there on the couch. She had pulled out my cock and was riding me right there while blowing me up with that Vicks inhaler. That was one of the best fucks I ever had. I guess the mixture of the drugs and what she was doing to me just mixed right. About one o' clock in the morning I left the house and walked back to the dealership while carrying a set of bolt cutters with me that I had taken from my friend's house. Once I got to the dealership, I had to cut through the padlock holding a chain across the entrance to the lot. After this was done, I walked to where the Silverado was that I had tested that afternoon. Using the keys I had copied, I let myself in and started the truck before driving out of the lot to the nearest gas station to fill the tank. Driving up the East Coast alone gave me time to think about everything. I had no set destination in mind, only to get the fuck out of Florida. I drove through Atlanta, Georgia and both South and North Carolina and into Virginia before making my way over to Cincinnati and then turning a bit north and going into Detroit, Michigan. For some dumbass reason I still cannot understand, I made a stop at a gas station in Calhoun County in Michigan which is in Belding,

Michigan. After going inside to pay for the gas, I was waiting inside the truck and staying warm while the tank was filling. Next thing I know, I'm surrounded by cops. They have their guns out and pointing at me in the truck screaming at me to show my hands and exit the truck. Exiting the truck with my hands held high in the air to show they're empty, I am instructed to kneel on the ground and interlock my legs over each other with my hands behind my head. Once this is being done, they run up to me grab my hands while throwing me to the ground face first, and dropping a knee into my back and pulling my hands down and behind my back to place me into handcuffs. Being placed into the back of one of the cop cars, I watched as the truck was placed onto a flatbed tow truck and taken to the impound yard (I was told). While I was driven to the jail in the next county over. Other than the truck being stolen I had no idea why I was being arrested right then. Nor did I have any idea why so many cops had shown up with their guns trained on me. Any thought I had of fleeing was out of the question as there were too many! It was while I was being booked into the Montcalm County Jail, which was in the next county over from the one I was busted in (don't know why they take me to the next county). But some female that I had had a one-night stand with and had heard stories about me afterwards from people she hung out with. Decided to go to the police and take out a PPO (Personal Protection Order) against me without me knowing. While I was inside paying her for the gas, she recognized some of my tattoos and called the cops. I sure in the hell didn't recognize her, guess that was why she was so pissed and had to call the cops, eh? So, I was arrested for violation of a PPO and two counts of FTA (whatever the hell that is). I was sentenced to a $175.00 fine and had to do 17 days in jail. I was released on, May 9th, 2004. Upon leaving the jail, I took notice that these hicks left my ass stranded way out in the middle of nowhere. The stolen truck was in the next county over and the nearest town was ten miles away. In the distance I could see some apartments and made my way in their direction. Once there, which was further than it looked, I was freezing my ass off. I made small talk with this country boy who was working on his truck and asked him if he could give me a lift into the next county over to get my truck out of the impound yard. He said he could but wanted to know what I was in their jail for. I told him that I had violated a PPO that I didn't know someone had out on me. He laughed at that and said he'd been there a time or two himself. He finished up and we got into his truck which was a Ford F150 that looked beat to shit with rust everywhere. When he dropped me in the next county at the impound yard, I thought it was going to be a yard but was a local truck shop. I went inside and asked about my truck and was told that it was in the back and covered with a tarp. I owed $100.00 to get it out. I paid the fee and got the keys and left. Tell me that's not some seriously slick shit. Knowing this truck is stolen and still going to get it and drive it away! I drove it into downtown Belding and found my way to a local carwash. Nope, I didn't get the truck washed because I didn't want anyone to get a clear shot of my plates. Sitting in the parking lot I started thinking and realized that there was someone in that town I knew and could get some serious cash from, until I found out what I wanted to do and where I wanted to go. I walked over to a telephone booth and grabbed the phone book. Looking under lawyers I found who I was looking for. Yep, there's crooked lawyers everywhere if you know where to look for the bastards at. In the case of this one he worked for a time for Danny when he was alive and his associates when they were near Michigan. I don't owe this fool one thing. His name was and is Pete Fry, Attorney at Law in Belding, Michigan. No shit, look this asshole up. See, Pete had a drug problem and got into some serious debt with Danny and friends to keep his life and job he was bought and paid off. Pete had a nice house on the Lake with a new Chevy Tahoe and a car along with his old model Z240. So, I looked old Pete up and got some cash and went to catch some sleep at his house while he remained at work for a while. Pete gave me some information to some locals that were in the market for some cocaine and I went around to their place only to catch them in a party.

Inviting myself inside, I spoke to a few people and found myself looking into the eyes of this long-legged beauty named Lisa Wagner. Lisa and I got to talking and she asked me what kind of drugs I had on me. I told her that I didn't have anything on me, but could get it within the hour if it was needed. She said she really just enjoyed smoking some weed and asked if I could get her some and we could just go off on our own and smoke and chill. I told her to come on outside with me and we got into my truck. I drove her over to Pete's house and ran inside grabbing an ounce of weed and a half ounce of cocaine. Though she didn't ask for the cocaine, I figured I would introduce her to a primo if she was willing to try one. A primo is a joint laced with cocaine. After returning to the truck, I asked her where she wanted to go. She directed me to way the fuck out into the middle of the woods and onto a dirt track that led to her house. About two miles from her house in the woods, we pulled over and I rolled her some joints to smoke. I asked her if she wanted to try a primo and she said no. We climbed out and I opened the tailgate and we sat and talked. I got to know Lisa and the things she liked to do and a little bit about her family. She was a good girl and was doing small things like pot with no other drugs. She asked about myself and I told her some but not much. We started kissing and making out, but for some reason I stopped and lightly pushed back from her. She asked me why I was stopping and I told her that I didn't want to just fuck in the bed of this truck as it was too fucking cold! She laughed at me and said she was use to this cold weather. I explained that I was from California and Florida and I didn't do cold, not even for some sex. She told me to get my ass in the truck and to drive her home which I did so. Thinking that this was it, I waited for her to get out but she just sat there asking me what I was waiting for. I said what do you mean? She said she wanted me to come inside with her as nobody was home, she wanted me to stay over and show her how guys from Florida and California had sex. Sorry people, but I'm not going to share the details of my sex life with Lisa with you. Even though she and I don't have contact, I still hold her in respect and know she has a family of her own now. Long story though, we hit it off and Lisa and one of her male friends ended up leaving with me from Michigan in another stolen truck, though this time I brought her friend Scot Nash into it. Made Scot take his license into a dealership and take out a new truck for a drive while Lisa and I waited across the street in my stolen truck. Once Scot brought the truck around, I changed plates and we left. I had to make some stops before leaving Michigan to pick up some guns and a few other things, then we were on our way. Somewhere in or around the states of Indiana and Kentucky we got pulled over for speeding. I pulled to the side of the road and watched the officer come up alongside of the truck. Not once did I place the truck into park or take it out of gear. I had my foot on the brake though. When the officer came up, I gave him one of my old licenses and he went back to his car to run it. When he came back, I took notice of how he had his hands on his gun now. I didn't want to get into a shooting match with Lisa and Scot in the truck, nor did I want to shoot the cop. I did the only thing that popped into my mind at the time. I took my foot off the brake and fled. I saw in my mirror that the cop was running back to his car to give chase. I told Lisa and Scot to put their seatbelts on. I drove like the wind. As the cop was coming up on us, I took notice that an 18-wheeler that was ahead of me was swerving all across the highway trying to assists the cop by getting me to slow and stop. Wasn't going to happen. I swerved onto the exit ramp and took it and raced us out into the middle of nowhere. As we came upon the woods, I got out of the truck after telling Lisa and Scot to remain inside. See, I had pulled the truck off into the woods and was now waiting for the cop to show up. He never showed, thus I started thinking that he called off the pursuit. After two hours or so I got back into the truck and made it back onto the highway. I never really thought about it much back then, but I'm sure you're all wondering if I would have shot that cop if he came up and found us. Probably, but I'm glad I never had to find out. Throughout the road trip I never allowed either Lisa or Scot to drive the truck. Not because they couldn't, but because if there was ever another incident like with the cop pulling us over, I had tons of experience with driving and evading from when I drove for Danny and friends. My plan was to drive over to California and then maybe go see my older brother Greg, who I think was living in or around Portland at the time. Right then though I was taking us to visit with my sister Kristina, who was living in some little town called Killeen in Texas. She had gotten married to her high school sweetheart, who in my rightful opinion is nothing more than an asshole, even if he did serve in the military and was stationed at Fort Hood Military base. But when we went to see my sister, I hadn't seen her in years because I had been in prison in California and then right on over into jail at Fort Myers, Florida. Once we got into Texas, I contacted my sister at her work because I didn't have any of her information like house address or numbers, but I knew where she worked, at least the name of the company. So, I looked up the number in the phone book and called her there. I explained when she got on the phone that I and two friends were there in Killeen and if she could visit for a few minutes? She gave me directions to her job and we met in the parking lot and she met both Lisa and Scot. It was the first time I had seen my older sister Kristina in over four years and some change. She told me that she got off work in a couple of hours and that if I wanted to, we could meet at her house that she gave me directions to. We did that and, in the end, she allowed us to stay with her for a couple of nights. After our short visit, we left with my sights set on California. We traveled through this big ass State of Texas for what seemed like hours and hours before coming upon and going through New Mexico and the city of Albuquerque. From there we drove onto and through the State of Arizona and onto and through the State of Nevada and into California. Along the way we made tons of stops for both rest and gas and to eat. When we got closer to Turlock, I decided to take a chance and contact my dad just for the hell of it. He agreed to meet with us at a local restaurant for lunch. After meeting in the parking lot and introducing both Lisa and Scot to my dad we all went inside and ordered lunch. I excused myself to use the restroom and while I was gone either Lisa or Scot took it upon themselves to explain to my dad that I had guns. When I came back to the table, he asked me to talk with him outside for a minute. I did this not having a clue what he wanted to talk about as I had no love for him as a dad. To me he was just another person, but I was still curious about what he wanted to talk about. When we got outside, he said that he knew I had some guns and wanted to know if I wanted to sell them to him or his friends? He wouldn't tell me which one of the people inside had told him about them, but there was a touch of fear that I would hurt someone with one of them (isn't that what guns are for!?). I told him that I didn't mind getting rid of one of them and sold him for $150.00 the Ruger 9mm, though I kept a 45mm S and W. After lunch, we all parted ways and the three of us continued on our way up the coast of California. Though I promised myself I would never have the love for my brother Sean like a sibling I decided to also contact him in the Bay area as that was where I understood him to be living with his girlfriend who would later become his wife. When we got closer to San Francisco, I got on my cell phone and called information for his telephone number. When his girlfriend picked up, I kindly asked to speak with Sean if he was there. A second later he came on the phone.

I explained that for some reason or another I was coming through Frisco and wanted to know if he wanted to visit? I was shocked when he said yes and instructed me to his condo. I was told to enter the underground parking. Driving into an underground parking lot in a full-sized Chevy truck was a tight ass fit and even more so when I decided that I wasn't going to be parked nose in and instead backed into a spot on the third floor. When my brother met us at the elevator in the garage, I introduced to him both Lisa and Scot. Sean and I shook hands and he led us into the elevator and took us up to their condo. He and his girl had a really nice place and I was happy for him, but I never told him so. Sean and his girlfriend Laura asked us if we would stay for dinner and then for the night. We accepted. Lisa and I slept on a foldout bed and Scot took the other couch. In the morning, before we left Sean asked me where I was going? I told him I didn't know (though I did). Before we left, he gave me some money that I didn't ask him for. The three of us got into the truck and left. Before leaving San Francisco, I thought to show Lisa around and to walk on Pier 51, as she had never been out of Michigan before this. We found another underground parking lot and paid the fee to enter. While I was getting ready to exit the truck, Lisa being a little slick ass called my name, and when I turned my head towards her, she took my picture! The picture found in this book is the one she took and it's the last picture anyone would ever see of me before I made the biggest mistake of my life back in Texas. We all walked around and enjoyed ourselves before it was time to leave. Back on the road and in turn the freeways. I took us to the Oregon State line and in we went on our way to find my oldest and last sibling, Greg. At the time my older brother was married and he and his wife Tabitha were living around Portland, Oregon. When we got closer to them, I called my brother up from the hotel we were staying at. He came out and we all met and talked. Greg asked me if Lisa was my girlfriend and I told him yes and that Scot was a friend of hers from Michigan. He asked me what our plans were and I told him nothing really, though I would like to find a job for a bit. He thought it over and the next night he and his wife Tabitha asked if I wanted to stay with him for a little while. Greg said he would get me a job working for his partner as they were doing concrete work. I asked about Lisa coming with and then what about Scot. They were welcome for the time being. We drove over to my brother's apartment complex and he showed us around. Tabitha met us and gave me a hug and I introduced her to Lisa and in turn Scot. She and Lisa hit it off. Scot and I ended up going to work for my brother and his partner for Maui's Construction. I had done construction work before when I was younger and not into so much crime, so this was nothing new to me, but for Scot, he didn't last long and before we knew it, it was decided that we would send Scot back to Michigan on a flight. One-week later Scot was flying home to be back with his loved ones while Lisa would remain with me for the time being. While working for my brother and his friend at Maui's Construction, I drove the heavy dump truck and the skid (Backhoe and Bobcat) for them. About two months into our stay, my brother helped me get a place for myself and Lisa, while Lisa was working with Tabitha during the days and I was working with my brother. It was hard work but it paid cash at the end of each week around $700 to $800.00 each week. Greg talked me into leaving the truck in a parking lot with the keys in it after contacting the law in Michigan and explaining to them where I was leaving the truck for the car dealership to recover it if they still wanted it. I made sure to wipe it down really good so there were no fingerprints, as they still had no idea who took their truck. I also got rid of my gun. Things were working out great for a while and then as usual my past found me and I started making money the other way and left working for my brother and his friend. Lisa tried her best to get me to do good and leave that kind of life behind and I honestly wanted to. In the end I just couldn't do it though. Lisa and I broke up, even though our feelings for one another were really strong, we both thought it best that she returned home to Michigan (to this day from my understanding she is married with a couple of kids. I wish her the best).

After Lisa was gone for good, I started going backwards in my life again, doing drugs and mixing with the wrong crowd. I knew where to look for the things I wanted to enjoy, and while I greatly enjoyed the help of my older brother and his wife at the time, I just couldn't deal with life like that. I needed the fast life and the drugs to run. One-night while having people over to my place, my brother and his wife entered and I was caught with drugs all over the place and people enjoying themselves. The things that seriously broke me inside though was the fact that my older brother had seen his little brother fucked up on dope. Had he and his wife entered a minute earlier, they would have caught me shooting up a major hit of cocaine. I was so fucked up back then that I was driving one day and while sitting at a stoplight, I was caught slipping and this fool attempted to car jack me after hitting me full in the face through my window with brass knuckles. I kept my piece of shit car but I ended up in the Emergency Room at the University Hospital South. (Please see that back of this book for medical papers and criminal papers).

After my carjacking incident, I and my brother got into it a bit, and I ended up leaving Oregon and traveling back into California and the Bay area of Oakland to a friend's place there. Once again back into this area of California, I located a friend that drives 18-wheelers for a living. I just happened to catch him at home and talked him into giving me a ride out of the State. He took me with him to Salt Lake City, Utah, where I caught a flight for Killeen, Texas. My friend tried to talk me into staying in Salt Lake City and working for the same company he drove for, but I knew there was no way I could do this with my criminal past and no CDL. Told him thanks and left. Upon landing in Killeen, Texas, I contacted my sister Kristina and asked if she could please pick me up and if I could stay with her for a few days before leaving. She came and got me and with her she brought a surprise. My mom was now living with my sister while my brother-in-law was in Iraq fighting in this stupid war when they should have just nuked that country.

Chapter Six

Teazer's Gentleman's Club

After my sister and mom came to get me from the airport and take me back to my sister's house, I was told that my mom had just moved in at my sister's request for company while my brother-in-law, Matthew Martinez, was over in Iraq. I hadn't seen my mom for almost one year now. I explained to them both that I wasn't planning on staying that long, just long enough for my face to heal from where I was sucker punched with brass knuckles in Oregon, as I was still black and blue around my left eye and cheek area and my jaw was still swollen. My sister said that she didn't mind, but that I couldn't stay longer than that. I told her I understood. Everyone know that I wasn't one that could sit still for very long nor not get into any kinds of trouble. After about one week, I had flown back to meet and talk with my friend in Salt Lake City, Utah, the same one that had given me a ride in his 18-wheeler from Oakland, California. When he met me at the airport we drove back to his job and got into his truck. He had a big double sleeper Volvo, that was basically like a tiny house on the inside. While sitting inside and talking he asked me what I really wanted. It was then that I explained that while I had been driving all over the place on the run from Johnny Law and saying goodbye to my siblings and even seeing my dad. I got it into my mind that I wanted him to find someone for me so I could end it. He said who? I told him to find Terry Brotherton for me. I gave him all the information that I knew about him. He said to give him about one week and then to come back here. We parted ways and I went back to Killeen, Texas. When I got back, I called my sister and asked if she could please come and pick me up? She said no, but that mom would come and get me and not to make this a habit. I explained that I would be gone shortly, though that's not what happened. While I was staying at my sisters, she was allowing me to drive her Jeep Wrangler around and do whatever I needed to do. Seems like it never fails though as I found myself at this Club called Teazer's. I thought I would go inside and see what they had going on there. It was during the afternoon hours so it wasn't very busy inside the semi-dark club. Once you enter inside there is a bar to the right and a dance floor with pole to the left. Straight back between the two is a sitting area and to the right the restrooms and next to the restrooms is a set of stairs leading to the second floor. Up here there was more seating and a pool table and the dancers changing area. Aside from the entrance that I came through in the front, there were two others that were inside and out, but were only being used for emergency exits at the time the club was open. One was back at end of the club that opened onto a parking lot that was shared with the club behind it called Dollhouse, and the other exit was through the dancers changing room on the second floor. Back behind the bar and to the left were a small office where the money and safe were being kept along with a telephone if someone needed to make a call. While I was inside, I took a seat and thought while watching one of the dancer's do her thing on the dance floor and moving on the pole. Needless to say, she sucked and her body wasn't all that. While watching her a man I'll describe as Middle Eastern with dark-black hair came walking inside and barking orders to people here and there. His name I was told was Mohamed but everyone at the club called him by his middle name, Amine. Amine was part owner of Teazer's, and weeks later I would know more about Amine and he would know lots about me. I left the club about two hours later and returned to my sister's home. My sister at the time had been working for Dynamic Designs there in Killeen and my mom got a job working on base in the children's part of the hospital. Without being asked I kind of moved into my sister's place with the two of them, but not before obtaining everything that I needed to know about the where abouts of one Terry Brotherton and the fact that he was in a little town in Indiana, but had been returning to Las Vegas a couple of times recently. I wasn't planning on staying in Texas nor with my sister and mom. I had no real destination in mind other than finding Terry so I could kill him.

That day/night when I returned to my mom's place in Las Vegas and saw her battered and bruised face and neck from Terry trying to beat and suffocate her while she was sleeping. That shit broke something within me that could never be replaced. Nobody should ever have to see their mom, their pride and gold beaten down like a dog like that. Especially no kid who had already been living a fucked-up lifestyle. What kind of piece of shit puts their hands on a woman!? I'll tell you what kind: a fucking coward and a piece of shit who should be taken out in the woods and either beat the fuck out of or shot dead! Nobody has the right to place their hands on a woman for any reason. That shit not only hurt me, but pissed me off more when in the end my mom got back together with this piece of shit. And in all honesty, that is what sealed Terry's fate with me. For some crazy ass reason, I kept returning to Teazer's and before long Amine and I met and talked about something. I found out for example that Amine enjoyed doing cocaine but didn't have a supplier that he could get it form anytime he wanted it. He also liked to act like he had more money than he did, though he had bought a boat that was out on one of the lakes, had a nice house that he was sharing with his sister and was screwing his choice of dancers from the club. Before long, it came to my attention that Amine also bought stolen goods and he was in the market for some stolen stereos for his car and home.

I got to thinking and looking around, but the one thing about Killeen? There are cops everywhere! Plus, I had to be on the lookout for military police that would come off base for some reason or another. By this time, I had been screwing this woman named Wendy that was a dancer at the Dollhouse, which was the club directly behind Teazer's. Her boyfriend at the time was also in Iraq, and while over there he had left Wendy the use of his lifted Dodge Ram truck. This truck was too big for Wendy to be driving, so she allowed me to use it whenever I needed to. Using my cell phone, I contacted my friend back in Salt Lake City and asked him if he knew anyone on Fort Hood Military Base. I was told yes and given a name and number to call. Once I had this information, I called the reason, number I was given and spoke with the person on the other end. We decided to meet up at Taco Bell and discuss things. We'll call him Mike (because he's still in the military). I met up with Mike and asked him what kind of things he could help me with at the Base in change for some cocaine. Mike would turn out to be a gold mine. One week later, he and I met up outside the gate of Fort Hood Military Base's Airport and right next to this place called TGI Electric. A place that I would return to not far from then. Mike was doing a lot of work around ACP 9 Alpha, West Fort Hood, after work two days after we met, he brought me a set of military BDU's a pair of boots and tags along with a military ID. I was dressed as a soldier every day when I was going onto Fort Hood Military Base even thought I was not a military soldier. The reason for my being this way was I was dealing in illegal activities having to do with the property of the Department of Defense. Mike was getting me guns and military issued Kevlar along with other items of military goods that could be sold off base. While doing this, I went about my usual and bought up stolen stereos and other items with bad checks. A few times I had to drive to San Antonio, Texas, to pick up a kilo of cocaine for Mike. I ended up getting caught up with the police early and had to go downtown in Belton, Texas, to meet and talk with the district attorney. It was here that an offer was made to me to work in OCD (Organized Crime Division) as an informant to clear up my record with them and a few other places. All I was thinking was that I was stupid for showing up there and I took their offer so I could get out of there. My contact was Detective Tim Steglich assigned to the Killeen Police Departments, Criminal Investigation Division of Organized Crime. I had their numbers and they had mine. Once they let me go, I contacted Mike and my friend back in Salt Lake City, Utah.

Both of them told me I needed to leave Texas right away. After I hung up with them, I got a call from one of the dancers at the club that told me Amine was going around telling people that he could have my family killed for as little as $10.00, and that I was being kicked out of the club and no longer working for Amine. I was never really working for him in the first place like everyone had thought. As I left the parking lot of the District Attorney's Office from talking with the Defectives, I headed towards my sister's house thinking that I should go ahead and just leave, but something kept me back. I ended up staying longer than I should have, thinking that I could play the cops and find Amine for the money he owed me for the stolen stereos and the cocaine. In between everything I still went out with people to other clubs and I still did stupid shit. Screwing this chick that was a one-night stand and jacking her ex-boyfriend for his 9mm Ruger. In my mind, I needed to leave Texas, but I never made it out as I was too caught up in things and wanted to do something about Amine first.

Near Thanksgiving Day, I had gone to Fort Hood Military Base and signed this punk out of CQ (Confined to Quarters). This caused me to have to dress in my BDU's and grab my military ID I had gotten from Mike. I went onto the Base and signed out the punk from CQ and we left the Base. The year was 2004. About two weeks before Thanksgiving Day, I showed up at OCD and had my fingerprints and past ran through the NCIC (National Crime Information Center) before being wired up to go and make a buy for over $300.00 in cocaine. The buy went smoothly and I left OCD afterwards, returning back to Teazer's even though everyone was telling me Amine didn't want me there. Just as I was leaving in the lifted Dodge Ram truck, Amine was pulling in with a friend of his in a dark green Jeep. The guy that Amine was with was named Haitham, but I was introduced to him as Blue and he as Frank. He was nothing like Amine, this guy acted like he wanted to be anywhere else than where he was that time. I paid little attention to him and asked Amine when he was going to pay me the money he owed for the stolen stereos and the cocaine. I was told that he would have the money soon and that for the cocaine he would trade me this Jeep they had just showed up in. That is when it was brought to my attention that Frank owned a car dealership of used cars in Cameron, Texas. Frank acted like he wanted to say something but he never did because Amine cut him off. Frank got back into the Jeep and came out with a title and we talked it over (Amine and I) and then Frank signed the Jeep over to me there and then. I was now the owner of a used green Jeep. They walked into the club and I left with the promise from Amine that he would have my money for the stereos by that weekend. The weekend came and went and Amine couldn't be found anywhere. I ended up taking a couple of girls to my sister's house for Thanksgiving Day, afterwards we left and went back to this chick's house to party. Two of the guys I had been doing things with and they had been buying cocaine from me were there at the house and I asked them to leave with me. One was named Chris and the other was named Tim. Chris couldn't come because he had somewhere else to be, that left Tim riding around with me in the early morning hours of November 27th, 2004, or I guess you could say late night on November 26th, 2004, Thanksgiving night. By this time, I had taken the Jeep and traded it in for a midnight blue lowered Chevy S-10 with tinted windows and a sound system along with a bed cover. I had all kinds of drugs and weapons within this truck. Tim and I left and went looking for Amine.

We drove all over Killeen, Texas, and I called Amine on his cell phone numerous times and even went by his house where I ended up talking to his sister who was just getting home from being out with her friends. She said that she didn't know where her brother was but did try and call him with no answer. As we were leaving his house, he called my cell phone and explained that he and Frank were out at a club and they would meet me in one hour. I told them where to meet and it was set up. Tim and I raced back into Killeen and back to the party, where I traded trucks and then Tim and I went to the location that Amine was to meet us at. Now we were riding in the lifted Dodge Ram truck that belonged to Wendy and her boyfriend who was in Iraq. What Tim didn't know at the time though was that when we got into this truck, I had removed a 9mm Ruger from my lowered S-10.

Every time that I drove in any other truck or car, I would always be wearing these thin black gloves. I never took them off for any reason unless I was at my sister's house. When Amine was supposed to meet with us after one hour and he still hadn't showed, I called him on his phone. He answered and said that they would be there in another twenty minutes, that he was just picking up the money. It was now around 2:00am November 27th, 2004, and we were sitting outside the gate of Fort Hoods Military Base Airport and next to TGI Electric in a dark and secluded area with a field beyond it all. It was set back away from the main road.

When Amine showed up finally, he was with Frank in a white

Mitsubishi Eclipse. They pulled into the lot and then shut their lights, but this forced me to turn the truck around because I didn't want to have to get out of the truck for any reason unless I had no other choice. Once I got the truck turned around so that we were now parked driver window to drive window where we could talk through our open windows. I made small talk with Frank because Amine acted like he was too busy talking on his cell phone with someone. To my right, Tim is hidden in the shadows videotaping everything, even though this was not planned he was just doing it. For some unknown reason, Frank turned his head away from me and said something stupid to Amine about how Amine said he could kill my loved ones for $10.00. When he turned back around, Frank caught a slug from a 9mm Ruger straight through his head, he was dead before his head fell forward. Right after the shot was fired, Amine who was still talking on his stupid cell phone is now screaming on the phone, "What the fuck! What the fuck!" before he was able to fully finish the third what the fuck, he was shot with the same 9mm Ruger, but my aim caught him through his left hand which caused the bullet to go through his cell phone and out the back side of his head. Before I knew that I had said anything to Tim, he was getting out of the truck and walking over to their car. I dropped down out of the truck and opened the driver's door to make sure that Frank was dead and to have Tim pull him from the car. Once this was done, we slowly walked around to the passenger's side and opened the door to get Amine out. As I opened the door, I took notice of the floorboards and that there was a black bag along with a folded down SK-74 assault rifle. Smiling to myself, I looked at Amine who was still breathing but barely. He had his seatbelt on and I instructed Tim to cut him out and pull him out of the car, which he did so. Once Amine was out of the car and laying on his back, he tried to reach up towards the sky by pointing his finger and trying to talk or maybe it was just to gurgle like a bitch, either way I no longer cared about the money he owed or anything else, I was pissed that this fool had the nerve to show up with a rifle like he was planning to kill me. I walked over to Amine and noticed that Tim was still filming everything. Though he was also covered in Amine's blood from when he had to cut his belt off of him and pull him from the car. He even pulled him right out of his dress shoes. I rested the .9 mm Ruger on Amine's head and told him Fuck

Allah and that he no longer held the power before blowing his brains out. After killing Amine, I looked back inside their car and grabbed the black bag along with SK-74 and threw everything into the truck before driving back to the party.

Chapter Seven

Not Finished Yet

The next 24 hours would become one giant clusterfuck and things would get way out of control. After returning to the party and being idiots and showing the video to this broad I was screwing, I instructed Tim to get rid of his bloody clothing. He took off for parts unknown to dump his bloody clothes while I went to sleep. When the morning came, Tim dug a hole in the dirt to burn the tape, then we left to wash the truck and return it to Wendy. While we were doing this, I noticed that two of the shell casings from the shots fired were still inside the truck. I removed them and threw them into the trash. After the truck was clean, I drove back to the house we had stayed at and I got this girl's car and told Tim to take the truck to Wendy's place and drop it off to her and tell her I said thanks. We parted ways. I drove to my sister's house and while I was there, I was watching the news (something that I never did). While I was watching this, my sister showed up and started watching it along with me, because I guess she might have been curious as to why her little brother was watching something he never does? Who knows? Just then a breaking news story shot across the screen. Then the story of the shooting was on the news and my sister saw how I got really interested in it all. You could see footage from an aircraft had taken overhead pictures of the scene. You could see footage of many different departments of police all the way from the locals to DOD (Department of Defense) along with the DOA (Department of the Army) and MP's (Military Police) along with your EMS and other police departments. I think that my sister was able to put two and two together because after she looked at the news and then at her little brother, she knew. I made the mistake of looking at her and knew it was over. She, along with my mom who she was thinking about telling, started talking and telling me I had to turn myself in to the police. I got up and left the house in my lowered truck. Went around doing some things and thinking about turning myself into the law. As I was driving around, I got two calls on my cell. One from this fool out in East Killeen, talking about how he was going to catch up with me and kick my ass for fucking his chick. I asked him who the fuck he was and he said his name was Anthony from Detroit and that I was fucking his chick named Zoe who was a dancer at Teazer's. I told him I wasn't fucking his chick and that now was not the time to be fucking with me and hung up on him. The thing is, I knew who Zoe was and where she was staying and that was at this fool's house. The second call came from this other girl I was kind of seeing on the side that was also a dancer at Teazer's, named Tiffany Dotson. Tiffany started telling me about how she knew that I was the one who had shot and killed Amine last night and that everyone was talking about it and that Zoe's boyfriend was talking about giving me up to the cops. I asked her if his name was Anthony and she told me it was. I hung up with her and left for Anthony's house alone in my S-10, but not really alone. When I got over into the right neighborhood, I slowed down real slow and just kind of creeped through at first to locate the right house. Once I found it, I sat across the street for some time before finally driving around the block. When I came through on my second pass, I had my window down on my driver's side and the barrel of the SK-74 resting on it. Stopping in front of his house in the middle of the street, I unloaded everything in the clip into his house. Spraying his house from top to bottom and side to side before burning rubber out of the neighborhood. Not five minutes later my cell phone is ringing and its Anthony asking me if I was just by his house. In response I just laughed as he started screaming at me that I was a dead motherfucker. Leaving the neighborhood, I returned to my sisters after making a stop to rid myself of the SK-74 in a dumpster outside of Fort Hood Military Base. I dropped my truck and grabbed that chick's car I had driven over there from the party house. My plan was to go to the party house and get my shit together and then make one other stop. On my way over there though, Tim called me and said to meet him at the McDonalds because he needed to talk to me about something that was really important. I told him that I was just up the street and would be there in a few minutes. When I pulled into the parking lot, he was there with Chris and Tiffany, my side piece. Tiffany ran over to me talking about how she and Zoe were going to be leaving to go out of the State later on that night, then started asking me all kinds of questions about the shooting. I told her that I would talk to her later before they left and we would meet up. She said okay and got back into her friends black Jeep and that's when I noticed Zoe was sitting inside too. As they left, Tim started talking to me and telling me that Chris was looking for some cocaine and that his friends were wanting half a key (kilo). I told them that I would make some calls and then get back with Tim later on tonight and he in turn would contact Chris. We all left Tim in his truck with Chris and me in this chick's little red car. I made some calls to Mike and my Salt Lake City connect. Mike already knew what had happened and told me to get the fuck out. I told him I was leaving that night but had one more thing to take care of then I would be gone. In the meantime, I told him that the kids were looking for half a kilo and gave him Chris's number and then hung up. I drove to my sister's house and spoke with her and my mom and told them I would be leaving tonight, though they continued to tell me to turn myself into the police. I left telling them I loved them, and got into my lowered S-10 and drove it to a used car lot to sell. I sold it in Killeen, Texas, to this used car dealership off of the main street in Killeen for $2,500.00. He paid me in cash and then gave me a ride back to my sister's house, where I got into the little red car and left. By this time, it's already after 8:00pm on November 28th, 2004. I got in touch with Tim and told him to meet me at Fort Hood's 4th ID. We met up and he got into the car with me and we left Base, and were in route to hook up with both Zoe and Tiffany before they left the State. Tiffany called me while Tim and I were driving out to meet them at a gas station, she said that she wanted to see me before she left. I explained that Tim and I were coming out to the station to meet them but were about thirty minutes away so wait up. When we finally made contact with them, Tiffany asked me if I had any cocaine on me and I said a little bit, but that I would give it to her at the lake we were going to go to after we all got gas, I told Tiffany to drive ahead of us to Stillhouse Park which was about forty minutes from where we were at the moment. Once we get off the Highway and took the exit for Stillhouse Park/Lake, there is the road that you have to take that twist and turns way out in the middle of nowhere. It sits back from the highway and is in a wooded area some 3 miles from the highway and lots of road travel. After we rounded the last turn in the road there was the gate to the park but it was closed and locked, so we parked outside the gate. Tiffany and Zoe were in a black Jeep Wrangler. They got out and walked over to Tim and I as we were getting out of the car. It was a little chilly out and Tiffany had a large blanket wrapped around herself and Zoe had on a light jacket. They were telling us about how they were headed out to visit with Zoe's grandma in another State, but my head was nowhere near listening to what they were talking about. In fact, my head and my thoughts were already gone. I was filled inside with nothing but rage and hate towards everyone including myself. Zoe climbed back into the Jeep and Tiffany walked over to me to give me a hug and a kiss and tried to hold onto me like she knew something was going to happen. I pushed her away and told her to take care and to leave, but she didn't do it fast enough and after she was inside the Jeep and Tim was getting into the car, I stepped over to the driver's side and opened the Jeep where Tiffany was sitting. The look she gave me was one not of fear but deep sadness before I pulled the 9mm Ruger from behind my back and shot Tiffany numerous times in the head and upper body, before turning my gun on Zoe and finishing her off with the remainder of shots. When the slide locked back, I turned around and got back into the car and we left racing out of there at a little over speeds of 100 mph.

 Two hours and some change later and back in Killeen, Texas, I turned myself into the OCD even though they asked me to come in under a fake warrant. I still showed up, thinking about what I had done and that I could probably talk my way out of it all. In the end though after almost 15 straight hours of interrogation by detectives, I confessed to everything.

Chapter Eight

Bell County Jail

After my interrogation, I was escorted in handcuffs to the main part of the jail there in Belton, Texas. Instead of having me wait like everyone else being processed, I was taken right up to the booking desk and told to be processed right then and there. An officer took me into the fingerprinting and photo room, and my prints were taken along with my mugshot. Before coming out of there, I was given one telephone call and I used it to call my mom and sister. After speaking with my sister who already knew that I had been arrested as did my mom, I then spoke with my mom. She was crying the whole time, but I remember very clearly something she asked me. She said son, if you had the choice between life in prison and death which one would you take? I told her honestly that I would take a death sentence. She cried harder but told me thanks for being honest with her about that. We then had to hang up so they could finish processing me into the jail. I was not yet being charged with anything, but was placed directly into an isolation cell per the directions of the detectives. Throughout the following days, I would go through more and more interrogations by detectives before finally being taken to court for a bail hearing and to be told my charges. At the start of January 2005, I was escorted to the 27th Judicial District

Court of Bell County, Texas, where I was indicted on two counts of Capital Murder and given a 2-million-dollar bond. I was then escorted in handcuffs back to my single man isolation cell on the third floor of the Jail.

I would remain inside of the county jail for a little over two years while going to trail, but long before I started my trial I was getting into fights with the jailers and their Major. Around February of 2005, I was being escorted downstairs to talk to a bonds person because someone was willing to post my bond from the East Coast. Just as I was getting ready to be shown into the holding booth where the bonds person was, I was turned away and down a short hallway and into a small court room. Please understand that anytime I came out of my cell I was in both leg irons and handcuffs. Inside this little courtroom there were other inmates in both the orange that inmates wear and street clothes, as well as both male and female. However, I was the only one sitting inside with a three-officer escort. While sitting inside there and waiting for them to call my name for what I didn't know at the time. The Judge kept calling the names of others and setting their bonds at $500.00 here and I think one was around $1,500.00. Then my name was being called. As I stood up in front of this little shit of a hick Judge and he's saying my name, all of a sudden, my head whips around and looks right at him. He's telling me that my bond is being raised to another 2-million-dollars and that I was being charged with another two counts of Capital Murder. I totally lost my cool, and before I knew what I was doing I was both yelling at the Judge about how the fuck am I to post bond on 5 million dollars while trying my best to get at him! I was tackled down to the floor by the officers and many more that came out of nowhere and from around the corner. The inside of the courtroom became a clusterfuck of fighting along with me in the middle of the pile. Though I'm in cuffs and leg irons it didn't stop me from trying to fight with the officers and I did fight. After a while they were able to raise me up off the floor and get me off of two of the officers that were stuck on the bottom of all of us, before escorting me out of the courtroom (drag me). I was taken down in between the booking desk and thrown into a small holding cage with the restraints still on my body before they closed and locked the door. There was a small window that I could see out of and into the booking area, and a side from that there was nothing in the cell but a hole in the floor for someone to take a piss. Basically, I was thrown into a rubber room/padded cell because they had nowhere to put me and try to calm me down. Now they had a problem though because I was beyond pissed off. An officer named Smith who I remember well was a real laid back black guy, but that day when he came to the little window in the door and asked me to allow them to remove the leg irons and cuffs from me, I wasn't really feeling him or anyone else and what they wanted. I did allow them to open the door and under the instructions to kneel down I allowed them to enter inside and remove the leg irons, after the irons were removed, I was told to stay down until the door was closed and then to place my hands through the slot in the door so they could remove the handcuffs. Everything was going well until this point. I still couldn't believe that they had slapped me with another 2-million-dollar bond! I was on my fucking way out of that shithole and this sorry ass state called Texas! I decided that every day they were going to have to fight with me for everything! I refused to allow them to remove the handcuffs and instead removed them myself and showed them that I now had my own weapons and for them to come on inside and we could play. They tried to get me to come and place the cuffs on the slot for them. It just wasn't going to happen without them having to work for it. At this time, the administrator who is also the Major showed up and instructed them to suit up a 7-man team to go inside and remove the cuffs from the cell. The Major's name was Robert Patterson. He was this big ass corn-fed looking sum bitch with pink cheeks. As the team suited up to get ready to come inside and try to remove the cuffs, the area around the booking desk was shut down and the holding cells that could see everything were being secured. Everything was stopped while they were trying to deal with me. In the jail they didn't have gas (chemical agents) that were used on inmates. Nope, these people loved to use force and to hit with their batons. I got up close and personal with these things over the years I was there. Once their team was ready, the Major threw open the cell door and the 7-man team came inside. Contact was made and all anyone from the outside could see or hear was the contact from fist being made to all inside. I was finally taken down to the floor, but in doing so I had an officer underneath me, while an officer on top of me had me in a choke hold. The only way I could get him to let up so I could breathe was to do something I have never done in my life. I grabbed his nuts and squeezed as hard as I could! He let go really fast and breathe I was able to catch my breath, then before I knew it, I was being dragged out of the cell by my legs, where everyone that was outside looking in piled on top. I stopped fighting. I mean seriously what the fuck was I going to do against half a dozen assholes? The handcuffs that I had been using as a weapon were removed from my hands as I was using them like brass knuckles. Leg irons were reapplied and another set of cuffs were placed onto hands but they were interlocked and then placed on my wrist, so that I had no give in them to work with or to remove like I had that first time. I was then escorted by the 7-man team and many of the jailers to the third floor and placed into a new isolation cell that looked out across the downtown street and right at the courthouse clock. These assholes had a sense of humor, look at the time dickhead they're saying. You're fixing to get a lot of it!

A few days later I was taken out for court, and afterwards I was allowed to use the telephone for ten minutes each day. The only thing was that every time I came out of my cell, it was with the handcuffs on and interlocked so I couldn't get out of them nor do harm to one of the staff. In the Bell County Jail, they have an inside rec room that has a ping pong table and weights along with this hanging camera that watches everything you do inside this room. There are two ways in and that is through a huge steel sliding door on each side. Once you're inside, these doors are sealed shut. Looking through one end though and you find yourself looking into the control booth and through the control booth you can look into the visitation area. The visitation area is non-contact and has 8 telephone-like booths on each side, where your loved ones or friends will come up through an elevator, go to the control booth and give them their pass and tell them who they are there to visit with. Visits are for one hour only. While everyone else in there is free of handcuffs, anytime I was in there to visit with my mom and sister, I was always in handcuffs and leg irons. I remember this one time I was inside the inside rec room when my mom and sister showed up for our hour visit on the weekend. I watched them come up and exit the elevator, and then stand there waiting for me to be brought out to visit with them. While I was waiting for my escort team to come and cuff me up and take me out there, I watched another inmate pull his dick out and start jacking off while looking at my sister and mom. My sister turned away and my mom never noticed. Then there was my escort and I was being cuffed up and taken into the visitation area and told that I would be sitting in booth 4, so telephone #4. Just so happened that the guy that was jacking off on my loved ones was seated next to me and visiting with his either wife or girlfriend I didn't know which one.

I had a good visit with them and when they started to get ready to leave my sister told me to not do anything stupid. I just kind of laughed and told her all is good. I deeply loved and cared about my mom and sister, but inside jail a place they have never been they had no clue about how things are ran and that there are things you do and don't do within both jail and prison walls. Most inmates show respect, but this guy that didn't know I saw him jacking off on my loved ones didn't show I nor my loved ones the respect they should have been given, regardless if I saw or not. What he did is something that you should NEVER DO. As soon as my loved ones were on the elevator and had waved goodbye to me, I was in motion and standing behind the guy while he was still talking on the phone to his visitor. While I had been visiting with my mom and sister, I had been working a homemade handcuff key into the lock on the cuffs and removing them from my hands. So, when I stood up the cuffs were no longer on my hands. I did what most inmates or prisoners call stealing on another inmate. Meaning without giving this fool time to acknowledge that I was standing there behind him I hit him upside the back of his head with my fist holding onto the cuffs. When his head slumped forward on the desk of the booth, I grabbed his ass up and dragged him off the stool he was sitting on and went about beating the fucking shit out of him for jacking off on my loved ones! The steel door behind me slid open and many officers jumped on top of us in their attempt to pull us apart and to stop me from killing this fool. Once we were separated, I was taken back to my single cell and later on that night the Major of the jail advised me that my visitation was being suspended until further notice. I ended up losing my visitation for like two-and-a-half months. So, while I wasn't allowed to visit, I took my frustration out in other ways, namely on Timothy Doan Payne; my co-defendant.

Tim, as we all call him, ended up turning himself into the Killeen police department after his commanding officer at Fort Hood told him to.

While Tim was in the military, he was with the 4th ID located off of Old Army Tank Destroyer Road on Fort Hood Military Base. The sad thing was Tim was just about 19 years old when he fucked his life up by meeting me. While sitting here typing out this story about my life and the crazy shit I did to land here, I can't help but feel sorry for screwing up his life and many. others. But back then, I guess you could seriously assume that he was on my shit-list within that jail. When I was on my way to court one day and being escorted to the elevators on the third floor by two officers that would be driving me to court. We had to pass the library which you could see into from through the control booth in front of the elevators. I had been hearing back in my isolation cell that Tim was turning states evidence against me and that he was being offered a deal in turn for testifying against me. Whenever we stepped onto the elevator, the officers would have me turn around so that I was facing out instead of in. This way they could always watch my hands to make sure I wasn't trying to remove my restraints. This was fine with me because it always allowed me to see everything that was going on around me and when we would pass the other floors and dorms. This day though as we were passing the library and they instructed me to turn around. I noticed my co-defendant Tim standing next to my friend named Vernon Walker who on the streets we all called Big V. I had no idea that he was in this jail with me, but at the same time I took notice of my co-defendant. Big V noticed me in the elevator and waved his hand at me. I leaned down as much as I could and really fast like cut my hands the best I could across my throat while then pointing towards Tim. Tim saw this happen and his eyes got really big and if we had been anywhere else, I would have been laughing my ass off. As it was, Big V Looked directly at Tim and before I or the escorting officers could warn anyone in the booth, Big V started beating the shit out of this little white boy named Timothy D. Payne! By this time the elevator doors were closing and my escorting officers were screaming for the elevator doors to open, doing this by looking at the video camera inside with us that was being watched by an officer downstairs. Throughout my two-and-a-half-years stay in that jail, my co-defendant would come to get his ass beat almost daily regardless of where the Major and his screwballs placed him. I did my best to have Tim killed within that jail before he was able to testify against me.

After a while I started to be good because I wanted to see my mom and sister. Sometime in 2006, I was moved down stairs to the first floor and the single cells there. While being housed down here, you could see the park from the windows, you could also speak to the guys next to you on each side. Most days and nights we would be playing chess against one another or doing some kind of workout in our cells, but all together. There were about 15 of us together in those single isolation cells downstairs. After each weekend that my mom and sister would come to visit, they would drive to the park and get out of their car and walk over to this big oak tree that I could see from my cell and wave to me. I would always scream at them and they would laugh and wave more and when they wrote to me or we talked on the phones they would tell me that they could hear me. While I was in jail, I got tons of mail from people I didn't know and this one young woman wrote to me thinking she would say her peace and that would be that. Back then I was young and full of myself and I loved to talk shit. In fact, I still talk shit to this day, just not as bad or as much. Her name was and is Paula Dicky from Waco, Texas, though back then she went by the last name of Brown. I knew nothing about this woman, but she wrote to me one day and didn't bother to put a return address (not many people did, writing to a killer). What she wrote though not so much as upset me nor pissed me off, but it did bother me for some reason. So, not caring about the jail staff listening in on my phone calls I contacted a friend here in Texas and asked about looking for this woman for me so that I could return a nice response. Three days later I got a letter in the mail from my friend and he came through with not an address but a telephone number and the place she worked. The next day, I was allowed out of my cell to make a telephone call and did so by calling this young woman at her place of work. When she came on the telephone, I explained to her that my name was Blue and that I had placed her onto my visitation list and that she needed to come and visit later that night. She said she didn't know anyone named Blue, and I said that I was sorry. But was this Paula Ann Brown of Waco, Texas? She said yes, and I said well in that case we do know each other. My real name is Richard Tabler and you went and sent me a letter telling me how you knew Amine from when you worked at CityLights and Teazer's, and that even though you knew Amine to be abusive you didn't have anything done to him. You talk to me about shit like this but you don't know me or why he got his ass shot do you? Like I said you're on my visitation list, be here for a visit tonight and we'll talk. I hung up and returned to my cell. Paula Brown showed up later that night for a visit and we became friends! She would return over the next few months and she would even come and visit with both my mom and sister. Then one day she showed up to visit wearing some dark sunglasses and sweats. When she removed her glasses, I about hit the roof and became pissed off. Both her eyes were black and blue from being punched by her ex-boyfriend. She had just driven home from work and was walking to her door when he came out of nowhere and started to beat her. What is it with men beating up on women? Are you assholes out there that small-minded and small in the other parts that you feel the need to abuse those that God created for us to cherish and love? Motherfuckers like these make me sick. Paula started telling me that it was okay and that she had called the police and made a report. See, back then she was mixed up with this guy that was how can I say this nicely… There's no way to say it. He was a white supremacist kind of asshole who thought he was the shit because he had this huge swastika tattoo on his arm like a badge of honor or something. All this did was make it easier to identify him when someone was looking for his stupid ass. Paula left after our time was up and I was taken back to my cell. She drove to the park and got out to wave at me, but being that it was dark out now it was hard to see her, but she could see me and that was all that mattered then.

After she left the park, I spoke with the officer on duty for the first floor, Officer Smith, and asked him to please, allow me to get on the phone real fast. I told him that if he let me out, I wouldn't cause him any shit for the rest of the week. I just needed to make a fast telephone call nothing more then maybe ten minutes tops. He let me out without the handcuffs on and I got my ten minutes on the phone. I made call to another friend in Copperas Cove, Texas. I explained that I could use his and his sister's assistance in something please. I explained that I didn't want the guy killed but wanted them to carve his swastika tattoo off his body after beating him. We hung up the phones. Two weeks later after her eyes had healed and she was feeling better, Paula showed up for a visit that I was not expecting. The first thing out of her mouth was why did you do that to him? I told her at first, I didn't know what she was talking about. She told me that her ex was found in an alley in Killeen with his face a bloody mess and his tattoo cut from his arm. I said it sounds like some kind of race thing, how could I have anything to do with it? I'm stuck in jail and have more important things to worry about then some dumbass. That was the last time she came to visit with me for months. Some women just don't know how to appreciate things that are done on their behalf.

In cause number 57,382 of the State of Texas verses Richard Lee Tabler, around March 20th, 2007, I was found guilty of Capital Murder in the deaths of Haitham Zayed and Mohamed Amine Rahmouni. The time was 1:23pm.

Less than three weeks later, I would be sentenced to Death for the murders of both Haitham Zayed and Mohamed Amine Rahmouni in April of 2007.

Darkness cannot drive out darkness;
Only light can do that.
Hate cannot drive out hate;
Only love can do that.
-Martin Luther King, Jr.

Chapter Nine

Not even after 24 hours had passed since I was sentenced to death in the 264th District Court of Bell County, Texas, under the Honorable Martha J. Trudo, and I was entering the Polunsky Unit where Texas Death Row prisoners are housed. Upon exiting the van that transported me here from Huntsville, Texas, I was met with a seven-man Use of Force Team. This consisted of seven grown men in riot gear. Seems word was called ahead of my arrival that I was going to be a problem. This was totally untrue, but when someone at the Bell County Jail contacted the Texas Department of Criminal Justice explaining that I had constantly been fighting within their own jail with their staff, up until my actual day of trial, people just couldn't help themselves in assuming that I would continue to be an asshole once I got to Death Row too.

When I got here, I was met by Assistant Warden Timothy Lester, who was nicknamed "Little Hitler", and Major Nelson, who was this little blonde lesbian. So, along with a seven man team and these two, I was introduced to Texas Death Row. Where a normal inmate would be placed on a normal pod filled with single man cells from sections A-F, numbers 1 through 84, and would be allowed to go to commissary and purchase items needed to survive while being a Level-1 inmate, I was being downgraded and placed on Level-3. I would automatically be starting at the bottom and have to make my way to Level-1. All because some crackers in the Bell County Jail was caught in their feelings.

After going through the process of having all my tattoos taken pictures of in a small classification office here in 12-Building, I was then given a white jumper with the letters "DR" on the back and down the side of one leg. I was given a bed roll consisting of two sheets, one blanket, toilet paper, some tooth powder, 3 pieces of tiny green soap, and an inch long toothbrush, along with a pair of gray socks, and a pair of boxers that you had to tie on the sides like a man bikini! Tell me that's not some shit right there. I was then re-cuffed behind my back and escorted down to F-Pod where all the Level-3 prisoners were housed. On F-Pod, I was placed into Cell #74. Once the cell door was closed behind me, I was instructed to place my hands out through the food slot so the cuffs could be removed. Once this was done, the slot was closed.

One of the very first people I met was my neighbor in Cell #75 named Carlos Trevino. He had gotten together with everyone, letting them know I had just rolled up. Next thing I knew, an officer was opening my slot on my cell door to hand me a brown paper bag that was filled with a pair of shower shoes, writing tablet, pen, stamps, soap, toothpaste, a homemade stinger (to heat water), a coffee cup, along with soups and coffee and a few other things to get me started. I was thankful for this because I didn't have anything with me other than my address book and a few pictures of my loved ones. Over the next couple of days, I was also given a t-shirt and a pair of gym shorts. I was informed that I shouldn't have been placed on Level-3 and should have been placed on Level-1. Thus I and those around me figured out that I was being fucked with because of my past actions in the county jail.

Aside from meeting Trevino, I would also meet one of the Texas 7, Donald Keith Newbury, who everyone called Lizard. It would be Lizard who would take me under his wing to show me the ropes while I was there on Level-3. This was one individual who was always, and I mean always, having a major use of force, making the officers suit up so that he could run the team. It was almost like he loved doing his best to make them use chemical agents on him (though they never really bothered him.) He was a beast when it came to having a use of force. Once they had utilized as much chemical agents on him in his cell as they could (really making all of us eat gas along with him), they would have his door rolled open, and off they would go, running into his cell in an attempt to extract him from his cell while also throwing a few punches here and there where nobody could see. Since when is it right or fair to utilize chemical agents on a man inside of a cell, then use seven grown-ass men in full riot gear with a shield to do their best to beat him, with the excuse they were extracting him? How is one man who weighs around 220 pounds going to beat seven men with a combined weight of over 1500 pounds? This is how they were treating those of us on Texas Death Row. Let's be fair though, Lizard did his best every time to return the favor by striking each and every team member that entered his cell with one of his homemade shanks. One of the ones to get hit the worst was Sgt. Harlen Petty. Lizard ended up stabbing Sgt. Petty seven times. This was the same time that when the Team entered his cell on F-Pod #46 that the Number 3 man on the team, Officer Pope, did the only thing he could to get Lizard to stop fighting. He got a handful of Lizard's balls and started squeezing! Lizard stopped fighting, and they were able to place him in restraints and leg irons before removing him from the cell.

When I made my Level-2, I was moved from F-Pod F-Section Cell #74 over to D-Section Cell #43, which is right next to the shower on One Row, as well as the cross-over door that is used to go from one section to the next. I had been in this cell for about 15 days when in the middle of the night I was awakened by some dumbass screaming aloud. When I came to my cell door to find out what and who it was, I would encounter my first problem with another Death Row inmate by the name of Hank Skinner.

Skinner, as everyone calls him, is a known drunk and drug user. He's a loud-mouthed piece of shit. But hey, I'm getting ahead of myself. After figuring out who was doing all the screaming, waking everyone up in a disrespectful way, I got out there with him. I just couldn't help myself. I hadn't been on Death Row long, but after doing time in prison in both California and Florida, I knew enough that most prisoners wouldn't get out there in this way. Coming to my cell door, I yelled out to Skinner and said, "Look out, Skinner! Man, what's up with yelling and waking everyone up like this, man!?"

It got real quiet for a few seconds. Then, "Who the fuck is that hollering at me about waking everyone up!? Fuck everyone else and you, who are you?"

I said that this was Blue down in #43 Cage. "Man, why you disrespectin' everyone like this, waking us all up?"

"Man, fuck you Blue, and fuck your mama, biiitch!"

I told Skinner, "You know what, we are set to go outside tomorrow on this section, Skinner, why don't you and I go outside first round and we can clean this shit up?"

Skinner said bet that!

That was it, it was all set up. Lizard heard this fool, and Billy Mason heard this fool. The next morning we had Officers Nickerson and White working the pod. These two officers were as laid back as could be. When C/O (Correctional Officer) White came around setting up the rec for that morning, I asked that he place me outside with Hank Skinner up in #54 Cell on Two Row. He told me that we would be going outside third round. About one hour later, my cell slot was opened, and a brown paper bag was dropped into my cell, making a loud banging noise when it did. I didn't see who had opened my slot and dropped the bag in, but once I went to see what was inside of it, I knew who had sent me the use of what was inside. Inside the bag was an 18-inch long piece of steel that had been ground down on the concrete of someone's cell floor, into the shape and sharpness of a machete. The one end was wrapped with homemade rope for a handle, with a loop hanging off so that it could be looped onto one's wrist.

When it was time to go outside, C/O Nickerson came to get me. With the machete hanging off my right shoulder and my green prison jacket to cover it up from everyone else seeing it, I placed my hands out my slot and was cuffed behind the back and escorted out to the outside rec yard. This is a big two-caged concrete yard with a basketball hoop, a pull-up bar, and a urinal and water fountain on each side. One side has glass windows so you can see inside the pod from outside. To get outside you have to go through the green outside rec yard door, then into one of the rec yards, where a steel gate is closed behind you and the handcuffs are removed. Once I stepped into the yard and C/O Nickerson closed the gate and removed the cuffs, he went back inside, closing the green outside rec yard door behind him.

Once this was done, the C/O who was up in the control picket on

F-Pod opened the outside rec yard gate that I was in. I stepped out of the rec yard, closed the gate, and stood to the side where I would be behind the green rec yard door when it opened to bring Hank Skinner outside. The machete was now hanging loosely from my right hand by the loop. Waiting to hear the green door pop, I would then raise it in a grip to use on Skinner when he came through the door.

Instead, C/O White started beating on the glass windows to get my attention, letting me know that he was not going to come outside to rec. The gate to the yard was popped open, and I stepped back inside and closed the gate behind me. Nickerson came back out, and I asked that Lizard be placed outside with me, while handing him my green jacket, asking that he please return it to Billy Mason.

After a couple of months being on Texas Death Row and down on F-Pod, where I would end up spending most of my time my first one and a half years, I would meet my court-appointed lawyers who would be handling my direct appeals. They were John Jasuta and David Schulman, out of Austin, Texas. One of my first meetings with them would be the deciding factor on not wanting to go forward with the whole appeal process. John told me right off that I had less than a one percent chance of ever getting off Texas Death Row. Knowing this, I honestly knew there would be no point in going forward when I had spent most of my life in prison anyway. I knew what the rest of my life would be like, because I knew the kind of person that I was.

Throughout my time spent in both California and Florida, I was constantly fighting with both prisoners and officers over the color of my skin. I look like a white guy, but my parents are mixed. My father was white, and my mother is full-blooded Jamaican. In prison in California, I was always being approached by the whites, also known as the wood pile or peckerwoods, to join up with them. This way I wouldn't have to constantly fight. Instead, I took a step when I first entered the CDC system in California at DVI. On my ethnicity, I put down black and was then celled after they made the mistake of housing me with a young white guy, who I ended up stomping on one morning and dragging down the stairs from Three Row. After that one time, I would always be housed with either black prisoners or Mexicans, or I was housed in dorms.

After leaving that legal visit with my lawyers and being escorted back down to F-Pod on 12-Building, which is where Death Row prisoners are housed at the Polunsky Unit, located in Livingston, Texas, I told myself that there was no way I was going to spend the rest of my life in prison nor fighting for my life through an appeal process while on Texas Death Row. I started sending legal letters to Judge Martha J. Trudo at the 264th District Court in Bell County. This was the same courtroom and judge that my trial was held before. I explained that I was wanting to waive my rights to further appeals and volunteer for execution. I saw no point in wasting time and effort in a lost cause because I was indeed guilty of the crime of Capital Murder. The two men I was convicted of killing I did in fact kill. There was never any questions about that, nor did I ever try to say that I was innocent of my crime. The truth is, even to this day I have deep regrets for my actions as a young and immature man back then who lost control of his temper. That though is no excuse for what I did. This was around August of 2008. Then I got a response somewhere in the first week of September, letting me know that I would be escorted by the County of Bell back to the 264th District Court of Judge Martha J. Trudo for a hearing to waive my rights to further appeals. This date was for September 30th, 2008.

During this same month of September, while I was waiting for the 30th to roll around, I was in E-Dayroom on F-Pod when I witnessed Sgt. Terry Valentine, C/O Robert Peters, C/O Michael McKnight, and C/O Robert Moss escorting an Ad-Seg inmate onto the pod and over into my old cell when I was Level-2 #43. This time around though, the Administration had turned F-Pod A-Section through D-Section into Ad-Seg housing, while those of us that were on Death Row and on Level-2 or Level-3 were housed on Sections E and F. While I was in E-Dayroom, I watched the above named officers escorting a black Ad-Seg inmate over and into Cell #43. Thinking nothing of it, I started to turn away from watching over there when I heard what sounded like someone hitting a piece of ground beef with a mallet. From E-Dayroom you can see a bit into Cell #43 when the cell door is opened. I could clearly see the Ad-Seg inmate's legs with his leg irons on and hear his sounds of pain as the officers continuously beat the inmate over and over with their riot batons while this prisoner is in both hand restraints and leg irons. The whole time I'm witnessing this, I'm hearing one of the officers yelling,

"You want to spit in my face, you fuck!?"

When I could no longer see the prisoner moving and the officers were done beating this man, they exited the cell without removing the restraints or leg irons, then slamming the cell door closed and walking away. Not one time while I was in the dayroom did I see someone come to remove the restraints from this man nor give him any kind of medical attention. I told my friend Lizard what I had watched/witnessed, and he told me that this happens all the time but there's really nothing that we can do about it aside from fighting back. And it's the price one pays for being stupid and spitting into an officer's face while he's in any kind of restraints.

A week later, I was being escorted off of F-Pod to a holding booth out in the hallway of 12-Building to be transported by the Sheriff's office back to Bell County for my court hearing that was scheduled for 10:30am on September 30th, 2008. Once there, the Judge held her little hearing, and the District Attorney said some things, and my counsel said some things before the Judge asked me some questions about my understanding what I was asking her to grant. That once I did this, there was a very good chance that I would not be able to try and pick my appeals back up, and that I would be executed. I explained that I understood and that I felt this would allow my victims' families closure, and that I was guilty of the charges and didn't want to spend the rest of my life in prison. The Judge was told during the hearing that I was competent and understood everything that was going on, and that I would indeed be executed if she granted this motion of mine, to waive my rights to further appeals, volunteering for execution. The Judge said that she was going to grant my motion to waive and volunteer for execution. After the hearing was over, I was transported back to the Polunsky Unit in Livingston, Texas, back on 12-Building F-Pod, E-Section Cell #61.

During the first couple weeks of October 2008, I was offered the use of an illegal cellphone to use that was the property of one of my neighbors there on E-Section. Having a cellphone on Texas Death Row had been unheard of and, in all honesty, never should have happened, but this is prison, and in prison you'll always find contraband of some kind or another, including all kinds of drugs. Most of the contraband found in prisons around the world are brought in by a corrupt prison officer. In order to use this other prisoner's smuggled-in cellphone, I had to be willing to have some prepaid minutes placed on it in exchange for using it. I had no problem with doing this, because the only thing I was thinking about was contacting my loved ones. Not one time was I thinking about doing harm to someone outside these prison walls or causing some kind of mayhem. I did however start to think back on what I had seen happen to that Ad-Seg inmate before I went back to Bell County for my court hearing.

After speaking with my loved ones who would be making the proper plans to come out and visit with me near the end of October because I would be getting an execution date, I started reaching out to some people in society that I knew might be able to help me get something done about the way we were being treated in prison. Had I thought about it thoroughly and what the repercussions might have been, I more or less never would have contacted the person I did. After explaining to someone in society what I had seen happen and who I wanted to contact in regards to the treatment and confinement of Texas Death Row and Ad-Seg prisoners, I was given the cellphone number for Texas State Senator John Whitmire. The first time I contacted this man without knowing that he was also a Texas Department of Criminal Justice Board member. I told him that I had witnessed several correctional officers beat the shit out of an inmate and then left him inside his cell with the restraints on and no medical attention at any time for 24 hours. We spoke several times cellphone to cellphone before he asked me to contact his office on a landline telephone. I never seriously thought about what I was doing other than the fact that I was going to be executed soon and wanting to bring to attention the beatings inmates were taking at the hands of those who were supposed to secure us and watch over us until our own execution dates arrived. Next thing I know as the days are going by, along with Little Hitler, O.I.G., and Warden Simmons, and some Directors of the Texas Department of Criminal Justice, my cell water was shut off, and I was escorted out of the cell and placed into the shower while my cell was searched by numerous officers, at which point a single Tracphone was found on the side of my cell bunk. All hell would soon follow.

Once the cellphone was found, I was then escorted down to the

Major's office in the front of 12-Building, where officers with O.I.G. started questioning me about the phone and how I got it and what I was doing with it. I was also informed that my mom was being arrested at the Austin, Texas airport for her part in buying her son prepaid minutes, though she nor my sister who O.I.G. also later placed a warrant out for her arrest (though she turned herself in.) My mom and sister, along with my grandma, were coming to visit with me because I had just ended my appeals, and we knew I would be getting an execution date soon. Throughout the day and coming following days that I was pressured into giving up the ownership of the cellphone and who brought it in and what it cost, I was told that if I worked with them that it would help my mom and sister. The two people I love more than anything in the world had been arrested behind some stupid shit I did. Neither my mom nor my sister had ever been in trouble with the law, and their arrest would eat at me for the rest of my natural born life that I was in prison here in this shit hole state people call Texas. I couldn't give anything to O.I.G. for the simple fact I didn't know anything, but after so much of their in my face shit and the threat towards my mom and sister, I admitted that the phone belonged to Obie Weathers, who was another Death Row inmate. That was the only information I gave to O.I.G., other than stating that I saw officers beating the shit out of an Ad-Seg inmate and leave him without medical attention for over 24 hours.

Not only did my actions with contacting State Senator John Whitmire cause the Texas Department of Criminal Justice to lock down the Polunsky Unit, but also they locked down their other 102 prisons throughout the state of Texas. The media did what they did the best: tell lies about what was really going on, and how I used the telephone to contact State Senator John Whitmire to get his help in visiting with my loved ones and help with my appeals. Rumors started flowing among both inmates and officers. I was transported for security reasons to a prison hospital called Jester-4 in Richmond, Texas, where prison officials said that I had attempted to hang myself after being caught with said cellphone. This was a bold-faced lie. Throughout my life and even while in prison in both California and Florida, it was known that I was what people in society call a cutter. This means that I would take either a sharp knife or a razor blade and cut myself to release my pain or anger or just to feel something. It didn't mean that I was suicidal, only that I liked to cut on myself. Not one time in my life have I ever tried to hang myself. If I didn't see some blood then I wouldn't start to feel better.

After returning from Jester-4 one week later to the Polunsky Unit/Texas Death Row, I was escorted to A-Pod, B-Section #26, which is located on Two Row. Each section of every pod on 12-Building consists of 6 sections starting from A-F, and on each section there is two seven single-cells per row. On Row One is seven cells and a shower, and on Two Row is seven cells and a shower. Out in front of the cells is a dayroom that is just a bigger caged-in yard but inside. This is where inmates go to rec inside for sometimes 1-2 hours per day alone. There is no contact with one another on Texas Death Row. Each prisoner is celled alone in a cell. There are no T.V.'s or telephones for us to use in the dayrooms nor inside our cells. However, after my return to 12-Building Death Row, and my escort to A-Pod, B-Section #26, where I was placed into this cell, I was instructed to place my hands through the slot so the handcuffs could be removed. At which time I did this, I was then instructed to strip out and hand all my clothing through the slot to the LT standing on the other side next to Assistant Warden Timothy Lester. Once this was done, the slot was closed.

While standing there butt-naked, I was told by Assistant Warden Lester that while I was in this cell I would remain butt-naked and on a 15-minute shakedown and one on one until further notice. This meant that aside from the video camera that they had placed in the cell above my sink/toilet, that would be monitored by the officers in the control picket but also the Warden's office, I would also have an officer, either male or female, sitting in front of my cell 24/7. They were to watch me 24/7 while either standing or sitting in a chair that was provided for them. They had with them a canister of chemical agents, along with C.O.P., a flashlight, a hand-held radio, and a log book/sheet. I was to remain inside that cell butt-naked with the AC blowing full blast while it was winter time. The officers inside the control picket were instructed to leave my inside cell light on 24/7 and that nobody was to enter that section unless they were an LT or higher. Where the section would normally house 14 grown single men, it now only held one single isolated prisoner of Texas Death Row, butt-naked, who was allowed no property, clothing, or anything else within his cell until further notice.

After being deprived of sleep and only being given a food-loaf to eat and two showers a week, while also being shook down no less than 20 times through the day and night in a 24 hour period, I requested to speak with someone from O.I.G. At this point, I was not only sleep-deprived, but was also starting to lose my mind. While I was at Jester-4, I was told by O.I.G. that if I worked with them, then it would be easier on my mom and sister. At this time I hadn't been told anything that was going on with my loved ones other than that they had both been arrested and had both bonded out after a little bit. This news on top of everything that was going on with my new housing situation was enough to cause anyone to start going insane. Instead of O.I.G. coming to see me, they sent a sheet of paper for me to write down what I wanted to say, along with a pen. It was now November 6th, 2008.

I wrote like a man without sleep and going nuts without a care in the world about what might come from the letter I was writing. I went off on O.I.G., and in my rant about them and everything I said something along the lines of 'fuck Senator John Whitmire and Mike Ward of the Austin American Statesman Newspaper.' That I wanted to see them put those two dicks into protective fucking custody behind O.I.G.'s fucking lies and their lies about why I contacted them. This letter not only brought me longer time butt-naked and isolated from everyone on Death Row, but it caused my mail to be watched even closer and for another set of charges to be placed against me for Terroristic Threats, along with the charges of a prohibited item in a correctional facility. My only interaction with anyone for the first six months I was butt-naked inside a cell was with the officers assigned to sit in front of my cell 24/7. Though it was after the first week into December 2008 that would bother me for the rest of my life on top of the trouble I caused on my mom and sister for loving me and for the trouble I ended up causing my fellow Death Row brothers.

While talking with C/O Rachel Alexander, who was this white chick with DD tits and a nice ass, with her one crooked tooth, an officer that usually always worked down on F-Pod came over to A-Pod and was allowed to enter B-Section and come up the stairs to Two Row to holler at me. His name was S.O. Woods. He was an older C/O that was really laid back and cool with all of us prisoners. It didn't matter what ethnicity you were or what your crime, he treated us all the same, and when you were on level he did his best to give you an extra tray of food or some extra rec time or pass commissary from one prisoner to another that wasn't supposed to have any commissary because he was on Level-2 or Level-3.

As he came up to my cell for just a few minutes, he said, "Tabler, I just want you to know that this had nothing to do with you or what is going on. Keep your head up and try to do your best, but know these people are going to fuck you over every which way they can. Again, this has nothing to do with you." Then he left. I looked at C/O Alexander like, what the fuck? I had no idea what he was talking about, as it was a little after midnight on a December night in 2008, and I was trying my best to keep my naked ass warm and not freeze to death in that cell.

Less than one hour later, LT Brown and a few other officers came up to my cell to shake me down and question me about what S.O. Woods was talking to me about. I explained that he didn't say anything to me other than to say that what was going on had nothing to do with me. C/O Alexander supported me in everything that I had said. What happened was that S.O. Woods had gone out to the parking lot on his break after leaving my cell and being the last person he spoke to. Once in the parking lot he got into his truck, opened his glove box, took his pistol, and blew his brains out, killing himself in the parking lot of the Polunsky Unit Prison in Livingston, Texas, in December of 2008. Even though he said that I had nothing to do with why he went out that night and took his own life, I would still harbor some guilt thinking that I was in some way or another responsible for his actions. It would be years later that I would hear from his wife, who was also an officer here at the Polunsky Unit, that he was having some problems out in society with their marriage and other issues, though it wouldn't help ease my mind any.

After six months of being butt-naked and shook down every 15 minutes, they issued me some state clothing and a mattress with sheets and blanket, and I was allowed a hot meal instead of food loaf. I was still being isolated and had to have an office in front of my cell while a video camera continued to watch me from within. Around the start of month seven, in 2009, every time they came to escort me to the shower, they would shake me down. I was still not allowed mail during this time other than legal mail from lawyers or the courts. I starting jacking the run every time I exited the shower. Refusing to walk back up the stairs to Two Row and my cell in #26. By sitting on the run and refusing to walk back to my cell, this would cause them to have to have a major Use of Force, because they would have to place me in leg irons and then carry me up the stairs to my cell and place me inside it, then remove the leg irons. This in turn would cause each officer that was involved in having to write up a Use of Force report while video was taken of them carrying me. My state of mind was, since they were going to continue with this shake down shit every time I came out of my cell to shower and that I was beyond any normal level and not allowed my own property, then there was no sense in me behaving and trying to do good. Fuck with me, and I was going to fuck with them. It was the only way I could hold onto some sort of my sanity without going batshit crazy from lack of sleep and total isolation from everyone other than the correctional officers assigned to sit in front of my cell 24/7. Texas Department of Criminal Justice prison officials had gone out of their way to devoid me of any kind of stimulation, intentionally trying their very best to drive me to the brink of mental collapse.

Once I was finally approved to go out to visitation to visit with lawyers, after months of not being allowed this, Assistant Warden Timothy Lester instructed the officers working on Death Row that I could only be escorted out to visitation by an LT or SGT, but not just the officers, and I was to be placed in leg irons because I was an escape risk. (Where the fuck am I going to run to? The electric fence?) As is always the issue with prison officers and those who operate the Polunsky Unit/Texas Death Row, people fuck up and just simply don't care. I had been escorted out to visit with my court-appointed lawyer, Kenneth Nash, for my charges of terroristic threats and prohibited items in a correctional facility. I was being escorted back by two OJT's (Officer Junior Training.) There was nobody with them other than myself. No LT, and certainly no SGT, nor any officer that I knew, and I knew a shitload of them cause they had been sitting in front of my cell every day for almost one year now. Walking back from visitation on the walkway that runs alongside of 11-Building from the visitation building, I had the urge to spit. So, leaning away from the officer and ahead of him, I spit in the grass on my right. Well, the dumbass on my left decided that my leaning away from his gave him the right to take his baton and strike me in the back of my legs, causing me to fall forwards into a kneeling position. This caused me to pull completely away now from both escorting officers because I was falling forward with no way to prevent myself from doing so because I was in leg irons and handcuffed behind my back. From that point on, they beat my ass on that walkway next to 11-Building with no give as if their very lives were depending on it. In the end, they didn't hit my face or head, but struck every part of my lower body and legs. A baton is made to jab a prisoner with; they are not made to beat the fuck out of someone with like you're going to a baseball game. I was placed on a gurney and returned to my cell on A-Pod B-Section #26 without any medical attention. In their eyes and my fellow inmates', everything that was happening to me I deserved 110%.

Then, on September 28, 2009, I was escorted out to the 258th District Court of Polk County, Texas, under the Honorable Elizabeth E. Coker. Under a plea deal I would accept, both my mom and sister only got probation and community service, and had to pay a fine. I pled guilty to a prohibited item in a correctional facility and to terroristic threats. I was sentenced to two ten-year sentences on top of my death sentence. Those twenty years were to run consecutive with my death sentence.

Once I was returned to my cell in total isolation, and under camera and the watchful eye of the officer assigned to sit in front of my cell, I tried to figure out a way to get a telephone call to my loved ones through the Administration. On November 1st, the mailroom brought me legal mail from the 264th District Court of Bell County, Texas and the Honorable Martha J. Trudo. Before the Texas Department of Criminal Justice or my own lawyers, David Schulman and John Jasuta, knew, I was served through the mail my own Execution Warrant, explaining that on May 20th, 2010 I was to be executed by the State of Texas until I was DEAD.

Chapter Ten

I don't know what it was about reading about my own execution/death that caused me to reflect on my time in the SHU (pronounced shoe) for 16 months up north in Crescent City, California. This is where one of the toughest prisons are to be found in the United States of America: Pelican Bay State Prison. The shit I went through while in there when, by all current records, I shouldn't have been. Whenever I try to explain things to my current lawyers, they look at me as if I have three heads and am speaking in another language they don't understand. Don't get me wrong, I have a wonderful legal team, but they're just too naïve about things and how a serious prison is run. What happens inside prison walls are beyond the imaginations of most lawyers who represent those of us who break the law and never really learn any better to change our ways. They don't understand that prison officials will and do cover up and doctor paperwork if they are aware that what they're doing is breaking the law themselves. The shit I went through at Pelican Bay when I was there would fuck with any normal person's head, regardless of how strong they think they are. When I first arrived there, I was left out in the snow in nothing but my boxers inside this fucking cage for hours, freezing my ass off and on the edge of hypothermia, before being removed from the outside to the inside. During my time there I saw prisoners get their legs broke, fingers broke, and guys shot point blank by guards. I've had my 7th rib broke, shoulder dislocated, and my ass beat down and while down on the ground repeatedly hit with an electronic stun gun.

The hardest thing for me in the SHU was mail time and being allowed to write and mail letters. Once a week, officers would roll a board up to my cell door with my incoming mail/letters and pictures stuck to the board with tape. They would then open the window on my cell door, allowing me to see out into the hallway where they would be standing, thus allowing me to see my property. I would be asked if I wanted to send a letter, and if I answered yes, they would hand me the letter without the envelope it came in, to read over. Once this was done I was told to hand the letter back. In return I would be given a 1 inch rubber pen and a single sheet of writing paper. I was granted one hour to write my letters in this fashion. Each time I finished a letter, I would have to hand it back to them, along with the pen, to read over. They would then in turn hand me a stamped envelope to address and hand back to them, along with the rubber pen. They would read it over, then seal it and place it in the pile to be mailed out. Once I was finished or my hour was up, whichever one came first, I would be instructed to return the pen and paper, the slot in my cell door would be closed and locked, and the window over my cell door would be closed. I was allowed to write letters and read mail only once a week, and that was only if I had been good without causing any problems that month or week, however they looked at it.

Unlike here in Texas where prisoners wear white and can purchase clothing while on level or in Ad-Seg from the prison commissary, while you're housed in the SHU at Pelican Bay State Prison, you're dressed in an orange jumpsuit and these ugly-ass yellow slip-on shoes. Pelican Bay was built and run to break the human spirit. You can find the prison on the Oregon border with California; the place is always surrounded in fog and huge-ass redwood trees and hills. While most politicians here in Texas want the public to believe that Texas Death Row and the General Population of its prison at the Polunsky Unit is the most secure facility, with only its one electric fence going around 12-Building as well as one on the roof, other than two twelve-foot fences topped with razor-wire, Texas security is trash. That's why there's always contraband of one kind of another being brought into its facilities.

If I remember correctly, the security while I was housed in the SHU at Pelican Bay State Prison consisted of seven layers of what was considered the most high-tech security there was back then. #1 is a pressure-detection system buried under the gravel border inside the first perimeter fence. #2, an above ground microwave detection system. #3, a twelve-foot fence, topped with razor wire. #4, a deadly electrical fence, capable of zapping a prisoner with 750 milliamperes of electricity (60 will do the job.) #5, another twelve-foot fence with razor wire. #6, a roving patrol that circles the prison twenty-four hours a day, seven days a week. #7, a coaxial cable connected to the first interior fence that detects when someone is trying to climb it.

Shortly before I had arrived at Pelican Bay, a U.S. District Judge had ordered that a Psychiatric Security Unit be built into the prison as well. The prison can hold around 3,800 prisoners and is divided into four parts within its grounds. The minimum security unit, a maximum security unit, the psychiatric security unit, and the security housing unit, also known as the SHU. The SHU alone housed 1,500 prisoners, though its prisoners were not the worst to be found within its walls. This honor would be taken by the guards that got away with literally murder within its walls. During my time there, guards were being charged with various crimes against prisoners. Violence beyond one's imagination, beatings, and even arranging to have a prisoner shot.

Some information about the Polunsky Unit, which was once called the Terrell Unit. 80 percent of the guards are white, though 82 percent of the prisoners are not. Virtually all of the guards come from small towns all over Texas, places like Diboll, Point Blank, Fred, and Kingwood, just to name a few. Back when the Terrell Unit was opened, a correctional officer could make a little over $22,000 a year, plus benefits like health insurance and a meal or two. Back then, this was more money earned than most people working in Polk County. At the time of its opening, Terrell Unit was supposed to be among the most modern and sophisticated prisons in Texas, a vast 463-acre complex capable of holding 2,250 prisoners. All of its doors are electronically controlled. Each cell block/dorm is bugged with listening devices and monitored by video cameras.

When the Terrell Unit was built here in Livingston, Texas, a Baptist stronghold in the heart of Polk County, one in every six people lived in poverty, one in every five lived in a mobile home, and fifty percent never make it through high school. To the people in Polk County, getting married, having a family, and living in a trailer home, then turning around and getting a divorce and paying child-support was the life for these so-called Texans of Polk County. While Texan prisons are vast places of inhumane conditions for those of us sent to them, for those of us sentenced to death and housed in 12-Building, along with those in Ad-Seg, it's a place of cruel and unusual punishment, but an economic salvation for those in society looking for jobs. Back in 1999, a federal judge found the Ad-Seg Units (12-Building) in Texas to be virtual incubators of psychoses. They inflicted such cruel and unusual punishment, he held, that confinement in them violated the Constitution. And yet, this is where we are caged like animals on Texas Death Row.

The thoughts running through my mind upon reading about my own execution, along with the feelings, were one of remembering and feeling what it was like to be on a roller-coaster once you reach the peak and drop down on the other side. The butterflies you feel, along with the touch of heat from a mixture of adrenaline and fear at the fact that you are now on your way to meet death face to face. Though this was something I had sought after, it still hit me hard to read about my own death. It made me think about all the times you're having a dream or nightmare while you're sleeping. You can see yourself running from something or someone, because your body is telling you to fear whatever it is that is chasing you. But when the time comes, and you know you've run into a dead end, your mind/body always wakes itself up before allowing you to see yourself dead. Isn't that crazy? Yet, here I was reading about how the state of Texas had been given the green light to kill me. That is beyond fucking crazy just sitting here thinking about it all. After two weeks, it no longer bothered me that I was going to be executed the following year on May 20th, 2010. I was content and had accepted it. I never realized just how much it had an impact on me reading that execution warrant though.

Not even three or four months later, the mailroom brought me some more legal mail, this time from a District Court Judge in Waco, Texas, named Walter S. Smith, Jr. It would seem that there were some lawyers out there in society that were putting pressure on my two lawyers that did what I asked, which was nothing, after I explained I wanted to waive my rights to further appeals and volunteer for execution. To this day, I still have no idea which lawyers placed pressure on them to do what they did, but I honestly wished that whoever the fuck they were, they would have minded their own fucking business. Without my authorization, nor talking to me about it, both David Schulman and John Jasuta filed an emergency motion to the judge in Waco, Texas, and this asshole judge granted their motion, which in turn gave me a stay of execution! I was served this stay of execution from Judge Walter S. Smith, Jr. in the mail. I sat my ass down and wrote out a letter to the judge, cursing his ass left and right, telling him nobody had any right to file something without talking to me about it first, and that he needs to remove the stay of execution he ordered. Fuck the lawyers that were placing pressure on my lawyers for doing nothing! In my mind, I couldn't understand why, why, why! Reading about my execution fucked me up, and now to know that I would have to remain in this shithole and continue living with the way these people were fucking me over was too much. I started making plans to end my life.

First I had to get one of the officers sitting one on one with me to bring me a razor or a box-cutter blade because I was still isolated on the section by myself. SSI's couldn't even come on that section to clean up, the officers had to do everything on that section. Everything I did I had to do through the officers. The first officer I tried to get to do this for me was this white girl with big ears that was named Deborah Hamilton. She was sitting on me during the day shift, and I thought, what the heck? I flat-out asked her if she would bring me a razor to shave?

"Are you out of your fucking mind, Tabler!?"

"What's the big deal? All I'm asking for is a razor to shave with. You're sitting right there, plus I got this fuck-all camera watching me inside my cell. What's up, Hamilton?"

"Fuck you, FUCK NO, TABLER!!"

See, not all officers will do just anything. I went through a shit ton of officers asking for someone to bring what I was looking for, and the person I least expected to help me with anything is the one that brought me what I needed. Sgt. Richard Hale was breaking out one of the officers that had been doing overtime and was watching me. Just shooting the shit with him, I told him that I was wanting to end my life, but some lawyers decided it was their business to pressure my lawyers into filing something without my say-so to a judge. Next thing I know, I'm being given a stay of execution I hadn't asked for. "Not like you seriously care though. If you did, you'd drop me a razor or box-cutter blade."

Twenty or so minutes later, the officer returned from her break, and Sgt. Hale left. Just before shift-change, the SGT returning with a johnny-sack for my dinner. I was supposed to be getting a hot tray but thought nothing of it cause I was in a funk still about everything and not knowing how I was going to be able to get the items needed to end my life. Sitting on my bunk, I opened the sack and started pulling things out: peanut butter sandwich, some prunes, a milk, and another sandwich. On the bottom of the bag was a brand-new box-cutter blade! I was as happy as pigs in shit, lol!

Sometime during the night, I was able to fall asleep, and when I woke up, the officer sitting in front of my cell was Officer Stanley Kimes. He opened my food slot and handed me a roast beef sandwich he had brought from home, and a Coke. In his own words, he thought it was fucked up the way they were treating me and singling me out from everyone. From everything that he was hearing, I was not the one talking and giving everyone up. I told him I knew this because, for one, I hadn't been here long enough to know the people who were getting busted, nor had I known any of them. But people are going to believe what they want to believe, regardless if it's the truth or not. Inmates here in Texas and officers don't do things the way we do it in prison in California or Florida, where you only go by the black and white, also known as paperwork. "It is what it is though. Thanks for the roast beef and Coke."

Officer Kimes and I spoke about a lot of shit that day and some following days. He said he couldn't understand how we could do time in prison as long as some of us had been doing it. He would have taken his own life or tried to escape a long time ago if the tables were turned. I told him there was no way for me to get outside this building; otherwise I damn sure would try to escape. Anything is better than sitting here waiting for that day you know is going to come. Just before he left to start working at another unit here in Texas, he asked me if I needed anything. I told him if he could get me some rubber bands, I'd appreciate it. Sometime before he left for good, he came around and gave me some big rubber bands. That was the last thing on my list that I needed supply-wise for how I was planning on taking my own life.

The morning of November 13th, 2009 came around with Officer Heath Beard working on the floor of A-Pod while also working with Officer David Aguero, and Officer Crystal Nettles working in the control picket. Just after noon sometime, the officers working the pod had taken their breaks and switched places. C/O Beard went into the picket while C/O Nettles came to work on the floor with C/O Aguero, so they swap out recs and slop trays. They were short staffed, so they didn't have an officer sitting in front of my cell all day, just for the morning. They figured I was under the watchful eye of the video camera inside my cell, and that should be enough. Standing at my cell door and waiting until I could see the officers were no longer working on this side of the pod and that C/O Beard was busy watching the officers on the other side of the pod, I turned away from my cell door and grabbed the rubber band from underneath my mattress and placed it up and around my bicep on my left arm to stop the blood from flowing in my arm and to pop up my vein. Once this was done, I reached under my desk and pulled the box-cutter that I had taped there down, turned around, and sat on my toilet. I turned my arm so that my left forearm was facing up towards me and slit my arm from my left wrist up to 1 ¼ inches from my elbow joint. I then pulled the rubber band off my arm as the blood started pouring out of my arm/body like a waterfall. Before losing consciousness, I threw up and heard the gate down by the opening to this section popping over and over and over as C/O Beard tried no doubt to get the officers' attention. One minute I was sitting on the toilet, the next I was on the concrete floor with my blood all over me and C/O Aguero banging on my cell door calling my name. "Tabler! Tabler! Wake the fuck up, Tabler!"

Slowly as I came around and noticed C/O Aguero, I also noticed the box-cutter still clutched in my right hand. Doing my best to stand up, I turned around, now facing the officer, and made one more attempt to finish myself off for good. This time I hit the main artery as well as the bone in my arm. C/O Aguero emptied his C.O.P. onto me, I guess in the hopes this would stop me from, what… dying? Lol. I found out later that I flat-lined twice when medical and security were able to get me out of the cell: once on the gurney on the way out of 12-Building, and once in 10-Building where the prison hospital was found.

Once I was considered stable and the on-call doctor showed up because security refused to transport me to an outside hospital, you found everyone inside the ER with me, from O.I.G. Terri Gardner, to Warden Simmons and Assistant Warden Lester, SGT. Chyrinie Youngblood, LT. Raymond Duff, and numerous other officers. The cut in my arm was 7 inches long and was closed with 15 staples. I was placed on suicide watch within the medical building for only twenty-four hours before being returned to that same cell, where I had to clean up all my own blood from the day before. This time though they made sure that I was with an officer watching me twenty-four seven now, as well as the video camera. After cleaning up the blood and my cell, I felt like there was nothing left inside of me. That my life had no meaning or purpose other than that the state of Texas would do anything to see to it that I was unable to end my own life, because they wanted the privilege of being the ones to insert the needle into my arm through lethal injection. In their eyes, they alone got this opportunity because, according to the status, by contacting that shithead state senator John Whitmire, I caused many heads to roll onto the plate before Governor Rick Perry as he called many of them to stand before him in the Governor's Office to explain how a Death Row Prisoner was able to get his hands on a cellphone within his cell to make such a call. Furthermore, it caused the State of Texas and the Texas Department of Criminal Justice to spend more than $60.2 million dollars on all new security for its 103 prisons, starting with the Polunsky Unit and its 12-Building where Texas Death Row prisoners are housed. I was informed that I would remain under video camera till the day I died while I was a prisoner within TDCJ-ID and on Texas Death Row, and that while Warden Simmons and Assistant Warden Timothy Lester were working this prison, I would never be allowed to make a telephone call to my mother or sister or anyone in my family; it didn't matter if there was a death in my family!

Knowing all of this while I was cleaning up my cell from my suicide attempt, I rolled my mattress up so that I could stand on top of it to see outside my cell window and look at the sky and watch the sunset in the west, while looking outside and thinking about all the problems I caused everyone since I came to Texas in August of 2004. The pain I caused certain families along with my own, the ache of loneliness and pain within myself, as well as all the built up anger and rage. Thinking about how my visitation was revoked with my mom, sister, and grandma, and everyone else until further notice. I seriously saw no point in remaining alive when in all honesty, I'm guilty of the crime and charges of Capital Murder and deserved to be where I was sent, Texas Death Row. Looking outside that window and watching the sunset, just barely moving my lips, as I was watching the clouds in the sky and the sunset, I spoke to God. I asked that if He was real, to please open my eyes and let me see something. To open my ears and allow me to hear something other than the emptiness. Please just give me some reason as to why I am here, why I should remain alive. Please, God, just give me a purpose. Show me anything to make me believe that you are real, God.

As soon as I said that, as I was watching the sunset, the sky took on a different shape and appearance. It was as if I was now up in the sky, looking down onto the land, where Jesus had parted the Red Sea. The clouds were blood red and had parted to reveal a city of nothing but gold as far as my eyes could see. I saw buildings with white light shining out of their goldenness, and a golden wall all the way around the city as far as my eyes could see. As soon as I said I saw, it all disappeared in a flash, as if it was never there. The next thing I saw, it was pitch dark outside. As I turned around to get off my bunk, I took notice of LT. Brown and a bunch of officers standing at my cell door watching me. I found out that I had been standing up there looking outside for 7 hours, and the officer that had been watching me said he had been trying to get my attention, but I had refused to acknowledge him or anyone else for all these hours. To me it seemed only minutes or seconds, if that. That night I slept for the first time in one year without any bad thoughts or nightmares.

I would remain on this section in isolation from everyone else and on a one on one security watch with a video camera inside my cell and cameras on the run for another year and a half before I would be moved. On the day, I was told during a minister visit, which were the only visits I was now allowed other than legal. On a day that was supposed to be good with the meeting of my spiritual advisor, Mary Hampton, for the first time. Other than my visit with her and knowing that someone cared enough to drive four hours to come and visit a total stranger, my world would start to be challenged in ways that no human should ever have to go through, regardless of the shitstorms he may have caused. Mary explained to me that she had spoken with my mom, and that early that morning, January 2nd, 2011, my mom's sister, who is my Auntie, lost her battle with breast cancer and died in the hospital out in Florida. After being escorted out of the visitation after our visit, I was informed that the prison knew about the death of my loved one and that the warden wanted me to know that I was not going to be allowed to contact my loved ones even though there had been a death in the family. They didn't care, they said; they did, however, have a surprise for me. I was moving to a new cell after 2 ½ years of being isolated in B-Section by myself. I was now being moved over onto the section better known as Death Watch. This is the section that houses the men with a set execution date. Each cell has its own in-cell video camera that watches the prisoner twenty-four seven. There are also video cameras on each run and in the dayroom. Death Watch is the only section to have video cameras inside the prisoner's cell. These cameras are monitored by the officers in the control picket on the pod, 12-Control, the Major's office, the Warden's office, and the Directors' office in Huntsville, Texas. Moving to this section was not better for me; it has become my hell on earth, and the most severe cruel and unusual punishment and constant restrictions, and punishment by the Directors of the Texas Department of Criminal Justice and the Chairman Patrick O'Daniel, as well as State Senator John Whitmire.

WITHIN THE SHADOWS OF LIFE

"If you gaze long enough into an abyss, the abyss will gaze back into you."
-Friedrich Nietzsche

Chapter Eleven

Death Row prisoners in Texas used to be executed with a three-drug cocktail that was designed to sedate and render the condemned unconscious, theoretically reducing the pain when the final fatal dose was administered. These drugs were sodium thiopental, pancuronium bromide, and potassium chloride. Now though, the politicians in Texas feel the need to cause the condemned as much pain as possible by using a one-drug cocktail call pentobarbital. This so-called drug is a sedative that's said to slow the activity of the brain and nervous system and is often used by veterinarians to euthanize animals.

As we move on to the next part of this book and my life story, I thought it would be best to start with the herein, as opposed to the very beginning of my moving onto Death Watch, where now the pain is fresh from the recent execution of Quintin Jones, also known as "GQ" to those who knew him and were his friends. His execution took place on Wednesday night just before 7:00pm, May 19th, 2021. May GQ rest in peace. Before moving into everything going on here at the Polunsky Unit, allow me to put a little spotlight onto what an individual goes through the day of his execution by the administration and the Directors of the Texas Department of Criminal Justice. Many people out there in society have no idea what the condemned go through, nor the humiliation by those that keep us within these walls, and what about if the condemned gets a stay of execution. Won't what he went through effect him upon his return to the Polunsky Unit/Texas Death Row? Turn the page to read about what Quintin Jones went through the day of May 19th, 2021.

Once you're removed from either being out at your last visit with family and friends, or you chose to remain on the pod and spent your time in the dayroom like GQ did, you're then escorted out into the hallway by an LT and SGT. In the case of GQ, on that midmorning of May 19th, 2021, he went out to the visitation for a little bit to visit his people before asking to return to the Pod and the dayroom, where he spent his last hour before they came to escort him off the pod where he was speaking to the guys on A-Section, also known as Death Watch.

In the case of GQ, one of the most disrespectful and undercover-racist officers came to escort him off the pod, LT. James D. Sliger. This officer, if he can even be called that, walks like he owns the world, and yet he refuses to even see to it that his clothing is starched and ironed like those of his co-workers. Usually you'll find LT. Sliger with his other trash buddy, SGT. Matthew W. Ruble. On this day though, it was a freshly new SGT that had the misfortune to be with LT. James D. Sliger. On his way off the pod, GQ hollered at many of the fellas on the other sections, some saying good-bye, and others keeping a positive attitude, saying they'll see him when he returns with a stay of execution.

GQ was escorted down to the metal cage that is out in the hallway between C-Pod and D-Pod, which is bolted to the floor. This is a heavy mesh cage approximately six feet wide and seven feet tall. Once you're locked in this cage and the handcuffs are removed, all your personal property you're wearing is taken away. You're then strip-searched by a lieutenant. Standing butt-naked in front of the head warden, assistant warden, regional directors, executive director, and many other prison officials both male and female, in a last resort to degrade and dehumanize you. You're instructed to run your fingers through your hair slowly front to back and on the sides. Turn your head to each side and run your fingers behind each ear. The lieutenant will produce a flashlight to look into your ears and even into your nose. You're instructed to open your mouth, wiggle your tongue, and pull your cheeks outward as the lieutenant looks into your mouth. Raise each arm so that he or she may inspect your underarms, then lift your penis and testicles, turn around, bend over and spread your butt-cheeks, lift each foot, wiggle your toes, run your fingers between each toe.

Then you're instructed to walk around inside of the cage, from corner to corner, butt-naked. They have this detection device outside of the cage at one corner. It's a gray plastic pole with a pyramid-like base that's nearly as tall as the cage, with small lights near the top. While you walk around butt-naked, if you touched the metal of the cage, the device will beep. After this done, you're given a new pair of prison whites to dress in before being handcuffed. Either a Captain or a Major will explain to the condemned the way they want you to place your hands to be cuffed. Your hands are to be cuffed with the backs turned inward and the thumbs pointing downward. Once the cuffs are double-locked in front of you, you're told to rotate your right hand until your hands are stacked on top of each other with the backs still facing each other, and your fingers now pointing to the opposite elbow. They do everything out of the sight of your friends to dehumanize and degrade you on the last day of your life. Once you're out of the cage, you're then instructed to kneel down so that leg irons can be placed on your legs. After the leg irons are secured, they assist you in standing up. Then a chain leading from the leg irons is connected to the handcuffs and locked into place with a padlock. This is to keep your hands from rising above your waist while standing. Most of the time they shorten the chain so that you have to shuffle along in a hunched over/stooped position.

These restraints are then checked by four officials. The Captain, which in the case of GQ would have been Captain Jekerria R. Carter, an assistant warden, senior warden Daniel D. Dickerson, and one of the transportation officers. You're then escorted out of 12-Building, where Death Row prisoners are housed, to a waiting van. Inside the van with you are four guards. An assistant warden from the Walls Unit sits in the front passenger seat, armed with an AR-15 rifle with a fully-loaded thirty round magazine. A Captain will be driving, armed with a 357 Magnum revolver. Sitting in front of GQ, turned sideways so they can watch him, is another Captain, also armed with a 357 revolver and a speed loader with six extra rounds. The ammunition used by the guards is hydro-shock man-killers. The final guard will be a lieutenant sitting in the rear of the van, armed with a 12-Gauge shotgun loaded with magnum loads.

The sad thing about this whole situation is that the young black man known as GQ to those of us left behind wasn't the same person that he was when he was locked up by the State of Texas. After twenty years in prison, GQ was a changed person, so how can you justify killing someone after twenty years from the time of his crime, when he's not the same person? Leave it to the State of Texas to start executing prisoners again, and who cares that there's a pandemic going on, and police all over the United States of America are killing unarmed black men and women. Still, Texas wants to be in the spotlight by executing a young black man as a way of making a statement... Slavery and Execution is what Texas is all about.

Furthermore, those in society never see what a prisoner on Texas Death Row sees out in the visitation or when they are escorting a Death Row man from visitation to 12-Building to strip-search him and chain him up before placing him in the van. On the walkway outside of 11-Building, a prisoner within one of the cells inside of 11-Building or on 12-Building B-Pod can view the officers and wardens and directors and other prison officials high-fiving one another, shaking hands, congratulating one another and patting each other on the back, celebrating the execution that is going to take place a few hours from then. Society fails to understand that 99.9% of Death Row prisoners are not the same people they were when they were first locked up. You're not executing the person a jury convicted and sentenced to death. How can we be, when it's been 17 or 20+ years from the time you sentenced us? Many of the men that are housed on Texas Death Row and here on Death Watch with me are talented. We've learned to draw, paint, make dream catchers, write poetry and books. We've taken classes through the mail because Texas refuses to rehabilitate us because those in society deemed us a continuing threat to society. That right there is why we've been sentenced to death. By being placed on Texas Death Row, we're considered in the eyes of the Texas Department of Criminal Justice and the Courts to be the worst of the worst; and yet it was Jesus Christ himself who worked with the criminal throughout the Holy Bible. Most of the prisoners are also very religious, though lately I have seen many prisoners give in to temptation and turn away from their religion to drugs, such as K2 which is a synthetic marijuana, as well as fentanyl, cocaine, and pills. In my opinion, the ones that turn to these are beyond weak and have no room to even talk trash about myself or anyone else. One day they claim to be a Christian, and in the very same sentence turn around and say they're a convict. How can you be both? You're either the one or the other, but what is worse is when someone's true colors come to the surface. Under pressure, (and trust me, the pressure comes when you're housed on Death Watch) a person's real feelings come out. They get into it with others, calling them names and being straight up disrespectful, and yet see nothing wrong with their actions. Seeing this has turned me away from claiming any one set religion. If people ask me what I believe in, I tell them that I have a relationship with God and that I believe in the Son Jesus Christ, but I no longer say I'm any one sect of religion, such as Christian or Catholic or Messianic or Jewish. I claim nothing because too many people are fake and hide behind the Word of God. What I do believe in though is Capital Punishment. I believe in the Death Penalty, and I strongly feel that all child molesters and sexually violent predators should be either taken out in the field and shot point blank by the family members of the ones they assaulted, or in the very least, given a sentence of death to be carried out within five years.

    Don't get this autobiography twisted thinking that this story is about how innocent I am or those around me are. Because you couldn't be further from the truth. I am not here to tell you about everyone around me, only myself and the shit I have gone through at the hands of the Texas Death Row administrators as well as its directors and the system as a whole that runs the Texas Department of Criminal Justice. Some of the shit I no doubt brought on myself, but for decades? Refusing to allow me to visit with my mother, sister, and grandma for 13 years because of my involvement with a cellphone?! Isolating me on a section that houses the men with set execution dates when I have not had an execution date myself since they placed me on this section as a means of punishment. How can they justify treating me in this way when other prisoners have been busted with cellphones numerous times and have never been charged with a free-world case? Have not lost their visitation for over a decade and counting. What about being given wrong information that my older sister died, when they knew this to be wrong. What kind of sick and twisted games are the prison officials playing at, by making me remain on Death Watch where my only contact is with men set to be killed by the State of Texas within three months to a year. Can you even fathom the pain and heartache I feel from watching guys I have gotten to know and even befriend some, to watch them walk off this section to go to their last visit knowing that in less than 10 hours they'd be executed. Over 100+ grown men have walked off this section since I have been housed on Death Watch to be executed from January 2nd, 2011, the day I was given news that my Auntie Donna Bird passed away from her loss with breast cancer. Information that was given to the wardens of this prison and who in turn refused to allow me to make a telephone call home, but moved me to Death Watch, until this very present day of 2021. I no longer fear what they can do to me or that more men I know will be taken from this section to be executed as much as I fear losing my sanity and my state of mind. I no longer suffer from the loss, but from survivor's guilt. Knowing that I have been left behind when I know in my heart and soul I deserve death more than the ones that have left before me. Numerous times I have tried but failed to end my appeals and volunteer for execution. Every time I think that I'm ready to have it all over, I become a sucker and allow my lawyers to talk me out of it for some reason or another, even though not one of my lawyers have ever been on this side of the wall and have no fucking clue what they're talking about. They don't understand that the reason I'm hated by the prison officials isn't only for my being caught with a cellphone on Texas Death Row, but because of that asshole Senator John Whitmire. This man claims to be religious and yet continues to hold his foot to my neck every time I write a letter to the Directors' Review Committee seeking to get my visitation reinstated with my mother and sister every six months. My Grandma passed away years ago, and again I was refused a telephone call home. I have been denied every time I seek to get my visitation back, and yet they never give a reason why. I could be a saint and never get into trouble, and they would refuse me, because of Board Member and State Senator John Whitmire. How can this man claim to be something and yet refuse to forgive me for my actions. It's not like I'm asking to be removed from Texas Death Row or even Death Watch. I am simply asking to be allowed to visit with my remaining family before they too die or something happens to them. And yet they have left me no other option other than to retain a law firm to file a federal lawsuit against them and Texas Death Row, which I have done.

Chapter Twelve

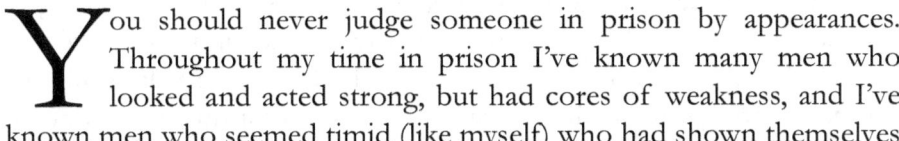

You should never judge someone in prison by appearances. Throughout my time in prison I've known many men who looked and acted strong, but had cores of weakness, and I've known men who seemed timid (like myself) who had shown themselves capable of great strength and of accomplishing terrible things.

Not every day in prison is a bad day, as we each make do with what we have. I try for the most part to treat everyone the same way. It doesn't matter to me if you're a prisoner or an officer. Unlike those around me who see the gray uniform that the officers wear as the enemy, I refuse to see them in that same light. How can I be mad at the officers for doing their job? They didn't put me in this place, my actions put me here. Each officer for his or her part is only doing this job to pay their bills, put a roof over their head or their family's head, and put food on the table. It's not my place to knock them for doing that, as it's more than I have done. My whole life I have been nothing but a failure in the eyes of family and friends, even in the eyes of some of my lawyers, though they refuse to say so. Kindness and compassion should start with us inside these walls, not the other way around. My fellow prisoners get pissed at me for talking with the officers so much, and in a form of retaliation they talk shit trying to get me pissed off. For the most part, I tune it out, though not every time. The old saying is you get more bees with honey than you do shit. Besides, we each have a heart that beats within our chest, it shouldn't matter if the person is black, white, Mexican, yellow, or purple. In stating this, I'm reminded of back in 2019 when Tracy Beaty, also known as "Tray", was housed over here on Death Watch in #5 Cage, and my amigo (friend) Fabian Hernandez, also known as "Spook", was housed over here in #7 Cage. Both of them had execution dates. For the record, my nickname is "Blue", and that is what most everyone calls me here. I was housed in #6 Cage like I am right now.

One day I was in the dayroom, and someone from over in B-Section sent some books over for Tray. I told Tray to shoot his line (fishing line made from braided thread or string) to the dayroom to get these books someone sent him from the other section. He said, "Well fuck, Blue, I ain't got no fucking line."

"Man, Tray, you a lazy ass muthafucker." I said, if I tossed them in front of his cell, could he get them in? Yes, he said. So I toss four books in front of his cell and go back to talking to Spook. As I'm talking to Spook, I notice that Tray was able to get the books up into the side of his cell door with a torn piece of sheet. The books are half in his cell but he cannot get them all the way in. Just as I point this out to Spook, the officer walks by and kicks Tray's door, and the books hit the ground. Tray starts going off on the officer and cussing her out. Spook and I are laughing our asses off, cause it's fucking comical all around. Tray looks like an older Albert Einstein with skin problems due to something he did during his crime. Tray hears us laughing and goes off on both of us, which causes us both to laugh all the more harder.

About three weeks later, we go on a lockdown and are now only getting showers once every other day during the week. Just so happens that the hot water is broke, so the showers are ice cold. Spook goes to the shower first, and you can hear him bitching about how cold the water is. He's telling me, "It's fucking cold as shit, Blue!" I'm not looking forward to taking a cold-ass shower, but I refuse to stink, and it sucks having to use your sink in the cell to take showers if you don't have a shower hose to plug into your sink. (Note: shower hoses made by us are coax cable, removed so you only have the rubber hosing. With this you place a pen top into one end and then jam the pen top into the sink, thus you now have a hose to wash off with.) The thing was, Tray would hardly ever go to the shower.

When the officers come and escort me to the shower, I get in, and that water is beyond freaking freezing! I'm now cursing Spook who's now laughing his ass off. I shut the water off and tell Spook to go along with me in a second. Starting the ice cold water back on and diving under the spray washing really fast, I start talking out loud about how hot the water is and how good it feels. I yell out, "Tray! Tray! Man, Tray, get your ass up, fool!"

"What the fuck, Blue?"

"Dude, you've got to come to the shower today, this shit is smokin' hot and feels really good."

When the officers come and escort me back to my cell, they get Tray next. I tell Tray as he passes my cell, just push the button on and dive under the water cause it's hot as hell. We hear the water come on, and next thing you hear is Tray, "Blue, you dick-sucking muthafucker, this water is fucking cold, muthafucker!! Fuck you, Blue, and fuck you, Spook!"

I'm laughing so hard I have tears coming out of my eyes. Tray comes out of the shower looking like Grumpy Cat, cursing up a shitstorm. Stops in front of my cell and looks at me, "FUCK YOU, BLUE!" Twenty minutes later he's laughing his ass off too cause someone else was now in the shower that was woken up by the officers for a shower and had no idea the water was freezing. We do our best to entertain ourselves within these walls. At least, I do.

Chapter Thirteen

I have decided to go about telling you everything in no set order. I find this easier than trying to deal with the past because some of the executions are too painful to remember, such as my best friend, Big Tai. What I do wish to explain is what happened to me on this past Friday, May 28th, 2021, at a little after 1:00pm. That racist shit LT. James Sliger was doing escorts along with fat OJT (Officer Junior Training.) I had double-checked with him when he came on the pod around noontime that I had a legal telephone call for 1:00 to 2:00pm with my litigation lawyer, David Lane, in Denver, CO. Thinking that by having this fresh in his mind he would come and get me in plenty of time. That ended up not being the case. LT. Sliger was still pissed at me for filing a sexual harassment complaint against him in 2020. I'll get to that in a few. Instead of coming to get me thirty minutes ahead of my scheduled legal call, this asshole waits until 5 minutes to 1:00, knowing that he still has to strip me out and then walk me out of 12-Building all the way to visitation. As he and the OJT are escorting me out of my cell, I simply say, can we speed it up a little. This fuck waits until we're off the pod and out of sight of the officers working the pod and the prisoners to stop me and start screaming at me in my face. Screaming with his spittle flying over the side of my face, that if I don't shut the fuck up he'll not only slam me but cancel my legal call with my lawyer! What could I say other than stay mute. We get out to my telephone call with my lawyer late. Once out there, I explain to my lawyer what this shithead said and did. What I don't understand though is this: how come all officers act tough against a prisoner only when we're behind a steel cell door or in restraints? The only time this fool ever talks shit is when I'm in cuffs!

Thirty minutes after he escorts me out to visitation to speak to my lawyer on the phone, he's back trying to talk to me as if everything is cool. Shit ain't cool, dicksucker. I told my lawyer that for a hot minute I thought about slipping off my handcuffs to stop on this piece of shit. What stopped me from doing so is I would have lost a lot, even though I would have felt better after the fact. I have no doubt though that before I'm executed by the State of Texas, sometime I will end up hurting that piece of shit. I mean really, how much shit am I supposed to take from this dude before I say enough is enough? His ranks are not going to do anything about everything he does. Truth is, the administration only responds to violence within these walls. Once, and only once, you assault staff do they come around trying to ask why you did this or that to their officers? What a crock of shit.

Then, Saturday morning I awake broken out in some kind of allergic reaction to the Pfizer vaccination shot I took on the 26th. Only when I awake this day, May 29th, 2021. From my head down to my toes I have broken out in a dark red rash-like symptom that not only itches but burns like holy hell, and my throat has swelled to the point I'm unable to eat and swallow foods and can hardly get down water or coffee. A SGT and Officer Karen Woodley come to escort me down over to 10-Building medical. When we get over there, there's this one lady who's always on the pods doing insulin. She asks what I'm there for, and when the SGT tells her, she says that's not an emergency. I stay silent for a second before another lady who is the charge nurse, named Martinez, asks me what the problem is. When I try to explain to her what all is going on and that it's hard for me to swallow, she checks my temperature and slaps a blood pressure cuff on my left arm. Both she and the first lady who spoke with me saying this wasn't an emergency remove my face mask to check my face, and then instead of placing it back on my face properly, just let it slap back half over my eyes and mouth. This is the first time I have ever dealt with either one of them face to face, even though I have been into the ER many times before for both cutting and for allergic reactions. What the charge nurse was supposed to do was call the on-call provider. Instead, she just said I can go back to my cell, that nothing was wrong with me, and that I would be referred to see the provider some time. Even though you can clearly see that I'm fucked up and my throat is swollen. As I'm walking out, I heard one of them say I wasted their time. I snapped and stopped walking to turn around and tell them they were a couple of bitches who didn't do shit for anyone unless someone has tried to kill themselves, at which time they send them on Mediflight. "You fucking cunts are worse than the hoes in the mailroom who don't do shit, fuck you bitches!"

At this point, Officer Karen Woodley decides to get up in my face screaming at me, "What the fuck you want them to do?" I want them to call the on-call provider like they should so I can fucking eat without choking, bitch! This chick is crazy! I was going to leave her out of this book, but her actions got her right in it. This chick is from the Islands and is always working the SSI's (Support Service Inmates) who come on the pods cleaning the showers, mopping up and sweeping, cleaning the bars, everything. The way this lady works these prisoners that come back here on Death Row from the general population is like they are fucking slaves. She's always in their faces, talking to them like they ain't going to do nothing but what she tells them to do. How do you expect to talk to grown-ass men who are in prison for anywhere between 10 years and life as if they aren't shit? Just like the men, she only talks her shit when someone is in restraints or behind a steel door. Though I would never put my hands on a female, I would be lying if I said that it's never crossed my mind with some of the females that work inside these prison walls. These women think that they can talk to prisoners any old way.

The thing that makes me laugh a little though is, all the officers only talk shit to prisoners that are locked behind a steel door like Texas Death Row and Ad-Seg on 12-Building. They don't talk the same tough-guy shit out there in the general population because they all know that they'd get their asses handed to them!

This morning I woke up worse than I was the day before, and still medical refused to do anything about the situation even though my throat is swollen and that more than half of my body is covered in a dark red rash that burns like crazy and has my body swollen. Unless I give in to temptation and cut on myself, thus forcing medical to have to see me and then attend to me, I will continue to suffer through the swelling and burning sensation of this allergic reaction from the Pfizer vaccination shot.

Part 2
TEXAS DEATH WATCH

Chapter Fourteen

The day that I was moved over to Death Watch on A-Pod of A-Section was the day that I'll always remember. I was having a spiritual advisor visit with this woman who over the years would become a very dear and great friend to me, named Mary. Once every month, she would drive from Austin, Texas, along with some other men and women that were a part of Friends Meeting of Austin, also known as Quakers. This was/is about a four hour drive one way. During our visit this day, she let me know that my mom wanted me to know that my auntie (Donna Bird) had lost her battle with breast cancer in the hospital in Florida. It was a great loss to everyone that knew her, moreso to her sister, my mom, who was at her bedside when she left to join Jesus in Heaven. After my visit and officers had escorted me back to A-Pod, I thought that I would be going back to B-Section where I had been housed alone for 2 ½ years, but instead I was escorted to Death Watch #14. This was their way of giving me something different to look forward to instead of being isolated now. I wasn't given a telephone call home to check in with my loved ones, nope. I was now being housed on a section that housed only the men with a set execution date. Everyone housed on this section was waiting to be killed by the State of Texas. It was January 2nd, 2011.

Besides myself, there was also at the time two other inmates housed on the section with me. They were ½ Deck and Tito. ½ Deck was housed on One Row in #4 Cell, and Tito was housed also on One Row in #7 Cell while I was upstairs alone. Out of a fourteen man section of single cells and one dayroom that is a bigger cage than our own cells that sits in the front of all the cells. There is also a video camera that watches everyone's moves twenty-four seven in each of our cells. These video cameras are able to be viewed by the officer in the control picket on the pod, officers sitting in the 12-Building control booth at the front of the building that houses Death Row and Ad-Seg, and also from the Major's office, Warden's office, and the Directors' offices in Huntsville, Texas. You never know who is watching you at any time of the day or night. If you're using the restroom, know that you are being watched. It does not matter if you're walking around in your cell butt-naked cause it's so hot in your cell; you are no doubt being watched. At first it took some time getting used to, but after a while, I don't even notice that it's really there, or maybe it's because I no longer care what they see. But back in January of 2011, ½ Deck, Tito, and I had fun with the cameras. Just like in the cells, on the runs (tiers) there are video cameras as well, and there's one in every dayroom that watches us. One day ½ Deck was in the dayroom and Tito and I were in our cells talking to him. We got the idea to cover up the security light out in the dayroom because during the night time when they turned off the lights on the run, that security light shined so bright we each thought it was directed into our cells. The only thing is, neither one of us had any glue at the time to glue something over it. I told Tito that I had some newspapers. If he could find something for ½ Deck to use to hold it up over the light, then shoot it to ½ Deck in the dayroom, I'll shoot him some newspaper.

"1/2 Deck, you feel like climbing up there to do it?"

"Yeah, why not?"

I shot him some newspapers from my cell by sliding it under the cell door to the dayroom bars, where ½ Deck climbed up on the bars to grab them. Tito said he had something in a clear bag that would work and shot it also out to the dayroom for ½ Deck to use. As ½ Deck is opening the bag of goo that Tito sent him to use, you could hear ½ Deck ask Tito, "What the hell is this?"

Tito said it was Colgate toothpaste! "Don't you brush your teeth!?"

"Yeah, but I use something else besides Colgate."

So ½ Deck grabs a page from the sports section of the USA Today that I sent him and the bag of Colgate and starts climbing the bars to the top of the security light. Once he's up there, he smeared a bunch of Colgate all over the light before spreading the newspaper over the Colgate. Seeing that the Colgate was in fact holding the paper to the light, ½ Deck spread more toothpaste over the newspaper and told me to send another page. After I sent another page of the paper to him, he climbed back up and pasted the second page of the paper over the first. Climbing back down, he went to the sink in the dayroom and washed his hands of the Colgate, then came to stand in front of our cells so we could all talk and laugh. ½ Deck was a young white guy, and Tito was on the chubby side for a Mexican, but he could cook! Lol!

Later on that day after ½ Deck was racked up and I was brought to the dayroom after him, I asked Tito if he wanted to cook some tacos for ½ Deck and I? Meaning he would cook for the three of us. He said yeah, but what did I have in mind? "Don't know, let me see what ½ Deck has to chip in with what I got and what you have." (Note: when any of us cook inside these walls, we do so with foods/pouches bought from the prison commissary.) ½ Deck had some cream cheese, jalapeno peppers, and two boxes of roast beef. I told Tito this and that I had some pouches of chili with beans, pickles, couple packs of tortillas, and some Mexican beef pouches. Tito said for us to send it all to him, and he'd hook something up for the three of us for dinner.

When I racked up after my rec time was over, Tito VR'd (Verbally Refused) his rec so that he could cook everything. Cooking food takes time for us. It's not like we have a stove or oven in our cells. Everything we do we do with the aid of our Hotpot bought from commissary. Unless you turn your Hotpot into a lava pot, meaning you bypass the thermostat so that water boils instead of just simply getting hot, to cook the food you place it inside of cook bags (empty chip bags or rice bags.) Also you won't find any knives being sold to us, so we make do with what they do sell us and what the officers give us (razors, broken down for the blades to use as something to cut with.) Using a broken down razor blade, we're able to cut our peppers and pickles and cut bags as well as other things. Everything that a prisoner needs to survive in prison is for the most part sold to us in the commissary. But to get such things to live, you have to have outside support to send you money to your inmate account. Otherwise you'll not only lose tons of weight, but probably get sick eating the food they serve prisoners in Texas.

When Tito was finished cooking that evening for ½ Deck and I, he had each of us shoot our line. This is the term used for us to fish with one another. Fishing consists of each of us using a line that was either spun or braided, that we added either a pole to the end of, or a slider to slide under our cell doors. Once out there, Tito or whoever you're running line with, would send his line to catch yours and pull it in. In my case, with Tito and ½ Deck being on One Row, I would use my fishing pole to shoot over the railing on Two Row. This meant it shoots out my cell door and over the railing to hit on One Row. Tito would then use his line/pole with hooks placed on the end to catch my line and pull me into his cell. His bottom of our cell doors used to have an opening that you could fit your fist out of, but now it's been welded over, so it's harder, but everyone still fishes with their friends or brothers. Like I was saying, when Tito was done cooking, he told ½ Deck to shoot his line. After doing this and being pulled into Tito's cell, Tito would loop on the line two chip bags with two tacos each inside the bags, and then send them out of his cell on ½ Deck's line, who would in turn pull his line into his own cell.

After Tito and ½ Deck finished, I was told by Tito to shoot my line. Practice makes perfect! Being in Cell #14 and him in #7 Cell directly beneath me with the dayroom bars right in front of both our cells, I had to send my pole/line at an angle out over the railing. Once I was sure my line had gone out enough and landed at the base of the stairs, I pulled the slack out of my line, just enough to give it one final hard tug so that it would pop back, and the weight of my pole would cause it to slide right up into the front of Tito's cell so he could grab it with his hand. Being that at the time my fishing line was braided, I was able to pull up a little weight. Tito was able to place both bags of tacos on my line, which I in turn pulled up and over the railing and into my cell. I thanked Tito, as did ½ Deck, and said I'd holler at him later. After putting away my fishing line and cleaning up, washing my hands, I sat at my desk, using my bunk as a seat and enjoyed the tacos my amigo (my friend) Tito made for us, while washing it all down with a can of Coke (wish they sold Pepsi!)

Texas Death Row prisoners do not have TVs, nor are we allowed access to telephones back then. To this day we still have no TVs and though we are allowed to make a five-minute telephone call once a week, this is only due to the Covid-19 pandemic. Before the pandemic, we could only get a telephone call once every 90 days (three months) and the call is collect. Inside of our cells, if you have outside support, you can purchase items such as a radio with headphones, coax cable to hook up to the radio to listen to, or a Hotpot with insert to heat water to drink coffee, make a soup to cook with or heat pouches of certain foods. Basically a Hotpot is our cooking stove/oven in one. You are able to purchase two fans to keep cool in the summer days or whenever you feel hot inside your cell to use. You can buy a nightlight to use to read by inside your cell instead of having to turn on the cell light which is always too bright or knocks out the radio reception when on. All your hygiene items, from soap, shampoo, conditioner, baby powder, lotion, etc., and art supplies for those that like to draw or paint, as well as all correspondence supplies and postage stamps to keep in touch with those on the outside. All kinds of foods and pastries, chips, bottled water, coffee, soups, meats, cookies, etc. Also you can purchase a typewriter and typing ribbons, though it's very costly for the typewriter, $360.00 and $6.50 for ribbons. You can purchase a lot, like I said. Your loved ones and friends can send you reading material from a bookstore or order it online through Amazon.com.

No doubt you're thinking this sounds good for prisoners or it's too easy. Think again. Did I mention that we live in a bathroom? Yeah, each of us sleeps and eats in our own personal restrooms. The same place you go at your home to use the restroom to poop or pee or, when drunk, throw up into the toilet. We have to sleep in one. Thus we're constantly cleaning our cells and the floors, walls, and wiping down everything. Who in their right mind wants to sleep with a toilet less than three feet from where he lays his head, or two feet from where he eats his food? If I were to sit on my cell floor here on Death Watch between my toilet and bunk, I can reach out and touch both as well as my desk. That is how close everything is together. If you don't keep your cell clean, as well as your own personal body, you will get sick, and those you come into contact with will also get sick, or vice versa. The laundry you purchase from commissary, such as t-shirts, gym shorts, boxers, and socks, you wash in your cell sink; they don't do anything for you within these walls other than give you hell or screw you over in whatever way they can get away with.

Besides cooking tacos and just spreading with one another, we can also play either chess or dominoes with one another, though not in the way you think. Each of us must purchase his own board, or 'Bones'. Dominoes must be played while one is in the dayroom and the other in his cell where he can see the 'Bones', thus we play that way. Chess, you each have a board, and it's numbered, and you call your moves by those numbers or some play by numbers and letters. We can pass reading material such as books back and forth, and newspapers and magazines. We share jokes with one another just to enjoy a sense of humor and laugh, because we all know that sometimes laughter is the best medicine for everyone. Sometimes though, even laughter cannot remove the pain and heartache one feels at the loss of friends and brothers. I would come to learn this over many executions in the months to come that would turn into years on end.

Though I had many great laughs with both Tito and ½ Deck, the execution of ½ Deck on February 15th, 2011, a little over one month after getting the news of my auntie's death, would be staggering. Nothing in my life ever prepared me for the pain felt within myself on February 16th, 2011 when I came to the dayroom and yelled out for ½ Deck, forgetting that he had just been executed the night before. Though we all knew of the executions taking place at the Walls Unit in Huntsville, Texas, where the condemned are sent from the Polunsky Unit, it's much more in your face on being housed with that same person who just the day before you were laughing with and eating with.

One week after the execution of ½ Deck, the administration took it upon themselves to start messing with me by moving me out of #14 Cell and over into #13 Cell right next door. No reason was given, and later the same night, another inmate was moved into #14 Cell, named "Youngblood", who had just gotten his own set execution date. Youngblood and I did not talk much, because he was under the impression that I had snitched when I was busted with that cellphone in 2008. He would tell me though that he thought it was fucked up that I had called the state senator asking for help with both my appeals and my visitation. This though, I was able to clear up with him, was wrong information, and I showed him paperwork to back it all up. That was always one thing that upset me with everyone. Everyone thought I had went to this fool for help with both my appeals and to see my loved ones. It never made any sense though, because the month of September comes before the month of October. If you all remember from the many previous pages in this book, I had gone back to court in the 264th District Court of the Honorable Martha J. Trudo on September 30th, 2008 to end my appeals and volunteer for execution. And though it greatly saddens me to say and still causes me great heartache and pain, my mom was coming to visit with me the day she was arrested at the Austin airport in October of 2008, for purchasing me minutes for a cellphone so we could talk on the phone. So, why would I be asking for help on either of these issues when I was finished with one and already had visits scheduled? People, even prisoners, will believe what they want to, regardless of the truth. If it was said in the newspaper or on the news, people automatically assume it's the gospel. Malcom X said it best: "The media's the most powerful entity on earth. They have the power to make the innocent guilty and to make the guilty innocent."

Though I kept my distance from Youngblood, we both still passed for one another when a kite (slang for note) came from another section while one was in the dayroom, as well as passing books or anything else that came from another section for each other. For about two weeks, I heard Youngblood asking the prison chaplain for a rosary, and yet he would always get the runaround from the then-chaplain. He even went to his friends that were housed on other sections to see if someone had an extra rosary he could please get. Nobody ever had one for him.

One day while I was in the dayroom, I had been talking to Tito when some volunteer chaplains came onto the pod/section to speak with the fellas on Death Watch, as well as myself. Some of the chaplains that would come around were always cocky, like they could be anywhere else and that they didn't really want to be there talking with us. This would always upset myself and some of the others there with dates. This day though, one of them came to talk with Tito and I by simply talking aloud without first saying "excuse me" or anything. Tito gave me a look that said volumes. He didn't want to speak with the guy and told him so numerous times. The volunteer chaplain just went on talking to Tito like it didn't matter what Tito wanted, he was going to say what he wanted to say. Having enough, and wanting to finish my talk with Tito, I asked the volunteer chaplain, loud enough so he could hear me from right there less than three feet away, what he called that book he was carrying? I was speaking about the Holy Bible he had in his hand but never once opened or tried to share anything from it with Tito. He told me that it was God's Word, the Bible. Being a smartass, and wanting him to leave us alone, I told him that he was wrong. I said something along the lines of it being a Book of Letters, 66 to be exact. How come he didn't open it and try to share anything from God's Word as he said with my friend? Instead of answering, he turned around and left Death Watch. Tito and I got back to our talk about ½ Deck's execution and how it sucked that he was gone now. Then the officer in the control picket yelled at me to let #14 Cell know that he had a visit. I did this, then thought to ask Tito if I could get his extra rosary he had, along with a piece of paper? He said sure and sent them both to me. I told him I'd be right back and sat at the dayroom table to write out a kite real fast to Youngblood. In the kite, I told Youngblood that I didn't expect him to be my friend, but I had been hearing him asking for a rosary and had gotten my hands on one. Here it was, and I hoped that it helped him relax and to have a good visit. I folded it up with the rosary inside and then climbed the bars and slid it under his cell door. Climbing down, I called his name and told him there was a kite in his cell. After picking up the kite, he asked who it was from, and I said me. He started to say he didn't want anything. I said, "Just read the damn thing, man," and turned away from him.

At that time, the officers that were escorting came onto the section to get him for his visit. As he's walking off the section, I took notice that he had the rosary around his neck and this huge smile on his black face! When he came back a little after two hours later, I was still stuck in the dayroom. He called me over to the front of his cell from up there on Two Row, and told me to climb up and grab the pictures he slid out there. I did as he asked, and he explained that he just had a great visit with his mom and that he wanted to show me the pictures of him and his mom. There in the two pictures is the rosary necklace around his neck, and Youngblood smiling huge with his mom! He told me thanks for the rosary and that it meant a lot to him. As he's speaking to me, he has tears falling down his face. I said that it was no big deal and that I hoped it helped him. He said that his mom and he are Catholic, and he'd been trying to get a rosary for some time but kept getting the runaround. After that, we became friends for the short time he was housed there with me and everyone else on Death Watch. We even cooked for one another and laughed together. On June 21st, 2011, Youngblood was executed by the State of Texas. Less than thirty days later I would lose another amigo, my friend and brother Tito, who was executed on July 7th, 2011. The loss and pain felt after getting to know these three men is something that goes beyond feeling, nor is it really explainable. All I can tell you is that it hurts knowing that someone you know and once laughed with is going to be dead and there is nothing that you can do to stop it or prevent it.

Not long after the execution of Tito, the administration moved one of the infamous Texas 7 into his cell. This would be George Rivas, who everyone just called Rivas. One of the things we all feared about Rivas while he was on Death Watch was him eating some beans with his food or tacos. One day during the month of February, after everyone was done for the day and starting to relax, out of nowhere you heard someone pass gas loud as hell! Nobody said anything like "excuse me" or whatever, then thirty seconds later the same person passes gas again even louder. The officer in the picket looks over to the section, and I guess George felt like something should be said. Right after he farts again, he says, "Exxxxxcuuuuuseeeeee mmmmmeeeeee!!"

When I tell you that everyone busted up laughing, I mean just that. Everyone on Death Watch started laughing so hard, and all of us were asking Rivas, "Dude, what the hell did you eat?"

Rivas: "Beans and more beans!!"

When Rivas wasn't farting around on the section, he could be sharing his skills with all. He was always good for some good jokes, and for hooking up TV on someone's radio. Since Death Row inmates were not allowed TVs, the next best thing for most of us was to hook up or have someone hook TV into our radios so that we could listen to TV throughout the days and nights. Some nights when all was quiet you could hear the sounds of COPS playing over someone's speaker (a speaker is something guys can make back here, and though it's considered contraband, we still make them.) I mean, come on, guys, COPS? Most times though it was some TV series or Judge Judy, or the Simpsons and Family Guy for laughter. One thing he taught me though, and I would use all the time, was how to knock out my video camera inside my cell so that I could have some privacy from the watching eyes of all.

The cameras in the cells back then were different from the ones that they have in our cells now. Back then though, you could take a piece of foil or something that would reflect the light back into the sensors on the camera. By doing this, I was able to knock out my camera whenever I would shut my lights off; it would no longer be able to see me in the dark because it shut off its own night vision.

Rivas wasn't over here for long before he too would be executed on February 29th, 2012. On March 1st, 2012, I was moved back into Cell #14 as a means to start harassing me with moving me into someone's cell that I was friends with or had just been executed. The thing is, that didn't bother me like they thought it would. Right after I moved and Rivas was killed, they moved into his cell a guy everyone called Sarge. Sarge was in the Army at one time for a while. He always had the same haircut when they offered cuts on Death Row by an inmate barber. High and tight was his cut. Sarge used to make so many of us laugh aloud with his sense of humor. Close your eyes and imagine this white guy that's got a high and tight haircut like a soldier, walking around in a dayroom with shorts on and a t-shirt with brown Rhino boots on. He's got this booming laugh. That was what Sarge looked like. He was funny, and yet he was one of the few who I got to know that was also very religious while he was here with us. He had numerous execution dates that never went through because he got stays of executions. I remember him telling us the story of the time he was driven over to the death house in Huntsville Texas. He was being told the way it's going to go down, yada, yada, yada, when he interrupts the Warden of the Walls Unit and says, "Look, I understand all of what you're saying, but let me say this. I'm a grown-ass man who served in the military. One thing I'm telling you that's NOT GOING TO HAPPEN is you putting a butt-plug in me. I'll wear the adult diaper but not a freakin' BUTT-PLUG." Sarge told us that when he said this to them, they all looked at him crazy before asking what the hell he was talking about? Sarge told them that one of the fellas who'd been over here before with a date said that you allow us to choose between the two before executing us. They told him that was not true. Sarge said to himself when he got back he was going to curse Balentine out for this bullshit. Telling us this story, we all started busting our asses up laughing so hard. I had tears falling cause I was laughing so hard. Balentine is another inmate named John Balentine, who no longer has an execution date but is still housed on A-Pod as I write this out to you. Fact is, he and I laugh a bit when we talk.

Another time while he was housed on Death Watch with me and the other fellas with dates, he was again in the dayroom walking around and just shootin' the breeze with us when we got word that a tour was going to be coming around onto the pod with the wardens and Rank. So we had to get our cells in order if they weren't already. Sarge is telling us all we need to act like fools so they don't come back. I told him to walk around like a dork in the dayroom, like Steve Urkle in that TV show where the young black kid with the big eye glasses is so smart and yet he has his pants pulled way up high and laughs funny. Before we know it, the tour is on the pod, and the wardens are talking about this section and how we all have execution dates and video cameras inside our cells. There are both men and women in the group. They turn around and are facing the control picket as the warden tells them how it's ran. When they turn back around, Sarge is sitting with his pants down around his ankles on the toilet, looks directly at the warden, and says, "Hey, Warden, can I get some shit paper!?" Then makes this loud-ass farting sound. We are all laughing so hard, the warden is turning red in the face, screaming for the officers to rack up Sarge and lock A-Section down for this bullshit! He can't get the tour off the pod fast enough. We were locked down on this section alone for two weeks for that. But when you think about it, to us it was worth it, and though they don't ask us, we don't like it when they bring tours around to this section to showboat everyone on this section. This is not a zoo where you bring people to see the animals, though that is exactly how they treat us… like animals in a zoo.

On September 25th, 2012, Sarge walked off this section for the last time, never to return to his friends and brothers on Death Row, let alone the rest who knew him on Texas Death Row. Not long after his execution, I was scheduled for a legal telephone call with a new appointed lawyer who was taking on my case. Seems she was appointed by the courts back in May, but I was too busy with the executions of my friends to take good notice. Her name is Marcia Widder, Esq. One thing that I was never good at was getting along with lawyers. I mean, who does, right? Over time though, she, along with some others who would also be appointed at her request to the courts, would get under my skin and become something more than just simple lawyers to me. At the time of her being appointed to work with me, she would be living in New Orleans, LA, and doing private practice for those dumb enough to land in prison or on Death Row in some states. More times than I care to remember, I would get into it with her about my current situation and remaining alive and fighting this losing battle with the State of Texas. However, trying to make her, or any other lawyer for that matter, understand that some people should just be allowed to waive their rights to appeals and volunteer for execution goes beyond her head and those that are with her. Deep down, she's a great person and means well and would do just about anything for someone she believes in or has befriended… such as I. Marcy, as she likes to go by, has been my lead lawyer now for 9 years, and I can tell you it's not been an easy nine years. Numerous times, when I felt that I had reached rock bottom and nobody would listen, I would go back to cutting on myself. Not to end my life, but to release my anger and frustration over the loss of friends/brothers, and over the situation I'm currently in. Being housed on Death Watch without a set execution date. Not being allowed to visit with my mom, sister, and grandma as a further means of punishment by the Texas Department of Criminal Justice and State Senator John Whitmire. When my grandma passed away from cancer years ago, I again was refused a telephone call home to my mom and sister. I took this hard, and feeling with no other choice, I cut myself because I felt something that I hadn't felt since California. I felt a homicidal rage within me to hurt someone in gray (Officer) or the Warden if I could get my hands on them. But deep down, I knew this to be the wrong way to go about something. Hurting the officers or even a warden that in my book deserved to be hurt wouldn't get me anywhere. It wasn't the officers' fault, so why should I take my anger out on them?

This is a way for them to put food on the table and a roof over the heads of their loved ones while also paying the bills. However, by harming myself, as they call it here, I was able to not only escape everything within myself when I saw my own blood bleeding out of my body, but it also allowed me to relax and be shipped off the Unit to another prison over in Sugar Land, Texas, called Jester-4.

This was and is a kind of prison hospital for prisoners that need to be there. I didn't go there to get fixed, I would either ask mental health to send me there and they would, or I would do something that would leave them no choice but to send me there. It allowed me to escape the death that I would continue to re-live day after day. People such as other prisoners that were doing time in other prisons throughout Texas had no idea who I was for a while. We were all butt-naked and in single cells. There were both men and women in the cells. The place sucked, and during the wintertime it was freezing, but the officers there treated all the prisoners like they mattered. It didn't matter what you were locked up for or how much time you had, you were treated like a human being and not an animal. Almost all of the officers over there are from Nigeria, and all of them are religious. I would stand at my cell door the first few times I was over there and just listen to the other prisoners talk to one another through their cell doors about how much time they had or what was going on in their lives. Some had lengthy sentences, while others were getting out in months, if not days. Some had serious issues where they snapped and lost their minds. They were smearing feces and urine on themselves or throwing it at other prisoners when they would pass their cells at their Units (Prisons.) To totally lose your mind in prison, I feel, would be the very worst place to do so. Prison is no hospice or hospital; the officers do not want to clean up after you when you crap all over the place, or when you lose the way to think and write because your mind went one way while your spirit went the other way and your body left you. To go insane within prison walls is death in so many ways; and what about the few that lose their minds other ways? Such as the ones who become violent because they're left no other choice but to fight for their own survival within the prison they're spending the rest of their lives? Don't think this happens? Well, then you've never been in prison for any length of time, have you? So you have no honest to gods idea of what you're thinking, just like lawyers. Right now, as I type out my story to you, I can feel the edge of the cliff at my feet. I can taste the edge of sanity going out of me and crazy wanting a place to live. Both of these I refuse to give into, before I lose it all one way or the other. I rather fight to have my appeals dropped, and if that doesn't work…

The real reason for this book though isn't just to share my story and what all I have gone through and continue to go through at the hands of those who keep me here, but hopefully also educate someone out there in society. If you know someone that is looking at going down the wrong path in their lives, be it your child or friend or a neighbor, brother, sister, nephew, niece, anybody, know this. Prison is not the place you want to do it from. This is no life, and when you hear your friends talk about this or that, just know that the minute your butt lands inside these walls, those same friends will no longer know you. Young guys think it's cool walking around with a loaded gun, talking a big game. Just know that when the pressure is on and you've talked yourself into a corner, you'll be tested and forced to do something you don't want to do. By that time it'll be too late to back down or get out of the situation you placed yourself into in the first place. You really want to go through with acting like a badass and carry a weapon of any kind? Then walk your tough little ass down to the local morgue and look at the dead bodies down there. Get up close and personal, knowing that this could very well be you one day, or your friend, or the person you place there. While you're there, listen to their loved ones that come in to identify their next of kin. Talk to the beat cops around your neighborhood about the things they've seen. Or if you really want to know, write to me, and I'll share with you much more than you'll ever read in this book or any other book. My information can be found at the end of this book. Whatever you do, don't throw your life away, cause it's not going to be worth it if you do.

The little control of things you do have out there in society, you'll no longer have within prison walls. Simple things like going to the shower and turning on the hot and cold water, that's gone. The water temp is set at one temp here, that's at 120 degrees, and when it's not set, it's freezing cold like ice water. When your toilet plugs up there in your home with your loved ones, you can contact a plumber to fix it or use a plunger to unplug it yourself. No such thing in prison. Your toilet will remain plugged until they find a plumber, or worse case, it's not only your toilet plugged, but a few of the guys on the run. The piping is screwed up and some idiot keeps flushing his working toilet, which is making the toilets that are plugged back up with feces and urine flooding all over your cell floor, so that you are now standing in it. Think someone is just going to come around and clean that up, you're wrong! You'll either clean up the sewage that came flooding out of your toilet, or you'll bask in it until you do. What about when there is a local water problem where you're at. They tell you to boil the water and you'll be okay, or go to the store and buy some bottled water. Not here in prison. The water goes off, we don't even know about it until it's too late. You wake up in the morning thinking you'll put on some water in your Hotpot to heat and brush your teeth, only you notice the freaking water has been shut off while you're sleeping. Or worse case than that is not only has the water been shut off while you were all sleeping, but before it got shut off something broke, and your cell is now flooded with water. You don't notice this though until you wake up and set your feet on the floor, only to set it right into freaking two inches of water that's running all through your cell and out the door!

Still want to spend your life in prison? Wait until they lock it all down, and you're given only a paper Johnny sack for breakfast, lunch, and dinner, food that wouldn't feed an animal, and this is what you'll get three times a day for weeks if not months, depending on how long they leave you locked down. Oh, and you only get to shower on Monday, Wednesday, and Friday, and that's only when they have enough officers to work and escort you to the shower. Not enough officers, and you're ass out. A homeless person lives better than some of us in prison. Want to spend your life in prison or on Death Row somewhere because you wanted to be accepted by your peers? Take your young ass and go sleep under an overpass like a homeless person. Learn to survive that way, and when you see that you don't like it nor ever want to live this way, take your ass back home and apologize to your loved ones for being an asshole. Take yourself back to school and get an education. Listen to those that love and care about you. I failed to do this. The highest education I got was up to the 11th grade and the streets and homelessness. It not only cost me relationships with family, but also good friends. I lost my best friend due to my stupidity. When he and his parents tried to get me on the right track, I paid no attention. In the end, he went on with his life, and I lost mine in so many ways. Wherever you are, Adam Enos of Turlock, California, I wish you and your loved ones the very best.

Lost many of my family members when they said they had enough and also turned their backs on me. My older brothers have nothing to do with me, even though I have tried to reach out to them to apologize. The only time both my brothers thought to come into my life was when I had my execution date. They asked me to place them on the visitation list so that they could attend my execution. That's all I am to my brothers now, something for their entertainment, to watch me be executed because I stole and hurt them so much. This is how I took it, my prison mentality is wired this way, yet I was told they only wanted to be there so I wouldn't be alone. I'm alone now, and they want nothing to do with me. The only ones to stick by me after everything, even when I don't deserve them or their love, is my mom, sister, and little niece. Though even my sister and niece have fallen away from me more and more lately, leaving only my mother. Being in prison is a hard and lonely life to live for anyone. Regardless of how tough you are, if you're not mentally tough, it will kill you from the inside of yourself out. People from all walks of life have at one point in time or another reached out to me, wanting to correspond, both men and women. They all talk a good game about how they each care about where you are and what is going on with you, only to break away because they truly do not understand, or they got what they wanted from you. They were fake and insincere in the end.

For the most part I have stayed away from pen-pal sites since I have been locked up in this sorry state of Texas. Only recently did I contact through one of my lawyers a pen-pal site to place my ad on their site. Not only have these two women been very professional to me, but they have treated me with kindness and compassion. Both of those things in my opinion I'm underserving of, because I'm unable to get over the hatred for myself, for the pain I caused so many and my own loved ones. The trouble I caused for my mom and sister when I was busted with that cellphone, that caused them to get arrested, will never part from my mind/heart. That shit eats at me every day and night of my life. Though my mom and sister have both told me that they forgive me and have moved on, I'm unable to forgive myself nor move on. It's one of the things that's slowly killing me from the inside out. Aside from my loved ones and the ladies who run the pen-pal site at Wire of Hope, Sigrid and Elodie, who can be found at www.wireofhope.com or contact@wireofhope.com, there are very few people in my life right now, because though I used to trust anyone, I am no longer like that, and prison will make you this way. I have become my very own worst enemy.

Chapter Fifteen

When Donnie was moved over to the Death Watch section after getting his own execution date, we said very little if anything to one another because he was also under the impression that I said more, because he was told by other pen pals that I had been talking. Finally one day, when I had had enough, I called him out to the yard so we could talk. The day we were finally able to get out and talk turned out great because he had been baptized recently and wanted to apologize to me about some things. Turns out Donnie was just going with the flow and assuming like everyone else that I was guilty. He told me that he knew just some of the other fellas, that the morning that they kicked in my cell door and found the cellphone, Billy Mason was seen sipping from a cup with no restraints on in the Major's office ten minutes before they busted me, thus letting me know that people knew that Billy Mason had snitched on me. It wasn't only my own stupidity that caused me to get caught by contacting that shithead Whitmire, but Mason too.

After the air was cleared between the two of us, we started playing dominoes on the outside rec yard a few times each week. Throughout the first month while Donnie was housed on Death Watch, I had heard him asking numerous people for a photo album, t-shirt, and an illustration board. Unable to obtain these things before his date that was getting to be three weeks closer, I went about helping him without his knowing it. He was out at a visit one day in early October when I had sent kites around the pod for the things he was asking after. I was able to obtain the t-shirt and illustration board, and the photo-album I took from myself because I had an extra one. Being housed in #14 Cell when Donnie got back from his visit, I yelled at him to shoot his line through the side of the door. Donnie was housed down the run on Two Row with me, but at the far end or near about. He was in Cell #9. Once he shot his line down to me and I pulled it into my cell through the side of my door, I tied on the things that I was able to get for him as well as the photo-album from myself. Once he got everything inside his cell, I told him that he didn't owe me anything and that I had heard him looking and trying to get these items weeks ago. He told me thanks because he needed them for something he wanted to leave his wife and daughter. The next week, after returning from another visit with his loved ones, he asked me to make a list for things to make tacos with for everyone on this section. He said that he would be doing his last spend in the morning, and that while he was at visit the last three days, he wanted to know if I would cook tacos for him, Lizard, Skinny, and myself. I told him that would be okay and went to writing out a list of everything needed. (Note: when someone is doing his last spend, that mean it'll be the last time TDCJ-ID will allow him to make commissary. That's 14 days from his date with death. He can purchase anything from the commissary, so long as he doesn't go over about $150.00. It's also during this time he's pulled out to talk to the Unit Warden and fill out all the proper paperwork, ie. who will be claiming his remains after his execution, picking up his property from the Walls Unit, who will he have witnessing his execution, etc…) When commissary came to deliver Donnie's stuff the next day after he spoke with the Warden and did his paperwork, he shot me everything early so that he wouldn't have to deal with it all later. It's hard work fishing everything through the side of one's cell door! Some things like bags of chips are a pain in the butt.

Before long, Donnie's three days were here. During the last 72 hours while he's housed on Death Watch, the officers have to check on him every thirty minutes and log it down on the paperwork in the control picket. Most of the times though, they do this by looking at the video cameras inside our cells. His last 24 hours, as it is with everyone who has a date, he's checked on both by the video camera inside the cell and by officers walking to his door to double check and to write down what he's doing. For the most part, the officers leave everyone on this section alone. While he was out at visitation, things went like they normally do back here. Loud and crazy. Officers slamming the gates that come onto each section, as well as the cross-over doors that lead from one section to another. Guys being escorted to the shower. Just because someone has an execution date doesn't mean time comes to a stand-still; if anything it seems like it speeds up! I also held up to my end and was cooking food throughout the last three days. On his final morning with all of us on the section, as he was passing by my cell going into the shower, he stopped and dropped some things in front of my cell. Once he was in the shower and the officers had left, I reached out and got the items. Before he started showering he asked me to pass those for him and to let everyone know he'd speak with them when he got out of the shower. I said cool. About that time, Lizard was just being placed in the dayroom, and I told him that I had a kite for him and one for Saint over in C-Section. "See if someone is over there yet, and I will pass it to him."

 I shot both kites for him and Saint to him in the dayroom. The last kite was addressed to me. I left it sitting on my desk, thinking that I would open it after Donnie left for the Walls Unit in Huntsville, Texas. Lizard read his, and when Donnie got out of the shower, he thanked him for the flags (stamps). Guess Lizard had loaned Donnie some flags, and Donnie not only repaid him, but twice as much. Don't know what he sent or said to Saint, but we heard that he got it and yelled back and thanked Donnie as well. Donnie asked me when he got back in the cell what I thought. I told him that I had not opened it yet. He said to open it and let him know. So when I opened the kite from Donnie, he not only wrote me a really kind letter telling me he was sorry for everything that I was going through and hoped that one day these people would let me see my mom and sister at a visit, but he also left me $120.00 in flags. I was beyond touched because I didn't expect anything from him, certainly not something like this. It just goes to show that not everyone on Texas Death Row is an asshole. A lot of us change over time, and for the most part, it's a better change from within ourselves. Donnie was executed later on that night of October 31st, 2012, Halloween night.

When I set out to tell my story in the form of this book, I didn't think it would be so hard to do. However, I'm finding it greatly painful to relive the memories of the guys that I got to know as human beings and not the animals the district attorney's office would have you believe we are. Therefore, I will share with you one more in depth who was my best friend back here on Texas Death Row/Death Watch. Before moving onto other topics about this prison and the people who get away with screwing us all over with things such as our legal and non-legal mail. But first allow me to introduce to you the men that have been escorted from this section I have been housed on as a means of further punishment and cruel and unusual punishment for my involvement of being caught with a cellphone back in 2008.

1) Michael Wayne Hall – Executed February 15th, 2011 (1/2 Deck)
2) Timothy Wayne Adams – Executed February 22nd, 2011
3) Cary D. Kerr – Executed May 3rd, 2011
4) Gayland Charles Bradford – Executed June 1st, 2011
5) Lee Andrew Taylor – Executed June 16th, 2011
6) Milton Wuzael Mathis – Executed June 21st, 2011 (Youngblood)
7) Humberto Leal Garcia, Jr. – Executed July 7th, 2011 (Tito)
8) Mark Anthony Stroman – Executed July 20th, 2011
9) Martin Robles – Executed August 10th, 2011
10) Steven Michael Woods, Jr. – Executed September 13th, 2011
11) Lawrence Russell Brewer – Executed September 21st, 2011
12) Frank Martinez Garcia, Jr. – Executed October 27th, 2011
13) Guadalupe Esparza – Executed November 16th, 2011
14) Rodrigo Hernandez – Executed January 26th, 2012
15) George Angel Rivas, Jr. – Executed February 29th, 2012 (Rivas)
16) Keith Steven Thurmond – Executed March 7th, 2012
17) Jesse Jo Hernandez – Executed March 28th, 2012
18) Beunka Adams – Executed April 26th, 2012
19) Yokamon Laneal Hearn – Executed July 18th, 2012
20) Marvin Lee Wilson – Executed August 7th, 2012
21) Robert Wayne Harris – Executed September 20th, 2012
22) Cleve W. Foster III – Executed September 25th, 2012 (Sarge)
23) Jonathan Marcus Green – Executed October 10th, 2012

RICHARD TABLER

24) Bobby Lee Hines – Executed October 24th, 2012
25) Donnie Lee Roberts, Jr. – Executed October 31, 2012 (Donnie)
26) Mario Rashad Swain – Executed November 8th, 2012
27) Ramon Torres Hernandez – Executed November 14th, 2012
28) Preston Craig Hughes III – Executed November 15th, 2012
29) Carl Henry Blue – Executed February 21st, 2013
30) Rickey Lynn Lewis – Executed April 9th, 2013
31) Ronnie Paul Threadgill – Executed April 16th, 2013
32) Richard Aaron Cobb – Executed April 25th, 2013
33) Carroll Joe Parr – Executed May 7th, 2013
34) Jeffrey Demond Williams – Executed May 15th, 2013
35) Elroy Chester III – Executed June 12th, 2013
36) John Manuel Quintanilla, Jr. – Executed July 16th, 2013
37) Vaughn Ross – Executed July 18th, 2013
38) Douglas Adam Feldman – Executed July 31st, 2013
39) Robert Gene Garza – Executed September 19th, 2013
40) Arturo Eleazar Diaz – Executed September 26th, 2013
41) Michael John Yowell – Executed October 9th, 2013
42) Jamie Bruce McCoskey – Executed November 12th, 2013
43) Jerry Duane Martin – Executed December 3rd, 2013
44) Edgar Tamayo Arias – Executed January 22nd, 2014
45) Ray L. Jasper III – Executed March 19th, 2014
46) Anthony Dewayne Doyle – Executed March 27th, 2014
47) Tommy Lynn Sells – Executed April 3rd, 2014
48) Ramiro Hernandez Llanas – Executed April 9th, 2014
49) Jose Luis Villegas, Jr. – Executed April 16th, 2014
50) Willie Tyrone Trottie – Executed September 10th, 2014
51) Miguel Angel Paredes – Executed October 28th, 2014
52) Arnold Prieto, Jr. – Executed January 21st, 2015
53) Robert Charles Ladd – Executed January 29th, 2015
54) Donald Keith Newbury – Executed February 4th, 2015 (Lizard)
55) Manuel Vasquez – Executed March 11th, 2015
56) Kent William Sprouse – Executed April 9th, 2015
57) Manuel Fernando Garza, Jr. – Executed April 15th, 2015
58) Derrick Dewayne Charles – Executed May 12th, 2015
59) Lester Leroy Bower, Jr. – Executed June 3rd, 2015

60) Gregory Lynn Russeau – Executed June 18th, 2015
61) Daniel Lee Lopez – Executed August 12th, 2015
62) Juan Martin Garcia – Executed October 6th, 2015
63) Licho Escamilla – Executed October 14th, 2015
64) Raphael Deon Holiday – Executed November 18th, 2015
65) Richard Allen Masterson – Executed January 20th, 2016
66) James Garrett Freeman – Executed January 27th, 2016
67) Gustavo Julian Garcia, Jr. – Executed February 16th, 2016
68) Coy Wayne – Executed March 9th, 2016
69) Adam Kelly Ward – Executed March 22nd, 2016
70) Pablo Lucio Vasquez – Executed April 6th, 2016
71) Barney Ronald Fuller, Jr. – Executed October 5th, 2016
72) Christopher Chubasco Wilkins – Executed January 11th, 2017
73) Terry Darnell Edwards – Executed January 26th, 2017
74) Rolando Ruiz, Jr. – Executed March 7th, 2017
75) James Eugene Bigby – Executed March 14th, 2017

Chapter Sixteen

"That's it, Slim! You are not beating me up anymore! You hear me, Slim!?"

"Dude, Big Tai, you called me out tonight and don't get mad cause I sunk your battleship once again! It's only right I'm kicking your ass right now after the beating you gave me in Hangman!"

"That shit still has me laughing, Slim!"

"Yeah, whatever, foo!"

(Note: Big Tai was the only one to call me by my nickname from Florida, Slim. Others call me Blue.)

We had been at it all month, playing games such as Battleship and Hangman while standing at our cell doors here on Death Watch. The two of us had known one another since I rolled up to the prison back in 2007. Big Tai, as we all who knew him called him, was a giant black guy about 6 foot 6 and around 240 pounds of muscle, with a shaved head that was so bald you could see your reflection, if you were tall enough, that is. He was also a Five Percenter. Though he was busted here in Texas, he was from Brooklyn, NY, and some family are still out there while some are here in Texas. While he was housed here on Death Watch with me, we had a rule between one another. He would always make the tacos or spreads or gumbo for the two of us, and I'd always make the cheesecakes and drink (hooch) for the two of us throughout his stay over here, in the hopes he would be getting a stay of execution. Also, when either he was in the dayroom or I was, we'd study together. Meaning he would bring his Qu'ran and Bible and dictionary to dayroom, and I'd have mine in the cell. For one hour each day we would study together as not just friends, but as Brothers. People are most afraid of what they don't understand, and too many people are quick to misunderstand another's faith, either cause they're cowards, or because they're ignorant to facts. Both the Holy Bible and the Holy Qu'ran tie into one another. If only people would take the time to study and read instead of passing judgement, life would be so much easier out there in society. But hey, I'm just another Dead Man Walking, so what do I know.

When Big Tai and I weren't studying, we could be found on the outside rec yard playing Run and Shoot with sweat pouring down our faces from busting our asses trying to beat one another for hours on end. Let me explain so you can understand better what the game is. The outside rec yards here on Texas Death Row's 12-Building are two big cages outside that sit side by side to one another. Probably about 30 feet by 15 feet. Each one had a basketball and hoop mounted up on the wall on one side, and a pull-up bar and a urinal/sink to drink water from. Other than that, there is open sky straight up that you can see through the bars. Standing at one end of each rec yard, at the start of the game, you would shoot the ball towards the basket. If you made it, that counted as one shot. You would run to the other end and do it again. The object of the game was to run and shoot points. First one to get ten points won the game. In the two hours we were outside sometimes, you would catch us playing between 60 and 100 games, with little if any breaks in between each set. The other thing that we would do would be when either one of us had a visit, either legal or spiritual in my case, and the same with visits from family with him, we'd bring back each other's favorite goodie/snack from a vending machine that we couldn't buy in the prison commissary. My thing was those freaking Rice Krispy Treats, and his were the Starburst Tropical flavors!

One thing that we couldn't buy in the commissary were game boards like for Battleship or Hangman. So we would make our own boards, and every Friday night he and I would have the music playing on one of our speakers while kicking each other's ass on one game or the other to pass the time when we weren't writing letters to home or lawyers.

One night that we had been planning for for two months came around. Usually it wouldn't be something either one of us would do, but with his upcoming execution date, we decided to get lit and have a good time with some weed and drink, along with some tacos he would be making. We were able to get our hands on three joints and a lighter, and I had made us three bottles of drink each, something that I hardly do because it's too risky. But this night was the only time we felt we could do it and get away with it, and just have fun blocking everything out and his upcoming execution that we both knew was going to go through this time. This night though, it was April 20th, 2017, and we had just finished eating the tacos he made and were sippin' on the second bottle of our drinks as we down the first one to get that good feeling going. Standing at our cell doors, talking with one another and laughing, it was like we were both thinking the same thing at the same time and called each other out for a game of Battleship. Let me tell you young and old people something, don't ever try to play this damn game while drunk and high. For a good many hours we both just talked shit before deciding to play Hangman instead. Standing at the door with a noose around my neck (on the board), it was the first time Big Tai said that a white-looking guy was being hung by a black dude! We both started laughing our asses off, and about that time, one of the officers working the pod decided to walk her rounds. When she made it to our cells there on Two Row on Death Watch, she stopped right in front of our Cells #14 and #13, with this look on her face that said she could smell the weed but wasn't saying anything. Big Tai and I just stood at our cell doors looking at her looking at us, before you hear me tell Big Tai, bet you can't do it again, and if you do I'm not telling nobody! The officer asked us what the hell we were doing up at 3:45am when usually we would both be sleeping by this time. Big Tai and I looked at her said that we were playing... HANGMAN!

That alone had us laughing like little kids caught red-handed, because when you honestly think about it, here you have two grown-ass men on Texas Death Row/Death Watch, and we're playing Hangman like everything is just one big joke or like we could care less about anything right at that moment. We were just enjoying life and the friendship we had.

On July 23rd, 2017, we were both out in the visitation with legal visits and were sitting right next to one another, when our lawyers did the old switch and started talking with us. I started talking with Big Tai's lawyer/paralegal, and he started talking with my lawyer/Investigator; both of us lucked out with two very beautiful women working for us and on our cases. Then, on the day of his execution, I had both of my Investigators come to visit with me so that I could, one, show Big Tai my support by being out in visitation with him when they came to escort him out, and two, because I wanted my legal team to feel what I was feeling and to see how we are truly treated like animals our last day by the administration of Texas Department of Criminal Justice. The day this sorry State executed my Big Homie was the day I felt something else break inside me. Just like when I decided to leave a party late one night with my co-defendant in November of 2004, and I shot and killed two grown men. Then I felt something leave me too. A part of me that I'll never be able to retain, and now this state not only executed someone's son, brother, uncle, dad, but they also took away the only hope and faith I had left in a system I had long been knowing was broken. When they executed my best friend Big Tai on July 27th, 2017 at a little after 6:30pm, making him #76 since I've been housed on this section as a means of further punishment, they might as well have strapped me down on the gurney too. Not a day goes by that I don't think of my friend and look forward to the day that he and I will meet again in Heaven with our other loved ones and friends that have left before each of us. Only now, I know what it is that I suffer from… Survivor's guilt.

77) Robert Lynn Pruett – Executed October 12th, 2017
78) Ruben Cardenas Ramirez – Executed November 8th, 2017
79) Anthony Allen Shore – Executed January 18th, 2018
80) William Earl Rayford – Executed January 30th, 2018
81) John David Battaglia – Executed February 1st, 2018
82) Rosendo Rodriguez III – Executed March 27th, 2018
83) Erick Daniel Davila – Executed April 25th, 2018
84) Juan Edward Castillo – Executed May 16th, 2018
85) Danny Paul Bible – Executed June 27th, 2018
86) Christopher Anthony Young – Executed July 17th, 2018

RICHARD TABLER

87) Troy James Clark – Executed September 26th, 2018
88) Daniel Clate Acker – Executed September 27th, 2018
89) Robert Moreno Ramos – Executed November 14th, 2018
90) Joseph Christopher Garcia – Executed December 4th, 2018
91) Alvin Avon Braziel, Jr. – Executed December 11th, 2018
92) Robert Mitchell Jennings – Executed January 30th, 2019
93) Billie Wayne Coble – Executed February 28th, 2019
94) John William King – Executed April 24th, 2019
95) Larry Ray Swearingen – Executed August 21st, 2019
96) Billy Jack Crutsinger – Executed September 4th, 2019
97) Mark Anthony Soliz – Executed September 10th, 2019
98) Robert Sparks – Executed September 25th, 2019
99) Justen Grant Hall – Executed November 6th, 2019
100) Travis Trevino Runnels – Executed December 11th, 2019
101) John Steven Gardner – Executed January 15th, 2020
102) Abel Revill Ochoa – Executed February 6th, 2020
103) Billy Joe Wardlow – Executed July 8th, 2020
104) Quintin Phillippe Jones – Executed May 19th, 2021

Chapter Seventeen

Not every officer that works for the Texas Department of Criminal Justice is a bad officer, nor are some of the ones that work on 12-Building's Death Row/Death Watch section. When this pandemic hit the world and caused widespread panic among society and the administration, you had some officers that would go out of their way to assist myself and many others here on Death Watch. After spending so many years locked up in isolation as a means of punishment, when everyone over here on Death Watch tested negative for Covid-19 during the 2020 and 2021 year, the administration moved prisoners that had tested positive over here with us. That made no sense to any of us, other than the fact that they were hoping some of us would also become sick with Covid-19. As long as the positive were being housed with us even though they shouldn't have been on this section, Death Watch was now being placed on a quarantine lockdown, which further caused much frustration amongst ourselves and those that worked here. It also allowed the Unit mailroom staff, namely Misty N. Sumner, to get out of doing her job and delivering all legal mail and packages to those of us housed over here, as well as for the whole pod. At some point in the past, the United States Supreme Court ruled that correctional officers were not allowed to handle legal mail from lawyers or their law firms that were being addressed to a prisoner. However, the Texas Department of Criminal Justice cares little about what some Justice of the Courts might say or order. By running to the assistant wardens of the Polunsky Unit and the Texas Department of Criminal Justice Mailroom Coordinator in Huntsville, Texas, crying about how A-Pod, and thus A-Section where Death Watch are housed and under quarantine lockdown are, she shouldn't have to go into the section nor anywhere on the Pod to deliver legal mail to us. They agreed with her and thus, she was now allowed to come to the front door of the pod and drop off all legal mail from lawyers and their firms, as well as all packages such as books and other periodicals that were ordered for us from either friends and family, or lawyers through Amazon.com or any bookstore. In doing so, many federal stimulus checks and other legal mail became missing or never made it to the proper inmates. One such piece of mail that had a $40.00 Western Union Money Order enclosed was addressed to my brother and friend Julius Murphy, who we all called Juju. It was stuck together with my legal mail, that wasn't delivered to me until Sunday night around midnight. This was four days after Misty N. Sumner of the mailroom dropped all the legal mail off at the front door to A-Pod. Juju wasn't even housed on this pod. He had been moved two weeks before and was now living on B-Pod in B-Section of that pod. When I tried to give the mail back to the officer that gave it to me, she refused to take it, stating that this shit wasn't even her job and she's not going to be held accountable for it. In the end, I ended up giving it to an LT. that had come walking the pod the next morning. He in turn took it to Juju on B-Pod, who in turn mailed it to one of his lawyers explaining what had happened. This was just one of the times that mail had been sent to the wrong person because the prison mailroom refused to do their job and instead passed off the duties to the officers.

Texas Death Row used to get tons of mail sent to each of us, but over the years the mailroom has either had much of that mail returned to sender or simply thrown it into the trash without the prisoners knowing this was being done with their mail. She's not the only one doing us this way in the mailroom. Her coworker, who was finally fired by the senior warden, Warden Daniel Dickerson, was also throwing mail out or not delivering it. Her name was Glenda McNiel. Her replacement is another bad apple that worked here before named Mrs. Allen. As well as Heather

Sczech-Smith. For the last five years, the mail has trickled down to almost nothing for each pod. Most times we're lucky if we get any mail out of the prison mailroom. Texas Department of Criminal Justice has a contract with www.jpay.com, where our loved ones can go online and send us an email that the mailroom is supposed to print out and deliver to us within 48 hours. This never gets done though. Whenever our loved ones send such an email, something they sat down to type out to their loved ones that they might never see again due to the Covid-19 pandemic or because he's given an execution date, and those same people pay a fee for the email, it matters not to the Unit mailroom staff nor the people in Huntsville, Texas. Unless we're willing to fight for these missing jpay's and risk going to legal and losing all personal property, even though we'd be in the right, we'll never see the email our loved ones, or friends, or even lawyers might send us. Their excuse is that they're busy or that they don't do reprints. Hold up, you mean that because you're busy sitting on your ass not doing anything or sending our mail to the wrong person, we're not going to get what's rightfully ours? Thus it's okay for you to break the contract that www.jpay.com has with TDCJ-ID, or that it's okay to screw us and those that send them to us over because in fact you are now stealing. Or what you're really saying is that even though we have been sentenced to Death by the Courts, that we shouldn't even be allowed to get mail that we're automatically being cast aside with no rights; that your life is more important than those of our own, or the officers that come on the sections and pods to feed us, do count each day and night, shower us. That your life, Misty N. Sumner, is more important than even Tracy B. Moye who is the Unit Grievance Officer and who is a young black woman. Your life is more important than hers. She not only does her job without complaint, but during the pandemic, she went along with everyone else by wearing PPE (Personal Protection Equipment) to pick up grievances from all prisoners. This woman goes out of her way to do not only her job, just as her one-time coworker Christina M. Norris had once done before being forced by the prison administration to quit her job, because people actually care about us on Texas Death Row and see us all as human beings. It's okay for the people like Misty N. Sumner and her mailroom coworkers to lie and screw people over in any way they can, regardless of fact or truth. People like the staff in the prison mailroom are no better than the lady that called 911 and lied about the black man who was bird-watching over on the East Coast. When he asked her to place her dog on a leash, this white woman wanted to lie, regardless of the fact that she was caught on video. If you think that you can get away with screwing myself and everyone else over in regards to their legal mail, jpays, and packages, you'll continue to do so, and the administration and the mailroom coordinator will continue to allow you to do this injustice against those of us condemned.

Yet, not all the officers and staff that work here at the Polunsky are bad apples. You have officers on both the day-shift and night-shift who do their jobs without making us feel like animals or worse. Officers that don't disrespect or name-call in an attempt to draw us out, allowing them to write us a false disciplinary case. I had thought about naming them in this book, but for the simple fact that most still work within these walls, that would not be a good idea on my part. I have no doubt that this book and what I say will be read by prison officials and will be banned from being allowed inside for others to read it. For that reason alone I shall leave their names out of it. They know who they are, and that is all that matters. In the end, they will each be rewarded for their kindness and actions towards myself and others from our Father in Heaven.

Though I'm no saint, I do try my best to have a relationship with God and His Son Jesus Christ. Back in 2019, I had been baptized by a Rabbi from an outside source that was allowed to enter into the prison for this special day. I had become a Messianic Jew. I honestly thought that this is what I was called to be because it felt right deep within my core; and yet not two years later I would be withdrawing from being one such religion because I was seeing how those around me and outside in society were acting and claiming to be the same religion. I would even be knocked down for becoming such, from people of the same religion, as well as Catholics, Christians, etc… Seeing how people were acting when they were any religion was screwing me up even more than I already am. It's not like I can get up and exit my cell to go to church or pick up a telephone and call a Rabbi/Pastor or anyone else for a study or questions. The people who I used to rely on and be able to talk about anything have been removed from my life through execution. The face of many people that they don't want you to see started coming to the surface and showing. The fact that many people both within these walls and out there in society are only hiding behind the Word of God and the Holy Bible is beyond sickening. It hasn't caused me to want to further my faith in any one religion, but has pushed me further away from claiming a religion as my own. How can people claim to be this or that, and then turn around and judge me for where I'm at. Truth is, even though I no longer claim a religion, I do in fact have a strong relationship with our Father in Heaven and His Son Jesus Christ. Daily as well as every night, I speak with Him and ask for His love and strength to get me through each day. I remember the "Footprints in the Sand" picture and poem/saying. When we see two sets of footprints in the sand, that is when we were walking side by side with God. When we saw only one set of footprints, that was when God was carrying us. Throughout my whole life, looking at that picture, I'm only able to see the one set of footprints, because God has been carrying me every step of the way. One day, I hope that I'll be able to make Him proud to the point I climb down off His shoulders, and He says, "Thank you, Jesus, Richard, for getting off. You're damn heavy, son!" One day, God, one day.

Chapter Eighteen

Though I know that my strength comes from our Father in Heaven, it also comes through the people who have remained by my side throughout my life and while I've been housed on Texas Death Row/Death Watch. Mary Hampton came into my life around ten years ago. She's with a group called Friends Meeting of Austin, also known as the Quakers. Once a month, she and others will drive down from Austin, Texas to visit with those of us on Texas Death Row. Slowly over the years, she and I would become great friends. Though I'm not allowed to visit with my mother or sister, Mary always brings me messages from them when she comes to visit so that I know what is going on and how they're doing. I can correspond with them, but I don't always get their mail or the Warden's office withholds my incoming as well as my outgoing mail to them for weeks at a time. When Mary and I visit, we talk about all kinds of things, even the bad times and the times we are frustrated with life in general. She's always been there to send me books from the local bookstore or take some pictures of us during our visit so that I can mail them home to my mom and sister and my little niece, as well as any artwork or property I am wanting to send home or to anyone else. Just as she is an anchor in life to her family, she has also become one for me. I'm thankful for having her in my corner, as she's not only been there for myself but for my mom too. No doubt that our friendship is not easy on her, because, trust me, I can be and am a handful! One thing she always talks about during our visits is her love for her family and their new dog, Daisy, being bossy. If it wasn't for her friendship, as well as the others I have made, though they are few, I have no idea where exactly I would be or if I would even still be here.

Because like her, there is also my long-time friend from Glasgow, Scotland, named John Dougan. For just as long as I have been friends with Mary, John and I have also been friends, and corresponding from overseas to here is no easy task. The mail system sucks, but when I'm feeling at my lowest and I reach out to John, he's always been there with his ear lowered and kind words to send back over the waters to me. He is also very understanding of what all is going on with me and how I have been and continue to be mistreated by the prison administration.

Patrick Pease, who is from here in Texas as well, but further up north. I first met Pat, as he likes to be called, when he reached out to Donald Newbury (Lizard), wanting to write him and see if he could attend his execution. Pat wanted to know what it would be like witnessing such a thing. Instead of responding to him, Lizard shot me Pat's letter, and I responded to him. Thinking I wouldn't hear anything back from him, I said a lot to him in the letter. I was in for a shock when a couple of weeks later I got a return letter. From that point on we've been corresponding back and forth and become friends. Pat even drove down from up north a couple of times for visits and to attend my federal court hearing back in 2018 in Austin, Texas. Pat is also a good person who has a huge family, tons of kids and grandchildren that he's always telling about keeping him busy.

Someone else that is special to me and reached out to me after my friend Big Tai was executed, only because I hadn't known he was doing so, but Big Tai reached out to this very special woman and told her about his little homie (Slim) and that if they went through with his execution, would she please be there for his friend. Her name is Sister Cordia Klein, of Germany. She is always writing to me and telling me that she has a candle burning in the Chapel for me and that Jesus loves me, as she does too. Though her English is not great, she does her best to translate the words from German to English whenever she writes. Whenever I get her letters, I can feel the love she has for our Father and that same love she sends my way. Though we've never met, I know that one day she and I will meet up with Big Tai once again when this life is over.

The lawyer who was appointed to my case back in May of 2012, Marcia Widder, she too has become more than just my lawyer. Let me tell you something about how far a lawyer will go to get what she wants. We all know tons of lawyer jokes, and we all know that most lawyers are crooks, some even worse than their clients. But, with Marcy, she brings a whole new caliber to the table. I had been fighting to end my appeals and wanting a hearing in federal court. I got my wish and was at a hearing in federal court in Austin, Texas before the Honorable Robert Pitman back in 2018. As I'm waiting for the U.S. Marshals to come and get me to escort me into the courtroom, being one of my lawyers, Marcy was allowed into the back with me to talk about things. She, along with a couple of my other lawyers and this other little doll named Cassandra, were doing everything that they could to get me not to go through with it. Marcy, seeing that I wasn't going to fold, pulled out a last minute stunt against me. Her daughter, Sasha, had hand-written me a card and drawn a picture on it, telling me that she didn't want me to be killed and that I should let her mommy continue to work on my case! Who in the hell uses their kid as a weapon like that to get what they want! That was a low blow, man. So now, as I'm sitting in front of Judge Pitman and others attending my hearing, I'm thinking about this little girl and the card she did for me, that her mother is using to get her way.

If that's not enough, also in the courtroom is another dear friend and lawyer/investigator named Cassandra Belter. If Sasha and her mother weren't enough, then Cassandra was the next best thing to get me to fold. When I first met Cassandra, I did everything within my power to push her away and not allow her to get close to me as a person. I went so far as to write a short story fiction urban book that I never published, but had her playing in a sex scene with me! I did everything I could to piss this chick off and keep her away, only to have her in the end and over the years become so close to me. That she is now invading my dreams and most of my thoughts. Though I know she is way off limits, we've become very close friends, and she, like Marcy and Mary, is someone that I'm able to go to for anything at any time when I need them/her. Her only fault is that she is a Georgia Bulldog fan, and she is a slave to her cat, Master Hopkins!

 Let me not fail to mention my friend Luis Batiz, who is also a part of my legal team and who at one time was my paralegal and has since become one of my investigators. He too has become more than just a legal team member. He was also friends with my Big Homie Big Tai, as was Cassandra through me. When I first met Luis, or I should say, when I heard he was my paralegal and that if I needed anything I should write to him at the Capital Habeas Unit Office in Philadelphia letting him know, I wrote to him asking that he please send me an S.A.S.E. (Self-Addressed Stamped Envelope) so that I could mail some legal documents back. He does this, but he also sealed the envelope he was sending me! How was I now supposed to send the legal documents back now with the envelope sealed shut. I in turn drew him a picture of a Rook upon a chess board and nicknamed him Rookie! From that point on, he and I would also become fast friends, and this would turn into more than him just being a part of my legal team. He, along with his wife and their daughter and the daughter's boyfriend, would become like an extended part of my own family. The story we share with one another when we're not talking about legal work or my appeals is truly one of a kind. Like myself, Luis also loves to ride motorcycles. During one of our visits one day, he shared with me about how his daughter accidentally hit a motorcyclist there in Philadelphia. I laughed so hard and told him it was a good thing he no longer rides while she's on the road! The stories that come from his family are one of a kind and truly special. I'm thankful that they are a part of my life. Though we honestly know who wear the pants in their house is his wife Joycet!

 The true ones that have also stuck by my side through the thick and the thin of it all, though sometimes they too have a hard time of doing so, and I wish they would be more in contact with me, is that of my mom, sister, and little niece. I know that my situation isn't easy on them and that they too have their own lives to live. I just wish that they would try to write a little more often than they do. However, I'm grateful for the time and effort that they have put into being there for me all these years, when God knows I don't deserve their love nor their continuing support. I cannot begin to imagine what it's like for them as they sit out there living their lives to their best ability, while knowing that one of their loved ones is guilty of Capital Murder and is sitting on Texas Death Row. Knowing that I have failed them in life though keeps me from doing better because it just eats away at my core and spirit, as it does when I think about how I've let so many others down in this life.

The last person to come into my life is my lawsuit lawyer, David A. Lane. I did an art piece for him after retaining him in my lawsuit against Texas Death Row/Texas Department of Criminal Justice. As my other lawyers that were appointed by the courts fight not only to keep me alive while also fighting against me fighting against them and the courts, David has become a friend who is more understanding about the crap I go through within these prison walls. He does his best to keep the peace between my appeal lawyers and I while also getting something done about the way I'm being treated on Death Row by all prison officials and not be allowed to visit with my mom and sister for over 13 years now. It's with his okay that at the back of this book I have added a copy of my current lawsuit as well as that of one with written permission of an Ad-Seg inmate also housed within the walls of the Polunsky Unit. This way you not only are able to read the hell I have gone through and continue to go through, but to read about how others are treated as well. I have never met Mr. Hope, nor do I know anything about him and his life. Word of mouth and his situation got back to me, and I took it upon myself to reach out to his lawyers.

It is my sincere hope that something in this book will help someone out there that is going through a bad time in life or is headed down the wrong path to stop, and know that it can always become worse than what you're currently going through in life. I have no idea what will become of my life, if I'll allow my lawyers to keep fighting to get me off Texas Death Row/Death Watch, or if I'll throw in the towel. At this point in my life, I want everyone to know about my side of the story about my life and what it was and is like for me to live it. Before I close this out, allow me to share one last thing with you from the book Just Mercy, written by Bryan Stevenson, that was sung to him by one of his first Death Row clients in Georgia and used here with permission:

"I'm pressing on, the upward way
New heights I'm gaining, every day

Still praying as, I'm onward bound
Lord, plant my feet on Higher Ground.
Lord lift me up, and let me stand
By faith on Heaven's tableland
A Higher plane, that I have found
Lord, plant my feet on Higher Ground."

The above is me taken by Lisa Wagner in 2004, before coming to Texas.

WITHIN THE SHADOWS OF LIFE

This is a picture of Big Tai on his last day of life visiting with one of his brothers
(R.I.P. Big Tai)

Mary Hampton & I during a visit. That's me holding my Jewish Bible

This is a picture of me taken in 2020 while visiting with Mary

This is a picture of my mom, sister and little niece having a day at the beach.

This is Marcy and her daughter Sasha who are my friends/support

RICHARD TABLER

My friend/lawyer/Investigator
Cassandra L. Belter & Master Hopkins

This is a picture
of my friend/Sister Cordia Klein

WITHIN THE SHADOWS OF LIFE

Lawsuits

RICHARD TABLER

Case 1:20-cv-00111   Document 1   Filed 03/16/20   Page 1 of 16 PageID #: 1

IN THE UNITED STATES DISTRICT COURT
FOR THE EASTERN DISTRICT OF TEXAS
LUFKIN DIVISION

RICHARD TABLER,) Plaintiff,)) v.)) LORIE DAVIS,) Director, Correctional Institutions) Division, Texas Department of Criminal) Justice, in her official capacity.) Defendant.)	Civil Action No. _____

COMPLAINT AND JURY DEMAND

Plaintiff, by and through his attorneys, David A. Lane and Reid Allison of KILLMER, LANE & NEWMAN, LLP, and Richard Burr, BURR AND WELCH, PC, hereby brings this Complaint and alleges as follows:

INTRODUCTION

1. For nearly a decade, Richard Tabler has been housed in the Death Watch section of the Texas Department of Criminal Justice's ("TDCJ") death row, at the Polunsky Unit. He has spent 22 hours per day alone in a small cell. His family is prohibited from visiting him. Besides guards, the people he has interacted with in the Death Watch section have been executed within weeks of their being housed near Mr. Tabler.

2. This is an extreme and torturous existence for any person, which is why those for whom Texas has scheduled an execution spend only a limited, determinate amount of time in the Death Watch section—typically no more than 60-180 days. Studies on prolonged solitary confinement have indisputably shown that such housing significantly damages a person's

physical, mental, and emotional health, while risking heightened levels of anxiety, depression, and exacerbation of pre-existing mental health problems. In recent years, Supreme Court Justices have recognized that prolonged solitary confinement "exact[s] a terrible price," "literally drives men mad," and "raises serious constitutional questions." *Davis v. Ayala*, 135 S. Ct. 2187, 2210 (2015) (Kennedy, J., concurring); *Ruiz v. Texas*, 137 S. Ct. 1246, 1247 (2017) (Breyer, J., dissenting). Justice Sotomayor has recently quoted Charles Dickens' observations that "very few" are "capable of estimating the immense amount of torture and agony which this dreadful punishment [solitary confinement], prolonged for years, inflicts upon the sufferers." *Apodaca v. Raemisch*, 139 S. Ct. 5, 9-10 (2018) (Sotomayor, J., statement on denial of certiorari).

3. For Mr. Tabler, this is a personalized torture, profoundly exacerbating his longstanding severe mental health issues. This cruel, protracted housing has not only significantly worsened his mental health, it has also led him to attempt to take his own life multiple times.

4. Mr. Tabler's continued, indeterminate housing in the Death Watch section: (1) is Cruel and Unusual Punishment, in violation of the Eighth and Fourteenth Amendments; (2) unconstitutionally denies him Due Process, guaranteed by the Fourteenth Amendment, to prevent the atypical and significant hardships he suffers in the Death Watch section; and (3) violates his rights under the Americans with Disabilities Act ("ADA"). He must be immediately transferred out of the Death Watch section.

JURISDICTION AND VENUE

5. This action arises under the Constitution and laws of the United States and is brought pursuant to 42 U.S.C. § 1983 and the Americans with Disabilities Act ("ADA"), 42 U.S.C. §§ 12101 *et seq.*

6. This Court has jurisdiction pursuant to 28 U.S.C. § 1331. Jurisdiction supporting

Plaintiffs' claim for attorneys' fees and costs is conferred by 42 U.S.C. § 1988.

7. Venue is proper in the Eastern District of Texas pursuant to 28 U.S.C. § 1391(b). At all relevant times, Mr. Tabler has been incarcerated within the State of Texas, in the Eastern District, all housing decisions made by Defendant affected him there, and all of the parties were residents of the State of Texas at the time of the events giving rise to this litigation.

PARTIES

8. Plaintiff Richard Tabler has been, at all relevant times, a state prisoner in custody of the TDCJ and housed in the Death Watch section of death row in the Polunsky Unit, Livingston, Texas.

9. Defendant Lorie Davis is the Director of the Correctional Institutions Division ("CID") of TDCJ. As Director of the CID, Defendant Davis is responsible for housing decisions, planning, direction, and coordination of all programs and operations of Texas state prisons, including death row and the Death Watch section at the Allan B. Polunsky Unit ("the Polunsky Unit"), located at 3872 FM 350 South, Livingston, Texas, 77351. Defendant Davis interpreted laws, policies, and operational procedures relevant to all employees at the Polunsky Unit and death row. As part of her directorship of the CID, Defendant Davis authorized and/or condoned the unconstitutional housing of Mr. Tabler. As such, she directly and proximately caused the constitutional and statutory violations set forth below. At all relevant times, Defendant Davis was acting under color of state law, as an official representative of the TDCJ.

FACTUAL ALLEGATIONS

I. Mr. Tabler's Cruel and Unusual housing

10. Mr. Tabler has been housed in the Death Watch section of TDCJ's death row at the Polunsky Unit since January 2, 2011.

11. The Death Watch section houses those TDCJ inmates who have an imminent

Case 1:20-cv-00111   Document 1   Filed 03/16/20   Page 4 of 16 PageID #: 4

execution date, scheduled within 60-180 days. Therefore, inmates spend only a limited, pre-determined amount of time in the Death Watch section.

12. Mr. Tabler does not have an execution date and has not had one scheduled at any point during his nearly ten years housed in the Death Watch section.

13. Mr. Tabler is in the Death Watch unit as punishment for his having been caught with a cell phone approximately ten years ago.

14. The restrictions within the Death Watch section are extreme.

15. Mr. Tabler is held in solitary confinement conditions for 22 hours every day, in a miniscule, 60-square-foot cell.

16. He is provided meals through a slot in the door of his cell.

17. He spends his limited recreation time in a pen separate from other inmates.

18. Mr. Tabler is allowed virtually no face-to-face contact with other inmates.

19. The harshness of these death row conditions, designed intentionally to limit human contact, is substantially exacerbated by Mr. Tabler's unusual status among death row inmates—though he is not scheduled for execution, he is housed exclusively among inmates who are within months of their own scheduled executions.

20. Death row inmates can communicate to a limited extent with other inmates. Given their years- and decades-long waits for execution, these limited communications allow inmates to form relationships and friendships, providing at least some human contact.

21. Perversely, aside from impersonal communications with prison guards, the only people with whom Mr. Tabler is permitted to communicate are sent to be executed within weeks of meeting him. Rather than the comfort that other inmates are permitted to draw from their limited society with one another, Mr. Tabler is confronted with an endless procession of men who are put to death as soon as he is able to form an attachment to them.

22. Indeed, while Mr. Tabler has been housed in the Death Watch section, TDCJ has executed over 90 inmates. Mr. Tabler had formed friendships with at least a dozen of those who were then executed. On average, once a month an inmate has been executed, after spending his final weeks housed in the Death Watch section with Mr. Tabler.

23. Though this bizarre and torturous circumstance would no doubt take a severe toll on the mental well-being of any inmate, Mr. Tabler's specific mental health problems are such that he suffers an unusually elevated level of stress and mental anguish from the loss of people to whom he has become attached.

24. The conditions for Mr. Tabler in the Death Watch section are so severe and have such a profound impact on his mental health that in 2011, a federal judge denied his request to drop his habeas appeals and be executed, after finding that his conditions of confinement coerced him to that decision.

25. Despite the judge's explicit finding that Mr. Tabler's conditions of confinement were so onerous as to coerce him into an effective suicide by dropping his habeas appeals, Mr. Tabler remains housed in the Death Watch section.

26. Mr. Tabler has never been afforded a meaningful process in which to challenge his housing in the Death Watch section and argue for a transfer to Texas' less restrictive standard death row, where he might at least find relief from his constant loss of friends to the death chamber under his current conditions.

II.   Mr. Tabler's severe mental health issues

27. Throughout Mr. Tabler's incarceration, TDCJ has known of his substantial mental health issues.

Case 1:20-cv-00111 Document 1 Filed 03/16/20 Page 6 of 16 PageID #: 6

28. Mr. Tabler has long been diagnosed with Fetal Alcohol Spectrum Disorder (specifically, Alcohol-Related Neurodevelopmental Disorder) and Klinefelter Syndrome. These diagnoses reveal that Mr. Tabler suffers multiple central nervous system dysfunctions, resulting in decreased impulse control, heightened anxiety, mood lability, low frustration tolerance, depression, and executive function impairment. TCDJ has been aware of these diagnoses for nearly five years.

29. With respect to his Fetal Alcohol-Related Neurodevelopmental Disorder, Mr. Tabler suffers difficulty with social skills, including lack of stranger fear, naivete and gullibility; inappropriate choice of friends; immaturity; difficulty understanding the perspective of others; and poor social cognition.

30. Mr. Tabler also meets the criteria for Bipolar Disorder and Attention Deficit Hyperactivity Disorder.

31. In addition to these significant mental health issues, he has suffered repeated traumatic brain injuries.

32. This particular combination of mental health disorders, resulting in emotional instability for Mr. Tabler at the best of times, leaves him without the emotional and cognitive ability to effectively process the loss of people close to him. In the Death Watch section, such losses are frequent and unavoidable and subject Mr. Tabler to undue suffering well beyond what a neurotypical inmate might experience.

33. Mr. Tabler has repeatedly expressed mental distress, including suicidal ideation, and has displayed physically self-harming and suicidal behaviors since his placement in the Death Watch section, often in connection with the frequent loss of friends as a result of their execution. What follows are a few examples of his significant mental health deterioration between 2011 and 2015 due to his housing in the Death Watch section.

34. On February 22, 2011, security and medical personnel contacted Mr. Tabler after he intentionally cut his right arm open.

35. In addition to his overt attempt to kill himself, Mr. Tabler made multiple suicidal statements during that contact with jail personnel.

36. A nurse who spoke with Mr. Tabler noted that she believed Mr. Tabler's suicidal statements might be genuine, and that he should be evaluated by a mental health professional.

37. Mr. Tabler asked the nurse for help with his suicidal impulses and was placed in a psych observation cell.

38. While housed in the observation cell, Mr. Tabler spoke with mental health staff. Mr. Tabler stated that a friend of his from death row had been executed a week earlier, and that another friend was being transported to Huntsville to be executed. Mr. Tabler discussed how difficult he found it to deal with the losses.

39. Asked whether he felt that other inmates' lives were more important than his own life, Mr. Tabler responded affirmatively. The mental health staff who interviewed Mr. Tabler noted that he was surprised by the question and that his eyes filled with tears as he answered.

40. Mr. Tabler recounted a conversation with another death row inmate during which Mr. Tabler voiced a desire to trade places with that inmate so that he could be executed.

41. On November 29, 2012, mental health staff noted that Mr. Tabler vented concerns about recent executions.

42. On February 20, 2013, mental health staff assessed Mr. Tabler after he made suicidal statements in a letter directed to his family and attorney, including a statement that he intended to complete suicide on March 11.

43. During the February 20, 2013 mental health assessment, Mr. Tabler indicated that one of the reasons he wanted to kill himself was that a friend of his was going to be executed the

following day.

44. On October 4, 2013, Mr. Tabler was assessed for urgent mental health needs after he threatened to cut himself with razor blades. Mr. Tabler informed mental health staff that he no longer felt that he was in control and asked to be transferred to the Jester IV inpatient psychiatric facility. The transfer was ordered the same day for the purposes of crisis management.

45. On October 8, 2013, during Mr. Tabler's stay at the Jester IV facility, Mr. Tabler informed staff that he remained very upset and needed to get some things off his chest. He stated that five out of six recently executed inmates had been friends of his, and that their loss had affected him deeply.

46. On October 9, 2013, still at the Jester IV facility, Mr. Tabler reported increased depressive symptoms, including irritability, disturbance of his sleep pattern, decreased appetite, and thoughts of hopelessness. During the same interaction, Mr. Tabler noted his concerns about his housing in the Death Watch section, the pod where death row inmates with imminent execution dates are housed. Mr. Tabler stated that he becomes close with the offenders housed near him, only to lose them to execution, and again referenced his friendship with five of the past six inmates executed. Mr. Tabler explicitly connected the loss of these five inmates with an increased sense of hopelessness and feelings of depression during this conversation.

47. On October 10, 2013, still at the Jester IV facility, Mr. Tabler again indicated his plans for self-harm to mental health staff, and he again explicitly connected his feelings of depression to the fact that several of his friends had been executed over the previous six months.

48. On October 14, 2013, still at the Jester IV facility, Mr. Tabler once more indicated that his poor mental health was connected to the loss of his fellow death row inmates, noting that he had seen 27 men executed.

49. On October 15, 2013, still at the Jester IV facility, mental health staff asked Mr.

Tabler to verbalize his principal problem that would be the focus of his clinical attention. Mr. Tabler asked staff to let him stay at Jester IV for a while rather than returning to the Death Watch area of death row, stating that he needed a break from Death Watch. He again expressed distress related to five of the past six men executed having been his friends. He told mental health staff that he would attempt to harm himself if and when he was returned to Death Watch.

50. Mr. Tabler also told mental health staff that he had been experiencing auditory hallucinations, hearing his friends who had been executed. He stated that he had most recently heard the auditory hallucinations the day after another offender had been executed.

51. On October 17, 2013, Mr. Tabler reported that his problems originated from his housing in the Death Watch section, and that he had seen 40 inmates executed over the course of his incarceration. He further reported that he had experienced auditory hallucinations in conjunction with his friends being taken to be executed, and stated that he felt upset that he would continue to live while his friends were executed. The mental health staff noted that Mr. Tabler's concerns appeared reflective of survivor's guilt.

52. On April 1, 2014, having returned to the Death Watch section, Mr. Tabler was seen by mental health staff after the facility's mail room again reported that Mr. Tabler had made suicidal statements in outgoing mail. Mr. Tabler once again told mental health staff that he was upset by being forced to witness other offenders being taken to die, an inevitable result of his housing in the Death Watch section. He indicated that he had been giving away his property as a precursor to an approaching suicide attempt.

53. On April 2014, Mr. Tabler expressed a desire to stop consuming food and liquids, noting that he was tired from watching executions. Mental health staff noted that Mr. Tabler appeared to desire to go into renal failure and seemed depressed.

54. On February 12, 2015, Mr. Tabler reported that he was feeling down about a

recent execution.

55. On numerous other occasions, and until the present day, Mr. Tabler's mental health has been substantially worsened by his housing in the Death Watch section, and he has continued to exhibit suicidal behaviors throughout his time in the Death Watch section.

56. Indeed, he attempted suicide and very nearly succeeded in June 2019. Mr. Tabler sliced his arm open from wrist to shoulder and nearly died. This was just the most recent in Mr. Tabler's established history of suicide attempts to escape his present torturous day-to-day experience in the Death Watch section.

57. As referenced above, the conditions remain so severe that a federal district judge has previously refused to allow Mr. Tabler to drop his habeas appeals, finding that his conditions of confinement were coercing him to seek execution rather than continue living in the Death Watch section.

58. Plaintiff has fully, properly, and timely exhausted all available administrative remedies in connection with the events described herein.

STATEMENT OF CLAIMS FOR RELIEF

FIRST CLAIM FOR RELIEF
42 U.S.C. § 1983 – Violations of the Eighth and Fourteenth Amendments
Cruel and Unusual Punishment

59. At all times relevant to this action, the Defendant was responsible for promulgating and implementing policies, practices, and procedures relating to inmate classifications and housing decisions.

60. The Defendant's decision to house Mr. Tabler in prolonged solitary confinement, among men due to be executed in mere weeks, in the Death Watch section has deprived and continues to deprive him of basic human needs. Mr. Tabler's continued, indeterminate housing in the Death Watch section is cruel and unusual punishment because this housing deprives him of

basic human needs, imposes serious and irreparable psychological and physical injury on his person, and violates present-day standards of human dignity.

61. The indefinite duration of Mr. Tabler's housing in the Death Watch section poses significant risks of incapacitating him and causing him permanent mental and psychological injury.

62. The Defendant's housing Mr. Tabler in the Death Watch section inflicts disproportionate punishment on him.

63. Housing him in these cruel conditions serves no valid, legal purpose and lacks penological justification.

64. The Defendant's infliction of mental and physical harm on Mr. Tabler strips him of his dignity and worth, transgresses civilized society's notions of decency, and is a practice that is disavowed in contemporary society.

65. The mental and psychological anguish inflicted on Mr. Tabler as a result of his housing in the Death Watch section are obvious to Defendant and any other reasonable person. Defendant knows that Mr. Tabler is suffering substantial and ongoing injury.

66. As a direct and proximate result of Defendant's constitutional violations, Mr. Tabler will continue to be irreparably injured. He will suffer irreparable harm unless Defendant is enjoined from continuing this unconstitutional housing decision.

SECOND CLAIM FOR RELIEF
42 U.S.C. § 1983 – Fourteenth Amendment Due Process Violation

67. Plaintiff Tabler incorporates all other paragraphs of this Complaint for purposes of this Claim.

68. Defendant has substantially increased the punishment suffered by Mr. Tabler by placing him permanently in the Death Watch unit.

69. Defendant has sporadically conducted hearings for inmates facing unusual increased levels of security within the prison system. The Defendant has created a liberty interest through the implementation of hearings, which give inmates the chance for less restrictive confinement and by maintaining a standard death row at the Polunsky Unit, as well as the Death Watch section in which Plaintiff Tabler has been housed for nearly a decade.

70. Plaintiff Tabler has this liberty interest in a due process hearing which may result in a less restrictive and torturous confinement and therefore must be afforded sufficient due process before the interest can be refused.

71. Plaintiff Tabler has not been provided sufficient process to argue for transfer to the less restrictive standard death row and exercise this liberty interest, in violation of his Fourteenth Amendment right to Due Process.

72. By denying him meaningful review of his protracted, indefinite housing in solitary confinement in the Death Watch section and never affording him the opportunity to be considered for transfer to the less restrictive death row, Defendant is denying Mr. Tabler liberty without due process of law.

73. Indefinite confinement in the isolated Death Watch section, with no prospect of meaningful review for transfer to the less restrictive death row unit, imposes atypical and significant hardship on him in relation to the ordinary incidents of prison life.

74. Every other prisoner in Mr. Tabler's Death Watch section has been promptly executed, and no other prisoner has ever been subjected to housing in this unit indefinitely.

75. Defendant's acts and omissions are the proximate cause of the violation of Plaintiff Tabler's rights under the Fifth and Fourteenth Amendments.

76. The acts or omissions of Defendant were conducted within the scope of his official duties and employment.

77. As a direct and proximate result of Defendant's acts or omissions, Plaintiff Tabler has suffered harm and is at risk of suffering harm going forward, until he is provided sufficient process to consider him for transfer to the less restrictive and torturous standard death row unit.

THIRD CLAIM FOR RELIEF
42 U.S.C. § 12132, *et seq.* – Violation of Title II of the Americans with Disabilities Act of 1990, as Amended
Unlawful Discrimination and Failure to Reasonably Accommodate

78. Plaintiff hereby incorporates all other paragraphs of this Complaint as if fully set forth herein.

79. The Americans with Disabilities Act (hereinafter referred to as the "ADA"), 42 U.S.C. §§ 12101 *et seq.*, and specifically 42 U.S.C. §§ 12131-12134, prohibits discrimination in public services on the basis of disability. 42 U.S.C. § 12132 provides:

> Subject the provisions of this subchapter, no qualified individual with a disability shall, by reason of such disability, be excluded from participation in or be denied the benefits of the services, programs, or activities of a public entity, or be subjected to discrimination by any such entity.

80. The ADA defines a "public entity" to include any state or local government or any department, agency, special purpose district, or other instrumentality of a State or local government, 42 U.S.C. § 12131(1). The Texas Department of Criminal Justice is a "public entity" within the meaning of the ADA.

81. Mr. Tabler is a person that Defendant knew had a disability, including severe mental health issues and suicidal ideation, that substantially limits his major life activities.

82. Plaintiff, with or without reasonable modifications to rules, policies or practices, met the essential eligibility requirements for the receipt of services or the participation in programs or activities provided by the Defendant. Thus, Plaintiff was a "qualified individual with disabilities" within the meaning of the ADA, 42 U.S.C. § 12131(2).

83. Plaintiff was qualified to participate in the services, programs, activities, and benefits provided to inmates in the TDCJ's custody within the meaning of Title II of the ADA.

84. Defendant was on notice regarding Mr. Tabler's serious mental health issues, suicidal state of mind, and repeated suicide attempts.

85. Defendant failed to reasonably accommodate Mr. Tabler's disabilities despite knowing of his suicidal ideation, and related impairments and conditions.

86. An obviously reasonable accommodation exists, that TDCJ has failed to provide Mr. Tabler: moving him out of the Death Watch section and back to death row.

87. Defendant's actions and inactions violated clearly established law under Title II of the ADA and its implementing regulations.

88. Defendant had no legitimate basis for violating Mr. Tabler's ADA rights.

89. Defendant's actions and inactions are objectively unreasonable in light of the circumstances.

90. Defendant's actions and inactions are the proximate and legal cause of Plaintiff's injuries.

91. Plaintiff has been and continues to be damaged by Defendant's unlawful conduct under the ADA.

PRAYER FOR RELIEF

WHEREFORE, Plaintiff respectfully requests that this Court enter judgment in his favor and against Defendant, and grant:

(a) Appropriate relief at law and equity;

(b) Declaratory and injunctive relief, as well as other appropriate equitable relief;

(c) Attorneys' fees and the costs associated with this action, including expert witness fees, on all claims allowed by law;

(d)   Any further relief that this Court deems just and proper, and any other relief as allowed by law.

PLAINTIFF HEREBY DEMANDS A JURY TRIAL ON ALL ISSUES SO TRIABLE.

Dated this 16th day of March 2020.

KILLMER, LANE & NEWMAN, LLP

s/ David A. Lane
David A. Lane
Reid Allison
KILLMER, LANE & NEWMAN, LLP
1543 Champa Street, Suite 400
Denver, Colorado 80202
(303) 571-1000
(303) 571-1001
dlane@kln-law.com
rallison@kln-law.com

BURR AND WELCH, PC

s/ Richard Burr
Richard Burr
Texas Bar No. 24001005
Burr and Welch, PC
PO Box 525
Leggett, Texas 77350
(713) 628-3391
(713) 893-2500 fax
dick.burrandwelch@gmail.com

ATTORNEYS FOR PLAINTIFF

CERTIFICATE OF SERVICE

The undersigned certifies that a true and correct copy of the foregoing pleading was served electronically upon Kristen Worman (kristen.worman@tdcj.texas.gov), General Counsel for the Texas Department of Criminal Justice and counsel for Respondent, this 16th day of March, 2020.

/s/Richard H. Burr
Counsel for Plaintiff

IN THE UNITED STATES DISTRICT COURT
FOR THE EASTERN DISTRICT OF TEXAS
LUFKIN DIVISION

RICHARD TABLER, Plaintiff, v. LORIE DAVIS, Director, Correctional Institutions Division, Texas Department of Criminal Justice, in her official capacity, Defendant.	)))) Civil Action No. 1:20-cv-111))))))

MOTION TO TRANSFER CASE TO PROPER DIVISION

Plaintiff RICHARD TABLER respectfully requests that the Court transfer this case to the Lufkin Division. The causes of action have arisen in the Lufkin Division. Undersigned inadvertently filed in the Beaumont Division.

Respectfully submitted,

s/ David A. Lane
David A. Lane
Reid Allison
Killmer, Lane & Newman, LLP
1543 Champa Street, Suite 400
Denver, Colorado 80202
303-571-1000
303-571-1001 (fax)
dlane@kln-law.com
rallison@kln-law.com

s/ Richard Burr
Richard H. Burr
Texas Bar No. 24001005
Burr & Welch PC
P.O. Box 525
Leggett, Texas 77350
713-516-5229
713-893-2500 (fax)
dick.burrandwelch@gmail.com

Counsel for Petitioner

CERTIFICATE OF SERVICE

The undersigned certifies that a true and correct copy of the foregoing pleading was served electronically upon Kristen Worman (kristen.worman@tdcj.texas.gov), General Counsel of the Texas Department of Criminal Justice, and counsel for Defendant, this 17th day of March, 2020.

/s/Richard H. Burr
Counsel for Plaintiff

IN THE UNITED STATES DISTRICT COURT
FOR THE EASTERN DISTRICT OF TEXAS
BEAUMONT DIVISION

RICHARD TABLER	§	
VS.	§	CIVIL ACTION NO. 1:20cv111
LORIE DAVIS	§	

TRANSFER ORDER

This action came on before the Court, and the issues having been duly considered and a decision having been duly rendered, it is

ORDERED and **ADJUDGED** that this action is **TRANSFERRED** to the Lufkin Division of this court.

SIGNED this 20th day of March, 2020.

Zack Hawthorn
United States Magistrate Judge

IN THE UNITED STATES DISTRICT COURT
FOR THE EASTERN DISTRICT OF TEXAS
LUFKIN DIVISION

RICHARD TABLER,	§	
Plaintiff,	§	
	§	
v.	§	CIVIL ACTION NO. 9:20-cv-00049
	§	
LORIE DAVIS,	§	
Defendants.	§	

**DEFENDANT LORIE DAVIS'S MOTION TO DISMISS PURSUANT TO FEDERAL
RULES OF CIVIL PROCEDURE 12(b)(1) AND 12(b)(6)**

Defendant Lorie Davis, Director of the Texas Department of Criminal Justice—Correctional Institutions Division (TDCJ-CID), as sued in her official capacity, files this motion to dismiss pursuant to 12(b)(1) and 12(b)(6) of the Federal Rules of Civil Procedure in response to Plaintiff's Original Complaint. ECF No. 1.

I. Statement of the Case

In his Original Complaint, Plaintiff Richard Tabler sues Lorie Davis, Director of TDCJ-CID, in her official capacity for cruel and unusual punishment in violation of the Eighth Amendment, denial of due process, under 42 U.S.C. § 1983, and for violation of his rights under the Americans with Disabilities Act ("ADA"). ECF No. 1. Tabler seeks "appropriate relief at law and equity," "declaratory and injunctive[1] relief, as well as other appropriate equitable relief," and attorney's fees and costs. *Id.* at 14. Tabler does not seek compensatory damages.

---

[1] It is unclear what form of injunctive relief Plaintiff is seeking. It seems that he is seeking to be moved out of the "Death Watch" section. See ECF No. 1 at 14 ("An obviously reasonable accommodation exists, that TDCJ has failed to provide Mr. Tabler: moving him out of the Death Watch section and back to death row.").

II. Statement of Facts

Plaintiff Richard Tabler is an offender in custody of TDCJ housed at the Polunsky Unit in Livingston, Texas. ECF No. 1 at 3. Tabler was sentenced to death on April 2, 2007 for capital murder. While he was at the Polunsky unit, Tabler was convicted of smuggling in a cell phone and using it to call and threaten Senator Whitmire. He was also convicted of retaliation. According to the Complaint, Tabler has been housed at the Polunksy Unit in the "Death Watch" section of death row since January 2, 2011. ECF No. 1 at 3. Usually, offenders housed in the Death Watch cells are scheduled to have an execution date; however, Tabler's execution date is still not scheduled. *Id.* at 4. Tabler asserts he has been housed on Death Watch as "punishment" for being caught with the cell phone ten years ago. *Id.*

In October of 2013, Tabler was transferred to TDCJ's Jester IV unit, an inpatient psychiatric facility, for making multiple suicide attempts. *Id.* at 7–8. Tabler remained at the Jester IV unit, where he told mental health staff that he would attempt to harm himself if he was returned to Death Watch. *Id.* at 9. Tabler asserts that his mental health issues originated from seeing 40 inmates executed over the course of his incarceration,[2] and mental health noted Tabler's concerns appeared reflective of "survivor's guilt." *Id.* After being housed at Jester IV for about 1.5 years, Tabler returned to the Death Watch section at the Polunsky Unit in April of 2014. *Id.* at 9. Tabler again was expressing suicidal ideations in went on hunger strike in April of 2014. *Id.* Tabler notes that on numerous other occasions, and until the present day, his mental health has been substantially worsened by his housing in the Death Watch section, and he has continued to exhibit suicidal behaviors throughout his time in the Death Watch section. *Id.*

Plaintiff Tabler sues Lorie Davis, the Director of TDCJ-CID, in her official capacity, alleging that she is responsible for housing decisions, planning, direction, and coordination of all programs

---

[2] Throughout his Complaint, Tabler makes many statements similar to being "tired from watching executions." ECF No. 1 at 9. The death chamber is not at the Polunsky unit, but rather at the Huntsville Unit, where Tabler would not witness any executions.

and operations of Texas state prisons. *Id.* at 3. Tabler further alleges that Ms. Davis interpreted the laws, polices, and operational procedures relevant to all employees at the Polunsky Unit and death row, and authorized and/or condoned the unconstitutional housing of Mr. Tabler. *Id.*

III. Standards of Review

Motions to dismiss under FED. R. CIV. P. 12(b)(1) are reviewed under the same standard as a motion to dismiss failure to state a claim upon which relief can be granted under Rule 12(b)(6). *Rivas-Hernandez v. U.S.*, EP-98-CR-345-DB, 2000 WL 33348738, at *1 (W.D. Tex. Oct. 30, 2000) (citing *Benton v. United States*, 960 F.2d 19, 21 (5th Cir. 1992)). Rule 12(b)(1) allows a party to move for dismissal of an action for lack of subject-matter jurisdiction. The party asserting that subject-matter jurisdiction exists bears the burden of proof on a 12(b)(1) motion. *Crowell v. Lahood*, CIV.A. H-09-1788, 2011 WL 147913, at *1 (S.D. Tex. Jan. 18, 2011) (citing *Ramming v. United States*, 281 F.3d 158, 161 (5th Cir. 2001)), *cert. denied sub nom. Cloud v. United States*, 536 U.S. 960 (2002). The court may determine whether subject-matter jurisdiction is lacking by any of three approaches: "(1) the complaint alone; (2) the complaint supplemented by undisputed facts evidenced in the record; or (3) the complaint supplemented by undisputed facts plus the court's resolution of disputed facts." *Ramming*, 281 F.3d at 161.

When evaluating a motion to dismiss under Rule 12(b)(6), the complaint must be liberally construed in favor of the plaintiff and all facts pleaded therein must be taken as true. *Leatherman v. Tarrant Cnty Narcotics Intel. & Coordination Unit*, 507 U.S. 163, 164 (1993); *Baker v. Putnal*, 75 F.3d 190, 196 (5th Cir. 1996). A complaint must nevertheless contain sufficient factual matter, accepted as true, to "state a claim to relief that is plausible on its face." *Bell Atlantic v. Twombly*, 550 U.S. 554, 570 (2007). This plausibility standard is not simply a "probability requirement," but imposes a standard higher than "a sheer possibility that a defendant has acted unlawfully." *Ashcroft v. Iqbal*, 556 U.S. 662, 679 (2009).

The standard is properly guided by "[t]wo working principles." *Id.* First, although "a court must accept as true all of the allegations contained in the complaint," that tenet "is inapplicable to legal conclusions" and "[t]hreadbare recitals of the elements of a cause of action, supported by mere conclusory statements do not suffice." *Id.* at 667–78. Second, "[d]etermining whether a complaint states a plausible claim for relief will . . . be a context-specific task that requires the reviewing court to draw on its judicial experience and common sense." *Id.* at 679. In considering a motion to dismiss, therefore, the court must initially identify pleadings that are no more than legal conclusions not entitled to the assumption of truth, then assume the veracity of well-pleaded factual allegations to determine whether those allegations plausibly give rise to any right to relief. If not, "the complaint has alleged— but it has not shown—that the pleader is entitled to relief." *Id.* (internal quotations omitted).

IV. Arguments and Authority

A. Plaintiff's 42 U.S.C. § 1983 claim against Ms. Davis in her official capacity must be dismissed for failure to state a claim and lack of jurisdiction.

Plaintiff Tabler claims that Ms. Davis's decision to house him in the Death Watch section has deprived him and continues to deprive him of his basic human needs, imposes psychological and physical injury on his person, and violates present-day standards of human decency. ECF No. 1 at 10–11. In sum, Tabler asserts that his housing inflicts a "disproportionate punishment"[3] on him, with no valid, legal purpose and lacks penological justification. *Id.* Additionally, Ms. Davis, is entitled to

---

[3] Plaintiff alleges he is housed on Death Watch as punishment for having a cell phone. A review of his public profile on the TDCJ "Offender Search" shows that he was convicted of capital murder and sentenced in 2007. https://offender.tdcj.texas.gov/OffenderSearch/offenderDetail.action?sid=07420770. While he was incarcerated, he was convicted of having a prohibited item in a correctional facility and retaliation; he was sentenced for 10 years for each crime in 2009. *Id.* To the extent that receiving the relief requested in this lawsuit, i.e., moving his housing, would invalidate his conviction or sentence, his claims are Heck-barred. *Heck v. Humphrey*, 512 U.S. 477, 487 (1994) ("[w]hen 'a judgment in favor of the plaintiff would necessarily imply the invalidity of his conviction or sentence,' . . . § 1983 is not an available remedy. . . . 'But if . . . the plaintiff's action, even if successful, will not demonstrate the invalidity of [his conviction or sentence], the [§ 1983] action should be allowed to proceed . . . '").

Eleventh Amendment immunity for the 42 U.S.C. § 1983 claims, and this Court lacks jurisdiction over the ADA claim altogether due to sovereign immunity. All claims are barred by the statute of limitations.

1. Defendant Davis is entitled to Eleventh Amendment Immunity for claims brought against her in her official capacity.

Title 42, United States Code, Section 1983 authorizes the assertion of a claim for relief against a person who, acting under the color of state law, allegedly violated the claimant's rights under federal law. *See* 42 U.S.C. § 1983. In Section 1983 suits, government officials may be sued in either their individual or official capacities. A claim against a state or municipal official in his official capacity "generally represent[s] only another way of pleading an action against an entity of which an officer is an agent." *Kentucky v. Graham*, 473 U.S. 159, 165 (1985) (citation omitted). Individual or personal capacity suits "seek to impose personal liability upon a government official for actions he takes under color of state law." *Id.* (citation omitted).

Plaintiff only brings suit against Defendant Lorie Davis in her official capacity. *See* ECF No. 1. Defendant Davis moves to dismiss the § 1983 claims brought against her in her official capacity because she is entitled to sovereign immunity pursuant to the Eleventh Amendment of the United States Constitution. *See Warnock v. Pecos Cnty.*, Tex., 88 F.3d 341, 343 (5th Cir. 1996) ("Eleventh Amendment sovereign immunity deprives a federal court of jurisdiction to hear a suit against a state."). The Texas Department of Criminal Justice, as a state agency, enjoys sovereign immunity under the Eleventh amendment. As previously mentioned, official capacity suits "generally represent only another way of pleading an action against an entity of which an officer is an agent." *Graham*, 473 U.S. at 165 (citation omitted). Thus, "an official capacity suit is, in all respects other than name, to be treated as a suit against the entity." *Id.* at 166. Consequently, the Eleventh Amendment bars suits against state officials and employees of state entities, acting in their official capacities. *See K.P. v. LeBlanc*, 627 F.3d 115, 124 (5th Cir. 2010) (citations omitted); *Green v. State Bar of Tex.*, 27 F.3d 1083,

1087 (5th Cir. 1994) (plaintiff cannot evade Eleventh Amendment by suing state employees in their official capacity).

a. Plaintiff Tabler does not meet the elements of the *Ex Parte Young* exception

The Supreme Court has carved out a narrow exception for suits for injunctive or declaratory relief against individual state officials. *Ex parte Young*, 209 U.S. 123, 155–56 (1908)); *see also Nelson v. Univ. of Tex. at Dallas*, 535 F.3d 318, 321-22 (5th Cir. 2008) ("Pursuant to the Ex Parte Young exception, the Eleventh Amendment is not a bar to suits for prospective relief against a state employee acting in his official capacity."). Under the *Ex Parte Young* exception, "claims against state officials for prospective injunctive relief under § 1983 . . . are not barred by sovereign immunity." *Kobaisy v. Univ. of Miss.*, 624 F. App'x 195, 198 (5th Cir. 2015) (citing *Nelson*, 535 F.3d at 324); *see May v. N. Tex. State Hosp.*, 351 F. App'x 879, 880 (5th Cir. 2009) (citing *Aguilar v. Tex. Dep't of Crim. Justice*, 160 F.3d 1052, 1054 (5th Cir. 1998) (stating that the *Ex Parte Young* exception "applies to suits that allege a violation of federal law that are 'brought against individual persons in their official capacities as agents of the state, and the relief sought must be declaratory or injunctive in nature and prospective in effect.'").

The *Ex Parte Young* exception only applies "when (1) the suit is against a state official and (2) the plaintiff seeks only prospective injunctive relief (3) in order to end a 'continuing violation of federal law.'" *Thomas v. Texas*, 294 F. Supp. 3d 576, 592–93 (N.D. Tex. 2018). Here, Tabler asserts in his Complaint that he "has suffered harm and is at risk of suffering harm going forward" and that he will "continue to be irreparably injured" until he is "provided sufficient process to consider him for transfer to the less restrictive and torturous standard death row unit." ECF No. 1 at 11, 13. However, as explained below, Tabler's relief does not fit the *Ex Parte Young* exception because he does not allege a continuing violation of federal law.

b. Plaintiff fails to state a persistent widespread policy or practice implemented or enforced by Defendant Davis

"[I]n an official-capacity suit the entity's 'policy or custom' must have played a part in the violation of federal law." *Graham*, 473 U.S. at 166. A § 1983 claim asserting a violation of the plaintiff's federal constitutional rights may proceed in federal court as long as the relief sought against a state official in official capacities is "declaratory or injunctive in nature and prospective in effect." *NiGen Biotech, L.L.C. v. Paxton*, 804 F.3d 389, 394 (5th Cir. 2015). "The failure of plaintiff to allege specific facts showing precisely how each of the named defendants was personally involved in the alleged [violations of a plaintiff's constitutional rights] does not furnish a basis for the dismissal of this action." *Barnes v. Givens*, Civil Action No. SA-17-CA-1071-XR, 2019 U.S. Dist. LEXIS 187059, at *13 (W.D. Tex. Oct. 29, 2019) (citing *Bagwell v. Livingston*, No. SA-15-CV-584-DAE, 2016 U.S. Dist. LEXIS 11173, 2016 WL 393553, at *2 (W.D. Tex. Feb. 1, 2016)).

To establish liability against a state employee in their official capacity pursuant to § 1983, a plaintiff must demonstrate that an official policy is the "moving force" behind the employee's allegedly unconstitutional act. *See Monell v. Dep't of Soc. Servs.*, 436 U.S. 658, 694 (1978); *Piotrowski v. City of Houston*, 237 F.3d 567, 578 (5th Cir. 2001). "To establish liability for a policy or practice, a plaintiff must prove that (1) the local government or official promulgated a policy; (2) the decision [or policy] displayed 'deliberate indifference' and proved the government's culpability; and (3) the policy decision lead to a particular injury." *In re Foust*, 310 F.3d 849, 861 (5th Cir. 2002) (citation omitted). An official policy is either a formal statement officially adopted by a municipality or a persistent widespread practice of municipal employees which is common and well established. *Id.*; *see Powers v. Clay*, No. V-11-051, 2012 U.S. Dist. LEXIS 184738, at *27-28 (S.D. Tex. Nov. 21, 2012) (dismissing claims against TDCJ defendants in their official capacities on the grounds that that plaintiffs failed to show that the policy in place for prison shakedowns do not reflect "deliberate indifference" and is "facially innocuous").[4]

Here, Tabler has not shown or alleged any specific TDCJ policy that deprived him of either a cognizable property or liberty interest. First, he has pointed to no state statute that creates property interest in his housing or classification. In fact, there is much law to the contrary as explained below. Second, Tabler has not stated a claim that Ms. Davis, or TDCJ, have deprived him of a cognizable liberty interest, because his classification on death row does not impose "atypical and significant hardship…in relation to the ordinary incidents of prison life." *Sandin v. Conner*, 515 U.S. 472, 483-484 (1995). Even if he did provide a policy, Tabler failed to allege that policy constituted deliberate indifference. Further, Plaintiff Tabler has failed to state an Eighth Amendment claim, as discussed below.

2. Plaintiff's allegations of conditions of confinement must be dismissed

Here, Tabler is essentially asserting a condition of confinement claim under 42 U.S.C. § 1983 by alleging that he has been deprived and continues to be deprived of basic human needs. The required substantial showing of the denial of a constitutional right must have some footing in the law. *Ruiz v. Davis*, 850 F.3d 225, 228 (5th Cir. 2017). The Fifth Circuit in *Ruiz* was not aware of any court that has found an Eighth Amendment violation occasioned by years on death row while a prisoner pursues his

---

[4] To the extent that Plaintiff seeks to sue Ms. Davis because of her supervisory capacity, he fails to state a claim. "Personal involvement is an essential element of a civil rights cause of action." *Thompson v. Steele*, 709 F.2d 381, 382 (5th Cir. 1983). There is no vicarious or *respondeat superior* liability of supervisors under section 1983. *Thompkins v. Belt*, 828 F.2d 298, 303-04 (5th Cir. 1987). *See also Carnaby v. City of Houston*, 636 F.3d 183, 189 (5th Cir. 2011) (the acts of subordinates do not trigger individual § 1983 liability for supervisory officials). "Supervisory officials may be held liable only if: (1) they affirmatively participate in acts that cause constitutional deprivation; or (2) implement unconstitutional policies that causally result in plaintiff's injuries." *Mouille v. City of Live Oak, Tex.*, 977 F.2d 924, 929 (5th Cir. 1992). Thus, a supervisor who is not personally involved is liable only if he has implemented "a policy so deficient that the policy itself is a repudiation of the constitutional rights and is the moving force of the constitutional violation." *Thompkins*, 828 F.2d at 304. "Mere knowledge and acquiescence on a supervisor's part is insufficient to create supervisory liability under § 1983." Doe v. Bailey, No. H-14-2985, 2015 U.S. Dist. LEXIS 136508, 2015 WL 5737666, at *9 (S.D. Tex. Sep. 30, 2015) (citing *Iqbal*, 556 U.S. at 677).

direct and collateral appeals. *Id.* The Fifth Circuit's jurisprudence on the subject is well-known: "[t]here are compelling justifications for the delay between conviction and the execution of a death sentence… [Prisoners who have] benefited from this careful and meticulous process . . . cannot [later] complain that the expensive and laborious process of habeas corpus appeals which exists to protect [them] violate[s] other of [their] rights." Here, it seems that Plaintiff Tabler's habeas appeals are still pending. ECF No. 1 at 5. Much like the case here, Ruiz alleged that he had been in solitary confinement for the majority of time he was on death row. *Ruiz*, 850 F.3d at 229. The Ruiz court dismissed his claims, citing several cases. *See Knight v. Florida*, 528 U.S. 990 (1999) (Thomas, J., concurring) (concurring in denial of certiorari in extended death-row confinement claims and, in response to Justice Stevens's "invitation to state and lower courts to serve as 'laboratories' in which the viability of this claim could receive further study," arguing that courts "have resoundingly rejected the claim as meritless"); *see also Stafford v. Ward*, 59 F.3d 1025, 1028 (10th Cir. 1995) ("We conclude that Appellant has failed to show that executing him after fifteen years on death row, during which time he faced at least seven execution dates, would constitute cruel and unusual punishment."); *Johns v. Bowersox*, 203 F.3d 538, 547 (8th Cir. 2000) (holding that, even if petitioner's *Lackey* claim were not barred, "[a]bsent evidence that the delay was caused intentionally to prolong the defendants time on death row, we [have] held that it [does] not even begin to approach a constitutional violation"); *Smith v. Mahoney*, 611 F.3d 978, 998 (9th Cir. 2010) (holding, in the context of AEDPA review, that "the Supreme Court has never held that execution after a long tenure on death row is cruel and unusual punishment"). *Ruiz*, 850 F.3d at 228, n.10.

Plaintiff Tabler has failed to state a claim that rises to the level of a constitutional violation because he has not identified any "basic human need" which he was denied for an unreasonable period of time. In *Crawford v. Epps*, No. 4:12CV38-M-A, 2014 U.S. Dist. LEXIS 68436 (N.D. Miss. Feb. 28, 2014), Crawford, a death row inmate, alleged a multitude of claims falling under the category of general

9

conditions of confinement. *Id.* Specifically, he alleged: (1) intermittently available hot water, (2) unsatisfactory laundry service, (3) lack of incentive programs for death row inmates, (4) unreasonably high prices at the prison canteen, (5) improperly conducted fire drills in the building housing death row inmates. *Id.* at *12. [T]he Eighth Amendment may afford protection against conditions of confinement which constitute health threats but not against those which cause mere discomfort or inconvenience." *Wilson v. Lynaugh*, 878 F.2d 846, 849 (5th Cir. 1989), *cert. denied*, 493 U.S. 969 (1989) (citation omitted). "Inmates cannot expect the amenities, conveniences, and services of a good hotel." *Id.* at 849 n.5 (citation omitted). It is clear that prison officials have certain duties under the Eighth Amendment, but these duties are only to provide prisoners with "humane conditions of confinement," including "adequate food, clothing, shelter, and medical care…" *Woods v. Edwards*, 51 F.3d 577, 581 n.10 (5th Cir. 1995) (quoting *Farmer v. Brennan*, 511 U.S. 825, 832 (1994)). The court in *Crawford* found that none of these claims amounted to a constitutional violation.

Specifically, as to the "fire drill" claim for death row inmates, the court wrote:

> A prison policy or practice will not be found unconstitutional as long as it is reasonably related to a legitimate penological objective of the facility. *Hay v. Waldron*, 834 F.2d 481, 487-87 (5th Cir. 1987). Though a different, more thorough, method of conducting a fire drill in Crawford's unit would be a more accurate measure of the ability of prison officials to evacuate the unit, the State's interest in the safety and security of both prisoners and prison staff is readily apparent. Transporting death row inmates is fraught with risk for both guards and prisoners. Therefore, the court will not second-guess the decision by prison administrators to use the procedure they have chosen to carry out fire drills.

Id. at *15–16. The court in Crawford found there was a legitimate penological interest in the State's interest in the safety and security of the prisoners and prison staff.

In another case, brought under the ADA but with similar complaints regarding the conditions of confinement on death row is *Scheanette v. Riggins*, No. 9:05cv34, 2005 U.S. Dist. LEXIS 41777 (E.D.

Tex. Dec. 14, 2005). In *Scheanette*, the plaintiff alleges there was a policy of discrimination against inmates on Death Row, including: the denial of access to television, the taking of blood samples in the dayroom, no spoons or cups are given to Death Row inmates, other inmates have been gassed while hanging themselves, inmates are not provided with any kind of educational programs, inmates are strip searched regardless of the weather, inmates are housed in segregation for 22 1/2 hours per day, strip searches are conducted every time inmates leave their cells, the medicine of an inmate Dione Summerlin was confiscated even though Summerlin had previously attempted suicide, Death Row inmates are locked down twice a year for shakedowns, Death Row inmates are moved from cell to cell yearly while inmates in general population stay in the same cell throughout their incarceration, Death Row inmates are not permitted to go to the law library, information about Death Row inmates is placed on the Internet, the Death Row inmates get clothes that say "D.R." on them, they are not allowed to practice their religion with other inmates of the same faith but must do it by themselves or with a minister at the cell, they are not allowed any inmate to inmate contact, and they receive different I.D. numbers beginning with 999. *Id.* at *6. In a *Martinez* Report provided by the prison officials, the prison officials stated legitimate, non-discriminatory reasons having to do with legitimate penological reasons to explain the conditions in which the plaintiff complained. *Id.* at *10.

The *Scheanette* court reasoned that the Fifth Circuit has held that indicia of confinement constituting cruel and unusual punishment include wanton and unnecessary infliction of pain, conditions grossly disproportionate to the severity of the crime warranting imprisonment, and the deprivation of the minimal civilized measures of life's necessities. *Wilson v. Lynaugh*, 878 F.2d 846, 848 (5th Cir.), cert. denied 493 U.S. 969 (1989). The Supreme Court has held, however, that to the extent that prison conditions are restrictive and even harsh, they are part of the penalty that criminal offenders pay for their offenses against society. *Rhodes v. Chapman*, 452 U.S. 337, 346–47, (1981). In compliance with the Supreme Court's opinion, the Fifth Circuit has stated that the Eighth Amendment does not afford protection against mere discomfort or inconvenience. *Wilson*, 878 F.2d at 849.

As to Scheanette's complaint regarding being housed in segregation for 22.5 hours a day, the court responded that inmates convicted of capital murder represent a significant risk to the security of the institution, and the segregation of such individuals, for the protection of staff, other inmates, and themselves, is reasonably related to a legitimate penological purpose. *Id.* at *24–25. The court dismissed Scheanette's claims as he failed to state a claim under the ADA.

This Court should apply the same standard. Tabler is not housed on death row in a restrictive cell to make friends but is a penalty that criminal offender pay for their offenses against society. Although his mental health has suffered in this environment, the Eighth Amendment does not afford protection against discomfort and inconvenience, and the removal of Tabler from the restrictive housing will do more harm than good to anyone.

3. Plaintiff's allegations of due process violation must be dismissed because he lacks a liberty interest in his housing.

"To state a Fourteenth Amendment due process claim under § 1983, a plaintiff must first identify a protected life, liberty or property interest and then prove that governmental action resulted in a deprivation of that interest." *Morris v. Livingston*, 739 F.3d 740, 750 (5th Cir. 2014). Prisoners have no constitutionally protected liberty interest in a particular housing assignment. *See Nathan v. Hancock*, 477 F. App'x 197, 199 (5th Cir. 2012) (no liberty interest is implicated by a prisoner's change in custody status, placement in segregation or lockdown and consequent restrictions on privileges). Liberty interests protected by the Due Process Clause are "generally limited to freedom from restraint which ... imposes atypical and significant hardship on the inmate in relation to the ordinary incidents of prison life." *Sandin v. Conner*, 515 U.S. 472, 483-484 (1995); *see also Meachum v. Fano*, 427 U.S. 215, 225 (1976) (no protected liberty interest in housing at a particular prison facility); *Nash v. Wilkinson*, 124 F. App'x 254, 255 (5th Cir. 2005) (no liberty interest in housing assignment); *Adeleke v. Heaton*, 352 F.

App'x 904 (5th Cir. 2009) ("Adeleke's allegations fail to state a claim for deprivation of due process of law arising out of his change in housing or arising out of the lockdown after the transfer of housing units. Adeleke's due process challenge to his transfer from one unit to another are without merit; prison officials exercise sole discretion over inmate unit placement, and inmates do not have a constitutionally protected property or liberty interest in housing in certain facilities.").

In *Bisby*, the punishments imposed on the inmate plaintiff, Bisby, included a reduction in classification status, a change in housing assignment, and the loss of 180 days good time credits. *Bisby v. Dir., TDCJ-CID*, No. 6:10cv358, 2010 U.S. Dist. LEXIS 139281, at *8 (E.D. Tex. Nov. 15, 2010). The punishments of reduction in classification status and a change in housing assignment do not impose atypical and significant hardships on an inmate in relation to the ordinary incidents of prison life. *Id.* (citing *Wilson v. Budney*, 976 F.2d 957, 958 (5th Cir. 1992) (no protected liberty interest in custodial classification); *Bradley v. Mississippi Department of Corrections*, 283 F. App'x 250, 2008 WL 2489905 (5th Cir., 2008) (no liberty interest in housing assignment); *Wilkerson v. Stalder*, 329 F.3d 431, 435–36 (5th Cir. 2003); *Moody v. Baker*, 857 F.2d 256, 257–58 (5th Cir. 1988)). In a similar case, in which a death row inmate complained about his custodial status, this Court found that the did not have a protected liberty or property interest in his classification status. *Robertson v. Thaler*, No. 9:12cv58, 2013 U.S. Dist. LEXIS 66135, at *11 (E.D. Tex. May 9, 2013). The inmate argued that the Death Row plan gave him a "state created liberty interest" in being present for his classification hearings, but this Court found that there was no constitutional violation in the fact that he was not allowed to be personally present at the classification hearing because he had no liberty interest in his custodial classification. *Id.*

Here, Tabler was placed in restrictive housing on death row due to smuggling in a cell phone and then using that cell phone to threaten a state senator. *See Tabler v. Stephens*, 588 F. App'x 297, 300 (5th Cir. 2014). An inquiry into the call ultimately led to an investigation into cell phone smuggling in the prison, which purportedly resulted in threats and harassment from prison staff and fellow inmates. *Id.* Due to his illegal actions of smuggling a cell phone, threatening a senator, and retaliation while he incarcerated in TDCJ,[5] prison officials exercised their discretion over Tabler's housing placement when he was placed in the restrictive housing area of death row.

B. Defendant Davis is entitled to sovereign immunity under the ADA.

Defendant Davis is entitled to sovereign immunity under the ADA because it's Eleventh Amendment immunity has no been abrogated. The doctrine of sovereign immunity "bars an individual from suing a state in federal court unless the state consents to suit or Congress has clearly and validly abrogated the state's sovereign immunity." *See, e.g., Perez v. Region 20 Educ. Serv. Ctr.*, 307 F.3d 318, 326 (5th Cir. 2002); *Kimel v. Florida Bd. of Regents*, 528 U.S. 62, 72–73 (2000) (stating that "for over a century now, we have made clear that the Constitution does not provide for federal jurisdiction over suits against nonconsenting States"); *Bd. of Trustees of Univ. of Alabama v. Garrett*, 531 U.S. 356, 363 (2001) (stating that "[t]he ultimate guarantee of the Eleventh Amendment is that nonconsenting States may not be sued by private individuals in federal court"). Congress, however, has the power to "single-handedly strip the states of their Eleventh Amendment immunity and thereby authorize federal court suits by individuals against the states." *Pace v. Bogalusa City School Bd.*, 403 F.3d 272, 277 (5th Cir. 2005). "When Congress does this, it is exercising its power to abrogate Eleventh Amendment immunity." *Id.* In addition to Congress' power to abrogate immunity, a state can also be sued if it has "waive[d] its Eleventh Amendment protection and allow[ed] a federal court to hear and decide a case" by consent. *See Idaho v. Coeur d'Alene Tribe of Idaho*, 521 U.S. 261, 267 (1997). In this case, it is undisputed that TDCJ is an arm of the State of Texas and can assert sovereign immunity as a defense from suit. *Sherwinski v.*

---

[5] See TDCJ Offender Search, https://offender.tdcj.texas.gov/OffenderSearch/offenderDetail.action?sid=07420770 (Last visited May 22, 2020).

Peterson, 98 F.3d 849, 851 (5th Cir. 1996). Here, Plaintiff has failed to allege any claims under § 504 of the Rehabilitation Act and thus has not stated a waiver of immunity for TDCJ-CID under the ADA.

1. Plaintiff fails to state a claim under the ADA/RA.

The Supreme Court has set out a three-part test to determine whether or not Title II of the ADA abrogates a state's sovereign immunity. *United States v. Georgia*, 546 U.S. 151, 159 (2006). First, the district court must consider which aspects of the State's alleged conduct violated Title II. *Id.* After making this determination, the court must ask to what extent such misconduct also violated the Fourteenth Amendment. *Id.* If the State's conduct violated both Title II and the Fourteenth Amendment, then Title II validly abrogates state sovereign immunity. *Id., see also Hale v. King*, 642 F.3d 492, 498 (5th Cir. 2011). If the conduct only violates Title II and not the Fourteenth Amendment, the court must then consider whether Congress' purported abrogation of sovereign immunity as to that class of conduct is nevertheless valid. *Id.*

Abrogation of sovereign immunity is not "absolute" in in a Title II ADA claim. *Brigham v. Tex. Dep't of Criminal Justice*, No. 1:15-CV-440, 2016 U.S. Dist. LEXIS 135674, at *16 (E.D. Tex. Aug. 29, 2016). The first step for the Court is to consider whether the plaintiff has state a claim for relief under Title II. Here, Plaintiff has failed to allege any violation of the Eighth Amendment or state a claim under Title II for the reasons set forth below. Thus, Ms. Davis retains sovereign immunity and this Court lacks jurisdiction over the ADA/RA claim.

To state a claim under the ADA or RA, the Plaintiff must allege that the decedent was (1) is a qualified individual; (2) who was excluded from participation in or denied the benefits of services, programs, or activities of a public entity; and (3) that the exclusion, denial, or discrimination was because of his disability. *See Blanks v. Southwestern Bell Communications*, 310 F.3d 398, 400 (5th Cir. 2002). Here, Tabler's Complaint fails to state a claim against Ms. Davis in her official capacity under the

15

ADA/RA because he fails to assert nothing but conclusory allegations and includes nothing but threadbare recitals of the elements needed to plead a claim under the ADA/RA.

a. Plaintiff fails to state a disability as required by the ADA.

With respect to the first element, the ADA defines the term disability as: (1) a physical or mental impairment that substantially limits one or more major life activities of such individual; (2) a record of such an impairment; or (3) being regarded as having such an impairment. 42 U.S.C. § 12102(1). Although the 2008 Amendment to the ADA statute provides broad coverage to the meaning of "disability," the Fifth Circuit has recognized that "it does not absolve a party from proving [a disability]." *Neely v. PSEG Tex., Ltd. P'ship*, 735 F.3d 242, 245 (5th Cir. 2013). Courts look to 29 C.F.R. § 1630 for detailed guidance on what constitutes a disability. *See* 29 C.F.R. § 1630.1–16. Section 1630.2 defines disability as "[a] physical or mental impairment that substantially limits one or more of the major life activities of such individual." A substantial impairment under the ADA is one that limits an individual's ability to perform a major life activity as compared to most people in the general population. *Garza v. City of Donna*, 2017 U.S. Dist. LEXIS 103118, (S.D. Tex. July 5, 2017) at *14 (citing 29 C.F.R. § 1630.2(j)(1)(ii)); *See also Weed v. Sidewinder Drilling, Inc.*, 245 F. Supp. 3d 826, (S.D. Tex. 2017) ("[T]o be substantially limited means to be unable to perform a major life activity that the average person in the general population can perform or to be significantly restricted in the ability to perform it."). "Neither the Supreme Court nor [the Fifth Circuit] has recognized the concept of a *per se* disability under the ADA, no matter how serious the impairment; the plaintiff still must adduce evidence of an impairment that has actually and substantially limited the major life activity on which he relies." *Salcido v. Harris Cty.*, No. H-15-2155, 2018 U.S. Dist. LEXIS 169034, at *141 (S.D. Tex. Sep. 28, 2018); *Griffin v. United Parcel Service, Inc.*, 661 F.3d 216, 223 (5th Cir. 2011).

Here, Tabler has alleged that TDCJ "failed to reasonably accommodate his mental health issues despite knowing his suicidal ideation and related impairments and conditions." ECF No. 1 at 14. Tabler asserts that an "obviously reasonable accommodation exists, that TDCJ has failed to provide Mr. Tabler: moving him out of the Death Watch section and back to death row." *Id.* Tabler alleges that he has been diagnosed with Fetal Alcohol Spectrum Disorder and Klinefeleter Syndrome, which effect his central nervous system, resulting in decreased impulse control, heightened anxiety, mood lability, low frustration tolerance, depression, and executive function impairments.[6] Tabler states that his combination of health disorders result in "emotional instability at the best of times" and "leaves him without the emotion and cognitive ability to effectively process the loss of people close to him. In Death Watch section, such losses are frequent and unavoidable…". ECF No. 1 at 6. Tabler has "repeatedly expressed mental distress, including suicidal ideation, and displayed physically self-harming and suicidal behaviors since his placement in the Death Watch section." *Id.* In his Complaint, Tabler then gave several examples of mental health deterioration between 2011 and 2015. *Id.*

Construing these allegations in the light most favorable to the Plaintiff, he has alleged that he suffers from mental health impairments that causes her to be potentially dangerous to himself and others. But allegations of suicidal risk are not sufficient, without more, to show than an impairment is disabling. *Wade v. Montgomery Cty.*, No. 4:17-CV-1040, 2017 U.S. Dist. LEXIS 216522, at *20-21 (S.D. Tex. Dec. 6, 2017); *see Garza v. City of Donna*, Cause No. 7:16-CV-00558, 2017 U.S. Dist. LEXIS 103118, 2017 WL 2861456 (S.D. Tex. July 5, 2017) (stating that "a person's 'risk of suicide' is not a life activity" sufficient to maintain an ADA claim); *Martin v. The Brown Schools Edu. Corp.*, Cause No. 3:02-CV-0144G, 2003 U.S. Dist. LEXIS 3942, 2003 WL 21077454 (N.D. Tex.

---

[6] Many of these symptoms, including his decreased impulse control and low frustration tolerance perhaps lend to more of a reason as to why Tabler should be watched and not let in to less restrictive housing.

August 6, 2003) (Fish, C.J.)(noting that the plaintiff "fail[ed] to even show how being 'suicidal' translates into a perceived impairment and to designate any major life activity in which she is substantially limited by the unidentified impairment"); *Steele v. Rowles*, 2009 U.S. Dist. LEXIS 80711, 2009 WL 2905903, at *10 (E.D. Tex. Sept. 3, 2009) (Crone J., adopting magistrate's recommendation) (holding that a plaintiff who expressed suicidal intent did not show that he was disabled), aff'd, 389 Fed. Appx. 347 (5th Cir. 2010). Similarly, allegations of depression, without any evidence that it substantially limits a life activity, are also insufficient. *Lottinger v. Shell Oil Company*, 143 F. Supp. 2d 743 (S.D. Tex. 2001) (noting that "depression . . . is not considered a disability per se" when it only occasionally affected the plaintiff's ability to sleep and eat) (citing *Schneiker v. Fortis Ins. Co.*, 200 F.3d 1055, 1061 (7th Cir. 2000)).

Tabler's allegations here detail several impairments, but they do not describe how those impairments substantially limit any major life activity. For that reason, Tabler has not alleged facts from which it can be reasonably inferred that he is disabled, as defined by subsection A of the ADA definition. *Hale*, 642 F.3d at 501–502 ("Absent allegations that [plaintiff's] ailments substantially limited him in the performance of a major life activity, [he] has failed to state a claim for relief under subsection A of the ADA's definition of disability."); 42 U.S.C. § 12102(1)(A) ("'disability' means . . . a physical or mental impairment that substantially limits one or more major life activities"); *see also Wade*, 2017 U.S. Dist. LEXIS 216522, at *21-22.

Tabler has also failed to allege sufficiently that she is disabled under subsection B of the ADA's definition of disability. A plaintiff proceeding under subsection B must allege that she "has a record of an injury or impairment" and that the "impairment limited a major life activity." *Dupre v. Charter Behavioral Health Sys. Of Lafayette, Inc.*, 242 F.3d 610, 615 (5th Cir. 2001). Plaintiff claims that he was diagnosed with mental illnesses before these events, so he has alleged that she has a record of impairment. However, as noted, Tabler has not alleged facts from which it can be reasonably inferred that those impairments substantially limited a major life activity. Again, for that reason, she has not alleged a necessary element to show that she is disabled under subsection B of the ADA's definition of disability.

> b. **Plaintiff fails to allege he was excluded from participation in or denied the benefits of services, programs, or activities provided by TDCJ-CID.**

Plaintiff Tabler has failed to adequately plead that he was denied access to any programs or services necessary to support an ADA claim. The Rehabilitation Act defines a "program or activity" as "all of the operations of…a local government." *Frame v. City of Arlington*, 657 F.3d 215, 225 (5th Cir. 2011) (citing 29 U.S.C. § 794(b)(1)(A) (2014)). As it relates to prisons, "[t]he Supreme Court considered the text of Title II as it is 'ordinarily understood,' and reasoned that 'prisons provide inmates with recreational 'activities,' medical 'services,' and education and vocations 'programs,' all of which at least theoretically 'benefit' the prisoners." *Frame*, 657 F.3d at 225.

Significantly, while a public entity may not deny a qualified individual the opportunity to participate in, or benefit from, an aid, benefit, or service, it also cannot afford a qualified individual with an opportunity to participate in, or benefit from, an aid, benefit, or service that is not equally afforded to others. 28 C.F.R. §35.130(b)(1)(i)-(ii) (2011); *see also Borum v. Swisher Cty*, No. 2:14-CV-127, 2015 WL 327508, at *9 (N.D. Tex. Jan. 26, 2015) (finding prisons not required to provide *new* services or programs for a disabled prisoner, but only that a disabled prisoner have meaningful access to *existing* services and programs) (emphasis in original). Furthermore, public entities responsible for the operation or management of correctional facilities shall ensure offenders are housed in the most integrated setting appropriate to their needs, and not be designated to a medical area unless actually receiving in-patient medical care or treatment while at the TDCJ Unit. 28 C.F.R. § 35.152(b)(2)(ii) (2011); 28 C.F.R § 35.130(d) (2011); *see also* TEX. GOV'T CODE § 499.055, Population Management Based on Inmate Health.

The only accommodation that Tabler alleges TDCJ failed to accommodate is placing him in a housing assignment that is less restrictive. This relief does not correspond to his disabilities, except to say that he "might" find relief from the loss of his friends. ECF No. 5 at 5. Moving him to less restrictive housing does not accommodate his alleged disability, but rather accommodates his lack of friends and loss he experiences therefrom.[7]

c. Plaintiff fails to plead a cognizable injury in fact.

A mere violation of the ADA alone does not establish injury. *DeLeon v. City of Alvin Police Dep't*, No. H-09-1022, 2011 U.S. Dist. LEXIS 1354, at *11 (S.D. Tex. Jan. 6, 2011). Rather, a plaintiff is obligated to show, by competent evidence, that a defendant's violation of the ADA proximately caused her actual injury before she can recover. *Id.*; *see Armstrong v. Turner Indus., Inc.*, 141 F.3d 554, 562 (5th Cir. 1998) (holding "that damages liability [under the ADA] must be based on something more than a mere violation of that provision. There must be some cognizable injury in fact of which the violation is a legal and proximate cause for damages to arise from a single violation."). Here, even if the Court finds that the Plaintiff properly plead he was disabled within the meaning of the ADA and he was denied services for which TDCJ was responsible, the Plaintiff has failed to establish the third element of his *prima facie* case because he has not plead sufficient facts that Defendants discriminated against him "by reason of his disability" or caused him any cognizable injury.

---

[7] "Discrimination" includes "not making reasonable accommodations to the known physical or mental limitations of an otherwise qualified individual with a disability who is an applicant or employee, unless such covered entity can demonstrate that the accommodation would impose an undue hardship on the operation of the business of such covered entity." *Id.* § 12112(b)(5)(A); *Daugherty v. City of El Paso*, 56 F.3d 695, 696 (5th Cir. 1995). Here, if TDCJ were to move the Plaintiff into a less restrictive housing area, it would put the rest of the prison and prison officials, and possibly the public at risk. Plus, it would be opening the door for any inmate who wants to get off death row or out of restrictive housing to bring a lawsuit to have their housing assignment changed for the possibility they may feel less anxious or depressed or be able to make friends.

C. Plaintiff is not entitled to injunctive relief because he cannot meet the standard required for injunctive relief.

To obtain a preliminary injunction, the applicant must show (1) a substantial likelihood that he will prevail on the merits, (2) a substantial threat that he will suffer irreparable injury if the injunction is not granted, (3) that his threatened injury outweighs the threatened harm to the party whom he seeks to enjoin, and (4) that granting the preliminary injunction will not disserve the public interest. *See Planned Parenthood of Houston & Southeast Texas v. Sanchez*, 403 F.3d 324, 329 (5th Cir. 2005). For a permanent injunction to issue the plaintiff must prevail on the merits of his claim and establish that equitable relief is appropriate in all other respects. *See Dresser-Rand Co. v. Virtual Automation Inc.*, 361 F.3d 831, 847 (5th Cir. 2004) (citing *Amoco Prod. Co. v. Village of Gambell*, 480 U.S. 531, 546 n. 12 (1987) (recognizing that the standard for a permanent injunction is essentially the same as for a preliminary injunction with the exception that the plaintiff must show actual success on the merits rather than a mere likelihood of success)). Injunctive relief in the form of "superintending federal injunctive decrees directing state officials" is an extraordinary remedy. *Morrow v. Harwell*, 768 F.2d 619, 627 (5th Cir. 1985). Here, Tabler seeks injunctive relief either in the form of due process by "sufficient process to consider him for transfer to the less restrictive and tortuous standard death row unit" or simply by "moving him out of the 'Death Watch' section and back to death row." ECF No. 1 at 13 (¶ 77), 14 (¶86).

In a similar case, the plaintiff, Watson, was an offender in custody of TDCJ who was placed in protective housing after he provided information to prison officials about illegal drug operation by a prison gang. *Watson v. Quarterman*, No. H-06-3260, 2008 U.S. Dist. LEXIS 15169, at *2 (S.D. Tex. Feb. 27, 2008). As a result, Watson was put on the gang's "hit list." *Id.* Because of the threats made against his life, Watson has been in protective custody since that time. *Id.* Watson filed suit under 42 U.S.C. §1983 against Nathaniel Quarterman in his official capacity as Director of TDCJ, along with the unit warden. *Id.* at *3. Watson complained that the conditions of confinement in protective custody are more restrictive than the conditions placed on inmates housed in general population. As a result of these restrictions, Watson complained that his constitution rights were violation in the follow manners: 1) he was denied "legal visits" with other inmates and therefore denied his right to access the courts; 2) he was denied access to adequate medical care for a hearing impairment because the transportation policy is unsafe; 3) he was denied routine mental health screening that is exempt from the co-payment prisoners are required to pay. *Id.* at *4. He also complained generally that in comparison to inmates housed in the general population, inmates assigned to protective custordy do not have sufficient access to a variety of privileges featured at the prison. *Id.* Watson sought injunctive relief in the form of changes to TDCJ policy concerning the privileges extended to inmates in protective custody. *Id.* The court denied his request for injunctive relief for failure to meet his burden on proving the elements needed for injunctive relief. *Id.*

In coming to its conclusion, the court in *Watson* noted several paragraphs of pertinent case law, which applies to the facts in the present case as well:

An inmate's placement in protective custody implicates the duty imposed on prison officials under the Eighth Amendment to the United States Constitution to maintain institutional security and to keep prisoners safe from conditions that pose a substantial risk of serious harm. *See Farmer v. Brennan*, 511 U.S. 825, 834 (1994); *see also Helling v. McKinney*, 509 U.S. 25, 33 (1993) (observing that a prison official's duty under the Eighth Amendment is to ensure "'reasonable safety'"). The Eighth Amendment standard associated with this duty incorporates due regard for prison officials' "unenviable task of keeping dangerous men in safe custody under humane conditions." *Farmer*, 511 U.S. at 846 (citations omitted).

The Supreme Court has explained that "[t]he very object of imprisonment is confinement" and, as such, "many of the liberties and privileges enjoyed by other citizens must be surrendered by the prisoner." *Overton v. Bazzetta*, 539 U.S. 126, 131 (2003). While an inmate is not "stripped of all constitutional protection as he passes through the prison's gates," *Jones v. North Carolina Prisoners' Labor Union, Inc.*, 433 U.S. 119, 137 (1977) (C.J. Burger, concurring); *see also Turner v. Safley*, 482 U.S. 78, 84 (1987) ("Prison walls do not form a barrier separating prison inmates from the protections of the Constitution."), it is well established that an inmate does not retain rights inconsistent with proper incarceration. *Overton*, 539 U.S. at 131. As the Supreme Court has repeatedly held, the United States Constitution permits greater restrictions on inmates' rights than it allows elsewhere and affords substantial deference to the professional judgment of prison administrators. *See Beard v. Banks*, 548 U.S. 521 (2006) (citing *Overton*, 539 U.S. at 132; *Turner v. Safley*, 482 U.S. 78, 84–85 (1987)).

Deference to prison regulations is required based on the recognition that "courts are ill equipped to deal with the increasingly urgent problems of prison administration and reform." *Turner*, 482 U.S. at 84 (citing *Procunier v. Martinez*, 416 U.S. 396, 405 (1974)). As the Supreme Court has acknowledged, "the problems of prisons in America are complex and intractable, and, more to the point, they are not readily susceptible of resolution by decree." *Id.* (quoting *Martinez*, 416 U.S. at 404–05). "Running a prison is an inordinately difficult undertaking that requires expertise, planning, and the commitment of resources, all of which are peculiarly within the province of the legislative and executive branches of government. Prison administration is, moreover, a task that has been committed to the responsibility of those branches, and separation of powers concerns counsel a policy of judicial restraint." *Turner*, 482 U.S. at 85. Further, where a state penal system is involved federal courts have "additional reason to accord deference to the appropriate prison authorities." *Id.* (citing *Martinez*, 416 U.S. at 405).

It is settled that safety and institutional security are legitimate penological interests. *See Washington v. Harper*, 494 U.S. 210, 225 (1990) ("There can be little doubt as to both the legitimacy and the importance of the governmental interest presented here. There are few cases in which the State's interest in combating the danger posed by a person to himself and others is greater

23

than in a prison environment, which, 'by definition,' is made up of persons with 'a demonstrated proclivity for antisocial criminal, and often violent, conduct.'") (quoting *Hudson v. Palmer*, 468 U.S. 517, 526 (1984) (citations omitted)). Accordingly, courts are required to show great deference to prison administrators' adoption and implementation of policies needed to ensure order and security. *See Pell v. Procunier*, 417 U.S. 817, 827 (1974); *see also Oliver v. Scott*, 276 F.3d 736, 745 (5th Cir .2002) (noting that prison administrators' judgments regarding institutional security are accorded "great deference").

In the present case, Tabler was placed in a section of death row for at least smuggling in a cell phone and threatening a senator. As stated above, safety and institutional security are legitimate penological interests. Washington, 494 U.S. at 225. The Complaint itself shows the danger Tabler presents to himself and others within the prison. Thus, courts are required to show great deference to prison administrator's adoption and implementation of policies needed to ensure order and security. *See Pell*, 417 U.S. at 827.

In assessing the elements needed for Tabler to obtain injunctive relief, he fails to meet the standard for a permanent injunction. The standard for a permanent injunction is essentially the same as for a preliminary injunction with the exception that the plaintiff must show actual success on the merits rather than a mere likelihood of success. *Amoco Prod. Co. v. Village of Gambell*, 480 U.S. 531, 546 n. 12 (1987). The first element being that he must show actual success on the merits, which he fails to do as illustrated by the argument made below.

As to the second element, Tabler does not show from his Complaint that he will suffer an irreparable injury if he is not taken off of "death watch." Tabler contends that being on death watch "imposes serious and irreparable psychological and physical injury on his person." ECF No. 1 at 11. This is because he has been suicidal in the past and due to the friendships he has formed and then lost on death row, his "specific mental health problems are such that he suffers and unusually elevated level of stress and mental anguish from the loss of people to whom he has become attached." *Id.* at 3.

24

In fact, he has been taken off death watch before, when he was at the Jester IV unit for 1.5 years, but allegedly still suffered suicidal ideations while at Jester IV and when he went back to Polunsky Unit. See ECF No. 1. Further, even if Tabler is given "due process" (to which he is not entitled because he has no liberty interest in his housing), it is still not guaranteed that he will be moved from death watch. Still, even if he was removed from death watch and housed in a general cell on death row, the offenders housed on death row are still sentenced to death but may receive an execution date and be moved to death watch at any time. Tabler includes no facts or assertions in his Complaint, other than pure speculation, the moving him into the "less restrictive" death row would help his mental health. In fact, Tabler states in his complaint that he seeks "transfer to Texas' less restrictive standard death row, where he *might* at least find relief from his constant loss of friends to the death chamber under his current conditions." ECF No. 5 at 5 (emphasis added). *See Kirby v. Johnson*, 243 Fed. Appx. 877, 2007 WL 2228616 (5th Cir. 2007) ("Injunctive relief is inappropriate when sought to prevent injury that is speculative at best.") (citing *Carter v. Orleans Parish Public Schools*, 725 F.2d 261, 263 (5th Cir. 1984)); *Taylor v. Milton*, 124 F. App'x 248, 2005 WL 352537 (5th Cir. 2005) (noting that, where a prisoner failed to allege any facts that would render the likelihood of a future injury any more than a remote and speculative possibility, he failed to state a valid Eighth Amendment claim for injunctive relief) (citing *Society of Separationists, Inc. v. Herman*, 959 F.2d 1283, 1285 (5th Cir. 1992)).

The third element that Tabler must overcome is that his threatened injury outweighs the threatened harm to the party whom he seeks to enjoin, which in this case would be TDCJ as whole (through his suit against Lorie Davis in her official capacity). As Tabler has been deemed a security threat through at least two crimes he has committed while in prison, and his free-world crimes put him on death row, his threat to the rest of the prison population and the threat he would pose to prison officers and officials would substantially outweigh the threatened harm to himself while in the custody of a more restrictive housing on death row. The Complaint does not state that he is not receiving medical and/or mental health treatment, nor that he is not allowed recreation time or showers, or access to the law library, or medical if he needs it. Instead, the Complaint actually states that he is allowed out of his cell 2 hours per day, he is provided meals, and that he is allowed recreation time.[8] ECF No. 1 at 4.

The fourth element Tabler needs to meet to qualify for injunctive relief is to show that the relief will not disserve the public interest. Again, as stated above, Tabler is capital murderer capable of many manipulation and violent acts and threats to other offenders and prison officials, even senators. Common sense dictates that it is not in the interest of the public that placed in less restrictive housing. There can be no dispute that inmates on Death Row are among the most significant security risks within the prison. *Scheanette v. Riggins*, No. 9:05cv34, 2005 U.S. Dist. LEXIS 41777, at *20 (E.D. Tex. Dec. 14, 2005); *See, e.g., Jeffries v. Reed*, 631 F. Supp. 1212, 1217 (E.D. Wash. 1986). Tabler's request for injunctive relief in the form of less restrictive housing should be denied.

D. Plaintiff's claims are barred by the statute of limitations

The Fifth Circuit determines the accrual date of a § 1983 action by reference to federal law. *Walker v. Epps*, 550 F.3d 407, 414 (5th Cir. 2008) (citing *Wallace v. Kato*, 549 U.S. 384 (2007)). Federal law holds generally that an action accrues when a plaintiff has "'a complete and present cause of action,'" or, expressed differently, "when 'the plaintiff can file suit and obtain relief.'" *Id.* (quoting *Bay Area Laundry and Dry Cleaning Pension Trust Fund v. Ferbar Corp. of Cal.*, 522 U.S. 192, 201 (1997) (citations omitted)). As the Fifth Circuit has stated, the limitations period begins to run "the moment the plaintiff becomes aware that he has suffered an injury or has sufficient information to know that he has been injured." *Piotrowski v. City of Houston*, 237 F.3d 567, 576 (5th Cir. 2001) (quoting *Russell v. Bd. of Trustees*,

---

[8] Ironically, Tabler complains that he has to spend his recreation time separate from other inmates and is allowed virtually no face-to-dace contact with other inmates, while at the same time he becomes too "attached" to these inmates, such that they become "friends" and he hears them in his dreams. ECF No. 1.

968 F.2d 489, 493 (5th Cir. 1992), cert. denied, 507 U.S. 914, (1993)). The Fifth Circuit in *Walker* held that there is no exception for § 1983 actions seeking only equitable relief. *Id.* at 414.

Because Congress has not adopted a statute of limitations for § 1983 actions, the limitations period is determined by reference to the appropriate state statute of limitations and coordinate tolling rules. *Board of Regents, Univ. of N.Y. v. Tomanio*, 446 U.S. 478, 483-84 (1980). In § 1983 actions, district courts apply the forum state's personal injury limitations period. *Moore v. McDonald*, 30 F.3d 616, 620 (5th Cir. 1994). The Texas general personal injury limitations period is two years. *Id.*; Tex. Civ. Prac. & Rem. Code Ann. § 16.003(a) (Vernon Supp. 2008); *see also Lee v. Valdez*, Civil Action No. 3:07-CV-1298-D, 2009 U.S. Dist. LEXIS 43381, at *8–9 (N.D. Tex. May 20, 2009). The two-year statute of limitations also applies to claims brought under Title II of the ADA. *Frame v. City of Arlington*, 575 F.3d 432, 441 (5th Cir. 2009).

In this case, Tabler alleges he has been housed in the Death Watch section of death row at the Polunsky Unit since January 2, 2011. ECF No. 1 at 3. According to the Complaint, the conditions in the Death Watch section are so severe that in 2011, a federal judge denied Tabler's request to drop his habeas appeals an be executed, after finding that his conditions of confinement coerced him to that decision. *Id.* at 5. Tabler alleges that TDCJ has known of his mental health conditions and detioration for five years. *Id.* at 6. Between 2011 and 2015, Tabler made several suicide attempts ad suicidal statements. *Id.* at 7. He was even seen multiple times by mental health where he apparently explained his issues with living on Death Watch. *Id.* Tabler stayed at a psychiatric facility, where he expressed his concerns regarding his mental health and the toll Death Watch was taking on him for over a year before he was transferred back to Death Watch in 2014. *Id.* at 9. The last specific event that the Complaint states happened on February 12, 2015, when Tabler reported he was feeling down about a recent execution. *Id.* at 9–10. Then, Tabler makes a vague and conclusory statement that "on numerous other occasions, and until the present day" his mental health has been substantially worsened by his housing in the Death Watch section. *Id.* at 10. Finally, Tabler reports that he attempted suicide in June of 2019. *Id.*

Tabler had notice of his §1983 the moment he became aware that he suffered an injury, which would be in 2011 when he entered Death Watch and the habeas judge found that his conditions of confinement made him want to commit suicide. Indeed, if it wasn't in 2011, Tabler had notice anytime between 2011 and 2015 during any of the events in which he alleged he expressed his mental health concerns, including in October of 2013 when he was transferred to the Jester IV unit for crisis management. Tabler filed this lawsuit on March 16, 2020. ECF No. 1. At the most, this lawsuit is seven years passed the statute of limitations. At the least, this lawsuit is four years passed the statute of limitations. Nevertheless, all of Tabler's claims should be dismissed because his claims were subject to a two-year statute of limitations and he far exceeded that date.

V. Conclusion

Plaintiff Tabler fails to state a claim under the ADA/RA, leaving this Court with no jurisdiction over those claims because TDCJ is entitled to sovereign immunity. Tabler also failed to state a claim under § 1983 for due process and conditions of confinement because he does not have a liberty interest in his housing. Tabler fails to meet the standard needed for the injunctive relief he seeks. Additionally, all claims are barred by the statute of limitations and should be dismissed with prejudice.

Respectfully submitted.

KEN PAXTON
Attorney General of Texas

JEFFREY C. MATEER
First Assistant Attorney General

RYAN L. BANGERT
Deputy First Assistant Attorney General

DARREN L. MCCARTY
Deputy Attorney General for Civil
Litigation

SHANNA E. MOLINARE
Chief, Law Enforcement Defense Division

/s/ Briana M. Webb
BRIANA M. WEBB
Assistant Attorney General
Texas State Bar No. 24077883
Briana.webb@oag.texas.gov

Law Enforcement Defense Division
Office of the Attorney General
P. O. Box 12548, Capitol Station
Austin, Texas 78711
(512) 463-2080 / Fax No. (512) 370-9814

Attorneys for Defendant Davis

Certificate of Service

I, Briana M. Webb, Assistant Attorney General of Texas, do hereby certify that a true and correct copy of the above and foregoing has been served via ECF/PACER to all counsel of record on May 26, 2020.

/s/ Briana M. Webb
BRIANA M. WEBB
Assistant Attorney General

IN THE UNITED STATES DISTRICT COURT
FOR THE EASTERN DISTRICT OF TEXAS
LUFKIN DIVISION

RICHARD TABLER, Plaintiff, v. LORIE DAVIS, DIRECTOR OF CORRECTIONAL INSTITUTIONS DIVISION, TEXAS DEPARTMENT OF CRIMINAL JUSTICE, in her official capacity; Defendant.	Civil Action No. 9:20-cv-00049

PLAINTIFF'S RESPONSE TO DEFENDANT LORIE DAVIS'S MOTION TO DISMISS
[ECF No. 9]

Plaintiff, by and through his attorneys, David A. Lane and Reid Allison of KILLMER, LANE & NEWMAN, LLP, and Richard Burr, BURR AND WELCH, PC, hereby submits the following Response to Defendant's Motion to Dismiss [ECF No. 9] (*"Def's Mot."*).

I. INTRODUCTION

Plaintiff Richard Tabler filed this lawsuit to achieve a very simple goal: to be moved from the nearly uniquely torturous housing he has been subjected to for almost a decade. He is not asking to be moved out of death row, altogether; he is not asking to be released. Reading Defendant's pending motion to dismiss could easily give the wrong impression of the very limited injunctive relief Mr. Tabler seeks. Viewed properly, Mr. Tabler has plausibly alleged violations of his federal constitutional and statutory rights that must be allowed to proceed to discovery.

II. FACTS ALLEGED

Mr. Tabler has been housed in the Death Watch section of the Texas Department of Criminal Justice's ("TDCJ") death row since January 2, 2011. *See Complaint* [ECF No. 1], at ¶ 10. The restrictions within this unit are extreme and include 22-hour per day solitary confinement in a tiny 60-square foot cell. *Id.* at ¶¶ 14-15. Mr. Tabler's meals are provided through a slot in the door, and he is allowed virtually no face-to-face contact with other prisoners. *Id.* at ¶¶ 16-18. The Death Watch section is reserved for prisoners who have an imminent execution date, scheduled within 60-180 days. *Id.* at ¶ 11. Therefore, every other prisoner that Mr. Tabler has had contact with in the last ten years has been killed by the state within mere months. *Id.* Mr. Tabler does not have an execution date and has not had one scheduled at any point during his decade in Death Watch. *Id.* at ¶ 12.

These conditions are designed to limit human interaction and do so to a severe degree. *Id.* at ¶ 19. However, there is a special cruelty in Defendant's treatment of Mr. Tabler, as the limited interaction he has is with prisoners who are at their last extremity and are only months away from being killed. *Id.* at ¶ 21. "Rather than the comfort that other inmates are permitted to draw from their limited society with one another, Mr. Tabler is confronted with an endless procession of men who are put to death as soon as he is able to form an attachment to them." *Id.* at ¶ 21. While Mr. Tabler has been housed in Death Watch, TDCJ has killed over 90 prisoners. *Id.* at ¶ 22. Mr. Tabler was able to form brief friendships with at least a dozen of these doomed men. *Id.*

These conditions are severe and would take a toll on the mental health of any prisoner. *Id.* at ¶ 23. But the conditions are particularly cruel to Mr. Tabler, because of his underlying mental disabilities, which are both obvious and well known to TDCJ and Defendant. *Id.* at ¶¶ 23, 27. Mr. Tabler suffers "an unusually elevated level of stress and mental anguish from the loss of people to whom he has become attached." *Id.* He has been diagnosed with both Fetal Alcohol

Spectrum Disorder and Klinefelter syndrome. *Id.* at ¶ 28. These mental disabilities cause Mr. Tabler "decreased impulse control, heightened anxiety, mood lability, low frustration tolerance, depression, and executive function impairment." *Id.* Mr. Tabler's mental disabilities also cause him "difficulty with social skills, including lack of stranger fear; naivete and gullibility; inappropriate choice of friends; immaturity; difficulty understanding the perspective of others; and poor social cognition." *Id.* at ¶ 29. Mr. Tabler also meets the criteria for Bipolar Disorder and Attention Deficit Hyperactivity Disorder, and he has suffered repeated traumatic brain injuries. *Id.* at ¶¶ 30-31.

Mr. Tabler's idiosyncratic combination of mental health disabilities leaves him completely unable to process the loss of people close to him. *Id.* at ¶ 32. The toll this housing has taken on him is so severe that he has experienced auditory hallucinations, hearing those who have been executed during his time in Death Watch. *Id.* at ¶ 50. His housing in Death Watch, therefore, subjects him to undue suffering well beyond what a neurotypical prisoner would experience. *Id.* at ¶ 32.

The combination of the conditions in Death Watch and Mr. Tabler's serious mental disabilities has compelled him to attempt to kill himself multiple times. *Id.* at ¶¶ 33-55. Mr. Tabler has repeatedly made clear to TDCJ that his mental health is being savaged by his housing in Death Watch and being forced to see over 90 people, including over a dozen friends, taken to be executed, soon after he meets them. *Id.* at ¶¶ 33, 38-41, 43, 45-54. These attempts have continued and include a June 2019 incident in which he sliced his arm open from wrist to shoulder and nearly died. *Id.* at ¶ 56.

In 2011, a federal judge found that Mr. Tabler's conditions in the Death Watch section were so severe that they were coercive as a matter of law—i.e. the conditions had effectively forced him into dropping his habeas appeals in order to be executed sooner. *Id.* at ¶ 24. These conditions have not changed, and Mr. Tabler remains housed in the Death Watch section in the same torturous conditions that the judge concluded coerced him into seeking a speedy death. *Id.* at ¶¶ 25, 57. Mr. Tabler has never been afforded meaningful process to challenge his housing in the Death Watch section and argue for transfer to TDCJ's less restrictive death row. *Id.* at ¶ 26.

Defendant has no valid penological justification to continue to house Mr. Tabler in Death Watch indefinitely, and his housing there inflicts disproportionate punishment on him. *Id.* at ¶¶ 62-63. Mr. Tabler's housing inflicts serious and irreparable psychological injury and violates present standards of human dignity. *Id.* at ¶¶ 60-61. Defendant's housing of Mr. Tabler indefinitely in Death Watch imposes atypical and significant hardship on him in relation to the ordinary incidents of prison life, and no other prisoner has been held indefinitely in Death Watch as Mr. Tabler has been. *Id.* at ¶¶ 73-74. Therefore, he is entitled to meaningful process to attempt to argue to be moved back to death row, and he has never received this process. *Id.* at ¶¶ 70-72.

III. Legal Standard

Federal Rule of Civil Procedure 12(b)(6) allows for dismissal of a complaint for "failure to state a claim upon which relief can be granted." "To defeat a Rule 12(b)(6) motion to dismiss, a plaintiff must 'nudge[ ] their claims across the line from conceivable to plausible' by pleading 'enough facts to state a claim to relief that is plausible on its face.'" *Wilson v. Bradshaw*, No. 9:16-CV-112, 2017 U.S. Dist. LEXIS 156993, at *3 (E.D. Tex. Aug. 10, 2017) (quoting *Bell Atlantic Corp. v. Twombly*, 550 U.S. 544, 570 (2007)). In reviewing a Rule 12(b)(6) motion, the Court "accepts all well-pleaded facts as true, viewing them in the light most favorable to the plaintiff." *Sonnier v. State Farm Mutual Auto. Ins. Co.*, 509 F.3d 673, 675 (5th Cir. 2007).

"It is axiomatic that a motion to dismiss an action for failure to state a claim upon which relief can be granted admits the facts alleged in the complaint, but challenges plaintiff's rights to relief based upon those facts." *Madison v. Purdy*, 410 F.2d 99, 100 (5th Cir. 1969). Under the appropriate standard, "[a] motion to dismiss on the basis of the pleadings alone should rarely be granted." *Id.* The same standard applies to Defendant's motion to dismiss Plaintiff's complaint under Federal Rule of Civil Procedure 12(b)(1). *See, e.g., Benton v. United States*, 960 F.2d 19, 21 (5th Cir. 1992).

IV. ARGUMENT

Plaintiff has plausibly alleged violations of his federal constitutional and statutory rights. Defendant's arguments in the present motion are founded on (1) minimizing the psychological torture that Mr. Tabler continues to undergo while housed in Death Watch and (2) implying that Mr. Tabler is asking for something more than transfer to death row and that a ruling in his favor would open the floodgates on litigation from other death row prisoners. This Court must reject Defendant's attempts to rewrite and contradict Mr. Tabler's allegations and must allow his claims to proceed to discovery.

A. **Plaintiff has plausibly alleged violations of his Eighth and Fourteenth Amendment rights.**

Mr. Tabler has plausibly pled violations of his right to be protected from cruel and unusual punishment in the conditions of his confinement. Defendant's continued housing of him in the Death Watch Unit is catastrophic for his mental health, Defendant has continued to house him there years beyond any penological reason for doing so, and Defendant's conduct for the last decade (as well as Defendant's argument in the present motion) make clear that Defendant has every intention of keeping Mr. Tabler housed there indefinitely.

"The Constitution does not mandate comfortable prisons, but neither does it permit inhumane ones." *Gates v. Cook*, 376 F.3d 323, 332-33 (5th Cir. 2004). Courts must analyze prison conditions according to "'the evolving standards of decency that mark the progress of a maturing society' and not the standards in effect during the time of the drafting of the Eighth

Amendment." *Id.* (quoting *Estelle v. Gamble,* 429 U.S. 97, 102 (1976)). As part of the analysis of humane conditions, a prisoner's "mental health needs are no less serious than physical needs." *Gates,* 376 F.3d at 332-33.

A prison official violates the Eighth Amendment when she "1) shows a subjective deliberate indifference to 2) conditions posing a substantial risk of serious harm to the inmate." *Gates,* 376 F.3d at 332-33. "Whether a prison official had the requisite knowledge of a substantial risk is a question of fact subject to demonstration in the usual ways, including inference from circumstantial evidence, and a factfinder may conclude that a prison official knew of a substantial risk from the very fact that the risk was obvious." *Id.*

"Conditions of confinement may establish an Eighth Amendment violation 'in combination' when each would not do so alone, but only when they have a mutually enforcing effect that produces the deprivation of a single, identifiable human need." Moreover, the Supreme Court has stressed that "the length of confinement cannot be ignored.... A filthy, overcrowded cell ... might be tolerable for a few days and intolerably cruel for weeks or months." *Hutto v. Finney,* 437 U.S. 678, 686-87 (1978). A plaintiff "need not show that death or serious illness has occurred." *Helling v. McKinney,* 509 U.S. 25, 32 (1993) ("It would be odd to deny an injunction to inmates who plainly proved an unsafe, life-threatening condition in their prison on the ground that nothing yet had happened to them.").

  1. *Mr. Tabler's conditions of confinement in Death Watch pose a substantial risk of harm to him.*

Mr. Tabler has plausibly alleged that Defendant housing him indefinitely in Death Watch is cruel and unusual punishment that violates his constitutional rights. Plaintiff's conditions of confinement are severely restrictive and cause obvious and well-known destruction to his mental health. *See generally Complaint,* ¶¶ 10-57. What limited human interaction he has had in the last decade has been almost entirely with men who are on the verge of being killed by the state. After certain of his fellow prisoners have been killed, Mr. Tabler has suffered auditory hallucinations, during which he hears their voices. These conditions have compelled him to attempt to kill himself multiple times during his housing in Death Watch. The conditions also led him to attempt to drop his habeas appeals so as to hasten his death at the hands of the state. Fortunately, a federal judge recognized the severe conditions of Mr. Tabler's confinement and found that the conditions had coerced him to such action. *Id.* at ¶¶ 24, 57.

Mr. Tabler's conditions of confinement are at least comparable to those found to violate the Eighth Amendment in by a court of this circuit in 1999. *See Ruiz v. Johnson*, 37 F.Supp.2d 855, 914 (S.D.Tex.1999), *rev'd on other grounds*, 243 F.3d 941 (5th Cir. 2001), *adhered to on remand*, 154 F.Supp.2d 975 (S.D.Tex.2001). In *Ruiz*, the court found violations of the constitutional rights of prisoners in TDCJ administrative segregation because the conditions cause them to "suffer actual psychological harm from their almost total depravation of human contact, mental stimulus, personal property and human dignity." *Id.* The court reasoned that it was clear in 1999 "that under American jurisprudence, deprivation of activity, exercise, mental stimulation and activity, at some level, is the denial of a basic human necessity." *Id.* The court quoted liberally and correctly from another federal judge, establishing:

> We thus can not ignore, in judging challenged conditions of confinement, that all humans are composed of more than flesh and bone--even those who, because of unlawful and deviant behavior, must be locked away not only from their fellow citizens, but from other inmates as well. Mental health, just as much as physical health, is a mainstay of life. Indeed, it is beyond any serious dispute that mental health is a need as essential to a meaningful human existence as other basic physical demands our bodies may make for shelter, warmth or sanitation.

Id. (quoting *Madrid v. Gomez*, 889 F. Supp. 1146, 1261 (N.D. Cal. 1995).

"As the pain and suffering caused by a cat-o'-nine-tails lashing an inmate's back are cruel and unusual punishment by today's standards of humanity and decency, the pain and suffering caused by extreme levels of psychological deprivation are equally, if not more, cruel and unusual. The wounds and resulting scars, while less tangible, are no less painful and permanent when they are inflicted on the human psyche." *Ruiz*, 37 F.Supp.2d at 914. Finally, the court noted that segregation and severe solitary confinement may be necessary in some circumstances for legitimate penological interests, but when conditions are so extreme as to violate the United States constitution and "the remedial powers of a federal court are invoked to protect the constitutional rights of inmates, the court may not take a 'hands-off' approach." *Id.* at 914-15.

Other courts in the years since *Ruiz* that have examined similar solitary conditions have made clear that "[t]he same standards that protect against physical torture prohibit mental torture as well - including the mental torture of excessive deprivation." *Wilkerson v. Stalder*, 639 F. Supp. 2d 654, 677-79 (M.D. La. 2007) (quoting *Ruiz*, 37 F.Supp.2d at 914. Regardless of what earlier cases said on similar subjects, "[t]he standard for determining whether prison conditions satisfy the Eighth's Amendment objective component, whether the condition is 'sufficiently serious,' is not static" and instead "focuses on whether the conditions are contrary to 'the evolving standards of decency that mark the progress of a maturing society.'" *Wilkerson*, 639 F. Supp. 2d at 677-79 (quoting *Farmer*, 511 U.S. at 833-34).

Specifically, the court in *Wilkerson* reasoned that:

> Such things as food, sleep, clothing, shelter, medical attention, reasonable safety, sleep, and exercise have been recognized by courts as basic physical human needs subject to deprivation by conditions of confinement. While the defendants urge the court not to recognize social interaction and environmental stimulation as basic human needs, the failure to identify them would be inconsistent with jurisprudence recognizing mental health as worthy of Eighth Amendment protection, and the requirement that Eighth Amendment protections change to reflect "evolving standards of decency that mark the progress of a maturing society." *Ruiz v. Johnson*, 37 F.Supp.2d 855 (S.D.Tex.1999), citing *Rhodes*, 452 U.S. at 346, 101 S.Ct. 2392. Additionally, recognizing social interaction and environmental stimulation as basic human needs is hardly going out on a radical limb, as defendants would suggest. In *Ruiz*, the district court found that the defendants were "deliberately indifferent to a systemic pattern of

extreme social isolation and reduced environmental stimulation," and social interaction and environmental stimulation have been identified as basic psychological human needs, either directly or indirectly, by other courts.

Id.

Since at least 1999, courts in this circuit have correctly determined that "in light of the maturation of our society's understanding of the very real psychological needs of human beings, courts have recognized the inhumanity of institutionally-imposed psychological pain and suffering" and that such recognition is not defeated by previous cases' focus on "the basic components of physical sustenance - food, shelter, and medical care." *Ruiz*, 37 F. Supp. 2d at 914. Moreover, courts around the country have rightly reasoned that it is not "rocket science" that "prolonged isolation from social and environmental stimulation increases the risk of development of mental illness." *Shoatz v. Wetzel*, 2014 U.S. Dist. LEXIS 9386, 2014 WL 294988, at *4, n.3 (W.D. Pa. Jan. 27, 2014) (quoting *McClary v. Kelly*, 4 F. Supp.2d 195, 209 (W.D.N.Y. 1998)); *see also Grissom v. Roberts*, 902 F.3d 1162, 1176 (10th Cir. 2018) (Lucero, J., concurring) ("[s]ocial interaction, environmental stimulation, and activity are basic human needs" and "[p]sychologically, solitary confinement is devastating."); *H'Shaka v. O'Gorman*, 2020 U.S. Dist. LEXIS 42908, *50-55 (N.D.N.Y. March 12, 2020) (collecting cases as establishing social contact and environmental stimulation as basic human needs for the purposes of the Eighth Amendment analysis).

Moreover, "[b]oth the Supreme Court and the Fifth Circuit have recognized that certain conditions that would pass constitutional scrutiny if imposed for a short period of time may be rendered unconstitutional if imposed for an extended period of time." *Wilkerson*, 639 F. Supp. 2d at 679; *see also Meriwether v. Faulkner*, 821 F.2d 408, 416 (7th Cir. 1986) ("[T]he duration of a prisoner's confinement in administrative segregation or under lockdown restrictions is certainly an important factor in evaluating whether the totality of the conditions of confinement constitute cruel and unusual punishment."). Mr. Tabler has suffered these conditions for nearly a decade, and there is no end in sight. Defendant obviously intends to keep him housed in Death Watch until he is either executed or succeeds on his still-pending habeas appeals. Whether or not being housed in solitary confinement and restricted to very limited human contact with only other prisoners who are soon to be executed would violate Mr. Tabler's constitutional rights, such housing for ten years and counting, with the expectation that such housing will continue for as long as Mr. Tabler is alive, is cruel and unusual punishment.

> 2. *Defendant is deliberately indifferent to the substantial risk of harm, and Defendant's Eighth Amendment arguments are erroneous.*

It is also clear (and does not appear to be disputed) that Defendant knows of the substantial harm to Mr. Tabler and yet persists in housing him in Death Watch. Indeed, "the extensive scholarly literature describing and quantifying the adverse mental health effects of prolonged solitary confinement that has emerged in recent years" strongly indicates that such risks are obvious. *Porter v. Clarke*, 923 F.3d 348, 361 (4th Cir. 2019) ("[g]iven [State D]efendants' status as corrections professionals, it would defy logic to suggest that they were unaware of the potential harm that the lack of human interaction on death row could cause."). Defendant is aware both (1) of Mr. Tabler's mental disabilities and recurring serious mental health crises and (2) that his housing in what amounts to solitary-plus (a place in which all of your peers are killed within months) is calamitous to his mental health.

In response to Plaintiff's allegations of torturous indefinite solitary confinement among those who are soon killed, Defendant Davis now indicates that Mr. Tabler has been housed in the Death Watch Unit for a decade in order to protect him from harming himself. *Def's Mot.* at 17 n.6. However, later in the same motion, Defendant Davis insists that "if TCDJ were to move the Plaintiff into a less restrictive housing area, it would put the rest of the prison and prison officials, and possibly the public at risk." *Id.* at 20 n.7. All of which is to say, Defendant Davis has no reason why Mr. Tabler must continue to be confined in the Death Watch Section, and Mr. Tabler has plausibly pled that others could be protected from his vague, ominous malice perfectly effectively in the normal Death Row (which is in no way un-restrictive). *See Complaint*, at ¶ 63. Defendant's lack of justification for continuing to house Mr. Tabler in Death Watch indefinitely also makes clear that this is exactly the type of "unnecessary and wanton infliction of pain" that is prohibited by the Eighth Amendment. *See, e.g., Hernandez v. Velasquez*, 522 F.3d 556, 560-61 (5th Cir. 2008); *see also H'Shaka*, 2020 U.S. Dist. LEXIS 42908, *50-55 (collecting cases for the proposition that indefinite confinement in solitary conditions "that is based on past [] conduct, and that fails to take into account a lack of more-recent serious disciplinary infractions over a lengthy period of time, suggests a violation of the Eighth Amendment."). Moreover, the question of whether Defendant has a legitimate justification for Mr. Tabler's indefinite housing in Death Watch is not one for this Court to decide on a motion to dismiss. *See, e.g., Wilkerson*, 639 F. Supp. 2d at 668-69 (accepting plaintiff's argument that defendants had no legitimate penological interest in continuing to keep them in solitary confinement for the purposes of the Eighth Amendment and rejecting defendants' generic assertion that the need for facility safety provided a legitimate penological interest under the circumstances).

Defendant also makes light of both Mr. Tabler's serious mental disabilities and the nightmarish conditions he has lived in for a decade, asserting without basis that allowing this suit to proceed into discovery "would be opening the door for any inmate who wants to get off death row or out of restrictive housing" to sue based on "the possibility they may feel less anxious or depressed or be able to make friends." *Id.* at 20 n.7; *see also id.* at 26 n.8 (finding irony in Mr. Tabler's nightmares). Plaintiff is not asking to be moved out of Death Row, altogether. He is not asking to be freed. And despite Defendant's baseless hints to the contrary, Mr. Tabler is not a threat to anyone else and certainly not to such a degree that he could not be comfortably managed in standard Death Row. Read correctly, Mr. Tabler's lawsuit does not threaten the parade of horribles that Defendant conjures.

Defendant relies heavily on *Ruiz v. Davis*, 850 F.3d 225, 228 (5th Cir. 2017) as dispensing with Mr. Tabler's § 1983 conditions of confinement claim. *See Def's Mot.* at 8-9. However, *Ruiz* has nothing to do with Mr. Tabler's case. There, a Death Row inmate sued on the eve of his execution, alleging that the significant delay between his conviction and execution the multiple previous stays of execution that he had been granted made the "ultimate punishment [of execution] cruel and unusual." *Ruiz*, 850 F.3d at 228. The Fifth Circuit denied him a certificate of appealability, noting that Ruiz had been granted two previous stays to consider his claims, and that his current argument amounted to an attack on capital punishment itself. *Id.* at 229-30. Importantly, the Fifth Circuit made clear that it did not "address the conditions death row inmates, in Texas or elsewhere, face generally. The solitary confinement of prisoners has long been at issue in suits challenging prison conditions." *Id.* at 229. The Court also noted that, "[d]espite being a named plaintiff in a § 1983 method-of-execution suit challenging Texas's lethal injection protocol filed last year, Ruiz voiced no concern regarding Texas's death row conditions of confinement, this at a time that would have allowed him to develop his claims in the district court. Had he done so, we might be properly situated to determine the merit of such claims." *Id.*

Read properly, *Ruiz* has no relevance to Mr. Tabler's claims; Mr. Ruiz sought relief declaring his imminent execution unconstitutional. He did not challenge the actual conditions of confinement of Texas' death row, let alone the even more restrictive and harsh conditions in Death Watch. Mr. Tabler is clearly not seeking any comparable relief in this case. For similar reasons, Defendant's string cite of purportedly similar cases has no relevance to Mr. Tabler's suit and cannot be grounds to dismiss his § 1983 claim. Mr. Tabler is not suing to be released from Death Row.

In general, the tone of Defendant's arguments regarding conditions of confinement make them seem as though they were written at least twenty years ago. *See Def's Mot.* at 11-12. For example, Defendant states that "to the extent that prison conditions are restrictive and harsh, they are part of the penalty that criminal offenders pay for their offenses to society." *Id.* at 11. Of course, this statement—citing a 1981 Supreme Court opinion as support—begs the question presented by Mr. Tabler's lawsuit. It is not, in fact, true as Defendant's definitive statement would make it seem that there are no conditions so restrictive and/or harsh as to violate the United States Constitution. Indeed, Mr. Tabler has alleged such conditions, and he has done so according to the evolving standards of decency that have progressed well beyond the state of the law in 1981. In recent years, courts around the country have recognized "that solitary confinement poses an objective risk of serious psychological and emotional harm to inmates, and therefore can violate the Eighth Amendment." *Porter*, 923 F.3d at 355-64 (collecting cases); *Reynolds v. Arnone*, 402 F. Supp. 3, 16-20 (D. Conn. August 27, 2019).

Finally, Defendant completely diminishes, misconstrues, and contradicts Mr. Tabler's allegations by stating that "the Eighth Amendment does not afford protection against discomfort and inconvenience" and that "removal of Tabler from the restrictive housing will do more harm than good to anyone." *Def's Mot.* at 12. Mr. Tabler has not alleged "discomfort and inconvenience;" he *has* alleged that he has been housed in a uniquely torturous environment for ten years and that there is every indication that Defendant intends to house him there for the rest of his life. For the reasons stated above, this Court should deny Defendant's motion to dismiss Plaintiff's claim of unconstitutional cruel and unusual punishment.

B. Plaintiff has plausibly alleged violations of his constitutional right to Due Process.

Mr. Tabler's conditions of confinement are some of the most restrictive and atypical that exist in any prison in this country. Indeed, his conditions of confinement are nearly unique among the living. By definition, his conditions are shared only by those who will soon be killed by the state. This existence continues to wreak havoc on his mental health and subject him to hardships that not even those in death row suffer. He has not been provided process to state his case to be moved from this terrible existence back to TDCJ's standard death row.

Defendant Davis now argues that Mr. Tabler has no liberty interest in avoiding these conditions by being housed in death row rather than Death Watch. *Def's Mot.* at 12-14. The Supreme Court has made clear that an inmate *does* have a protected Due Process liberty-interest in the conditions of his housing, if that housing "imposes atypical and significant hardship on the inmate in relation to the ordinary incidents of prison life." *Wilkinson v. Austin*, 545 U.S. 209, 222-23 (2005). "[T]he touchstone of the inquiry into the existence of a protected, state-created liberty interest in avoiding restrictive conditions of confinement is not the language of regulations regarding those conditions but the nature of those conditions themselves 'in relation to the ordinary incidents of prison life.'" *Id.*

In *Wilkinson*, the Supreme Court examined Ohio Supermax conditions, including the facts that "almost all human contact is prohibited, even to the point that conversation is not permitted from cell to cell; the light, though it may be dimmed, is on for 24 hours; exercise is for 1 hour per day, but only in a small indoor room." *Id.* at 223-24. In addition to these conditions, the Court noted that such housing was of indefinite duration and was only reviewed annually, and transfer to the facility eliminated an inmate for parole eligibility. *Id.* The Court was "satisfied that assignment to OSP imposes an atypical and significant hardship under any plausible baseline." *Id.* Finally, the Court noted that even if the harsh conditions could be viewed as necessary, "[t]hat necessity ... does not diminish our conclusion that the conditions give rise to a liberty interest in their avoidance." *Id.*

Mr. Tabler's conditions of confinement are similar to *Wilkinson*, as well as the other cases discussed in the previous section. He is subject to severe solitary confinement, with minimal human contact. Importantly, Mr. Tabler has been housed in Death Watch for nearly a decade, and it is clear that Defendant intends his housing there to be indefinite. This factor was fundamental to the Supreme Court's decision in *Wilkinson* and has been central to court's analyses of similar housing ever since. *See, e.g., Wilkerson v. Goodwin*, 774 F.3d 845, 855-56 (5th Cir. 2014); *see also Sandin v. Conner*, 515 U.S. 472, 486 (1995) (holding that there was no liberty interest in part because a 30-day period of disciplinary segregation was not of atypical, excessive duration). And like *Wilkinson*, even if a factfinder were eventually to deem this housing necessary, Mr. Tabler is still entitled to due process to avoid the severely restrictive conditions.

Mr. Tabler's conditions of confinement on Death Watch are also similar to those examined in *Wilkerson v. Goodwin*. 774 F.3d 845, 855-56 (5th Cir. 2014). In that case, the Fifth Circuit confronted prison conditions, including solitary confinement conditions for 23 hours per day, "significant limitations on human contact, and placement is indefinite." *Id.* The Court concluded that the conditions were sufficiently severe, despite the prisoner being allowed "some contact visits, telephone privileges, peer counseling, and correspondence courses." *Id.* Viewing the extended solitary isolation, limited human contact, and many years that the plaintiff had been subject to these conditions "collectively" the Court held that "there can be no doubt that these conditions are sufficiently severe to give rise to a liberty interest under *Sandin*." *Id.* The Fifth Circuit held that this conclusion was particularly true because the plaintiff's housing was "effectively indefinite," reasoning that this was a "significant factor" in the Supreme Court's decision in *Wilkinson*. *Id.* For the same reasons, Mr. Tabler's indefinite confinement in conditions with severely limited human interaction and 22-hour solitary confinement in a tiny cell pose "atypical and significant hardships" such that he has a liberty interest and a concomitant Due Process right to be afforded an opportunity to avoid such confinement and be moved to death row.

Defendant argues that Mr. Tabler has not pointed to a state policy that creates such a liberty interest. *See Def's Mot.* at 8. However, that line of reasoning has been outmoded for at least 15 years. In *Wilkinson*, the Supreme Court noted its previous, sometime, focus on what policies a state did or did not have regarding housing and transfer. *Wilkinson*, 545 U.S. at 222-23. The Court reasoned that such a focus "creat[ed] a disincentive for States to promulgate procedures for prison management." *Id.* Therefore, the Court adopted the "atypical and significant hardship" standard and explicitly rejected myopic examination of prison policies. *See id.* ("the touchstone of the inquiry into the existence of a protected, state-created liberty interest in avoiding restrictive conditions of confinement is not the language of regulations regarding those conditions.").

Defendant also cites to an unpublished Fifth Circuit case, dismissing a *pro se* prisoner's appeal as frivolous to contend that "[p]risoners have no constitutionally protected liberty interest in a particular housing assignment." *Def's Mot.* at 12 (citing *Nathan v. Hancock*, 477 F. App'x 197, 199 (5th Cir. 2012)). However, as in the previous section, this statement begs the question and is simply not true as a matter of law. As explained above, a prisoner does have a "constitutionally protected liberty interest in a particular housing assignment," when he can establish that his housing "imposes atypical and significant hardship on the inmate in relation to the ordinary incidents of prison life." *Wilkinson*, 545 U.S. at 222-23.

What each of the cases Defendant cites lacks is an indefinite duration of the severe conditions present here. Mr. Tabler has been housed in these torturous conditions for nearly a decade. And it is clear that Defendant intends to keep him in these conditions indefinitely. In examining similar conditions of solitary confinement and/or segregation, the Fifth Circuit has indicated that "two and a half years of segregation is a threshold of sorts for atypicality." *Bailey v. Fisher*, 647 F. App'x 472, 476-77 (5th Cir. 2016). The Fifth Circuit has also noted that eight years or more of such solitary confinement has been found sufficient to establish a liberty interest, especially where there is no prospect of transfer to less restrictive housing. *See Wilkerson*, 774 F.3d at 855-56.

Finally, Defendant's argument that Mr. Tabler's current and continued housing in Death Watch in 2020 is justified by the misdeeds that got him placed there in the first place (over a decade ago) makes clear that Defendant will never move Mr. Tabler. *See Def's Mot.* at 12-14. This exact argument has previously been viewed as establishing an indefinite housing decision, with substantial importance to the Due Process analysis. *See, e.g., Wilkerson*, 774 F.3d at 855-56 (holding that a review board's repeated insistence on continued confinement based on the original infraction made clear that the reason for such housing could never change and was in fact indefinite). For the same reasons, Mr. Tabler's indefinite housing in Death Watch poses atypical and significant hardships; he is, therefore owed due process to challenge his continued housing in Death Watch, rather than in death row with all other prisoners who, like him, have been sentenced to death but do not yet have an execution date.

C. **Defendant is not entitled to sovereign immunity.**

Defendant Davis is not entitled to sovereign immunity on Plaintiff's claims seeking injunctive relief for continuing violations of his federal constitutional and statutory rights. "Sovereign immunity is not limitless, and this case involves an important caveat—the *Ex parte*

Young exception." *Williams v. Reeves*, 954 F.3d 729, 735-36 (5th Cir. 2020). *Ex Parte Young* allows a plaintiff to sue a state official in her official capacity, as long as the plaintiff "seeks prospective relief to redress an ongoing violation of federal law." *Id.* "Though an *Ex parte Young* suit has an 'obvious impact on the State itself,' it is an essential mechanism for affirming the supremacy of federal law." *Id.* (quoting *Pennhurst State Sch. & Hosp. v. Halderman*, 465 U.S. 89, 104-05 (1984)).

The Fifth Circuit has noted three requirements for an *Ex Parte Young* suit—it "must: (1) be brought against state officers who are acting in their official capacities; (2) seek prospective relief to redress ongoing conduct; and (3) allege a violation of federal, not state, law." *Williams*, 954 F.3d at 735-36. As a fundamental matter, the state official who is named as defendant must have a "sufficient connection [to] the enforcement" of the unconstitutional acts. *City of Austin v. Paxton*, 943 F.3d 993, 998 (5th Cir. 2019).

Defendant does not appear to dispute that she has a "sufficient connection" to the federal constitutional and statutory violations Mr. Tabler has alleged; she clearly has the power to order Mr. Tabler moved. *See generally Def's Mot.* at 4-6. Instead, Defendant's argument that *Ex Parte Young* does not allow Mr. Tabler's suit is based on the conclusory assertion that he "does not allege a continuing violation of federal law." *Def's Mot.* at 6. The above facts and legal discussion should make abundantly clear that Mr. Tabler is absolutely alleging a continuing violation of federal law. And fundamentally, "the inquiry into whether suit lies under *Ex Parte Young* does not include an analysis of the merits of the claim." *Williams*, 954 F.3d at 735-36. If a complaint alleges an ongoing violation of federal law (as Mr. Tabler's does) and seeks relief properly characterized as prospective (as Mr. Tabler's also does), the suit complies with the requirements of *Ex Parte Young*. *See id.*

D. Plaintiff has plausibly alleged violations of his rights under the ADA.

Mr. Tabler has plausibly alleged violations of his rights under the Americans with Disabilities Act ("ADA"). Defendant again asserts that she is entitled to sovereign immunity. However, with respect to an ADA claim, the issue of sovereign immunity is bound up with the merits. *See, e.g., Hale v. King*, 642 F.3d 492, 497-98 (5th Cir. 2011). In such a case, a court considers "which aspects of the State's alleged conduct violated Title II [of the ADA]" and then determines whether the State's conduct "also violated the Fourteenth Amendment." *Id.* at 498. "If the State's conduct violated both Title II and the Fourteenth Amendment, Title II validly abrogates state sovereign immunity." *Id.*

"A plaintiff states a claim for relief under Title II if he alleges: (1) that he has a qualifying disability; (2) that he is being denied the benefits of services, programs, or activities for which the public entity is responsible, or is otherwise discriminated against by the public entity; and (3) that such discrimination is by reason of his disability." *Id.* at 499.

Mr. Tabler has plausibly alleged that he is an individual with a qualifying disability. Courts throughout this circuit have recognized that serious mental illness can constitute a qualifying disability for purposes of an ADA discrimination claim. For example, in *Williamson v. Larpenter*, the court determined that plaintiff had plausibly alleged a qualifying disability based on his mental illness, "including depression, suicidal tendencies, [and] mood and behavior alterations." No. 19-254, 2019 U.S. Dist. LEXIS 133628, at *35-36 (E.D. La. July 15, 2019). In reaching this conclusion, the court noted that "[d]epression and other mental illnesses can qualify as disabilities for purposes of the ADA." *Id.* (quoting *Stradley v. Lafourche Commc'ns, Inc.*, 869 F. Supp. 442, 443 (E.D. La. 1994)). The court also found that plaintiff's "history of depression and multiple suicide attempts indicate that his mental impairments limited his ability to engage in the most basic life activity there is — keeping himself alive." *Williamson*, 2019 U.S. Dist.

LEXIS 133628, at *35-36. Based on these allegations, the court determined that plaintiff's "impairments of depression and mental illness constitute a qualifying disability under the ADA." *Id.*

Similarly, in *Carter v. Cain*, the court considered claims that the prisoner-plaintiff was disabled due to his "mental illness, psychosis, paranoia, acute anxiety, [and] hallucinations," and that he "was at high risk of suicide." No. 17-201-SDD-RLB, 2019 U.S. Dist. LEXIS 27293, at *33-35 (M.D. La. Feb. 21, 2019). The court reasoned that such disabilities could substantially limit plaintiff's ability to engage in "major life activities," like "caring for oneself, performing manual tasks, walking, seeing, hearing, speaking, breathing, learning, and working." *Id.* The court specifically determined that "Plaintiff's allegations describe how Terrance Carter's mental illness caused him debilitating anxiety and even interfered with his ability to perceive reality," and that based on these allegations "a reasonable factfinder could conclude that Carter had a 'qualified disability' under the ADA." *Id.*

Lastly, a court of this circuit has determined that a plaintiff-prisoner plausibly alleged an ADA claim based on her housing in solitary confinement, despite her known mental illness. *See Wade v. Montgomery Cty.*, No. 4:17-CV-1040, 2017 U.S. Dist. LEXIS 216522, at *15-17 (S.D. Tex. Dec. 6, 2017). In that case, plaintiff alleged that her placement in solitary confinement constituted disability discrimination because it exacerbated her mental illness. *Id.* The court concluded that

> This allegation also plausibly states a claim upon which Plaintiff could recover. *See Wright v. Texas Dept. of Criminal Justice*, Cause No. 7:13-CV-0116-O, 2013 U.S. Dist. LEXIS 176222, 2013 WL 6578994 (N.D. Tex. Dec. 16, 2013) (holding that jail failed to reasonably accommodate inmate's mental disability when it placed him in a solitary cell where he was able to attempt suicide, and that was sufficient to show a prima facie violation of the ADA and Rehabilitation Act); *Lee v. Valdez*, Cause No. No. 3:07-CV-1298-D, 2009 U.S. Dist. LEXIS 43381, 2009 WL 1406244 (N.D. Tex. May 20, 2009) (noting that a jail's refusal to accommodate an inmate's mental health needs constitutes an impermissible

denial of benefits or services); *McCoy v. Tex. Dep't Crim. Justice*, Cause No. C-05-370, 2006 U.S. Dist. LEXIS 55403, 2006 WL 2331055, at *7, n.6 (S.D. Tex. Aug. 9, 2006) ("In the prison context, failure to make reasonable accommodations to the needs of a disabled prisoner may have the effect of discriminating against that prisoner because the lack of an accommodation may cause the disabled prisoner to suffer more pain and punishment than non-disabled prisoners.").

Id. The court then reasoned that "[b]ecause these allegations 'are to be taken as true,' they suffice to establish both the second and third elements of a Title II claim," and determined that "[a] fact finder could plausibly conclude from these allegations that Defendant discriminated against Wade by denying her benefits and services due to her alleged disability, and by not accommodating that alleged disability." *Id.* The court reached this conclusion, despite plaintiff not ruling out "benign explanations for her treatment," while stressing that "at this stage of the proceeding, [plaintiff] need not prove her claims, nor must she negate all potential defenses that the County may have. Wade need only allege facts that make her claim plausible." *Id.* (citing *McCoy v. Texas Dep't Crim. Justice*, 2006 U.S. Dist. LEXIS 55403 (S.D. Tex. Aug. 9, 2006) for the proposition that the reasonableness of the requested accommodations was a question for the jury to decide).

As a fundamental matter, pursuant to its statutory authority to issue regulations to carry out the ADA, 42 U.S.C. § 12116 (1994), the Equal Employment Opportunity Commission has refined the definition of "disability" to include "any mental or psychological disorder, such as . . . emotional or mental illness." 29 C.F.R. § 1630.2(h)(2) (1996). The EEOC has expressly characterized major depression, anxiety disorders, bipolar disorder, and personality disorders as disabilities under the ADA. *See* EEOC Enforcement Guidance: Psychiatric Disabilities and the

Americans With Disabilities Act, 2 EEOC Compl. Man. (BNA), filed after Section 902, at 15 P 1 (Mar. 25, 1997).[1]

With respect to exclusion from "services, programs, or activities," courts have been careful to stress that the "only reasonable interpretation of Title II is that law enforcement officers who are acting in an investigative or *custodial* capacity are performing 'services, programs, or activities' within the scope of Title II." *Williams v. City of N.Y.*, 121 F. Supp. 3d 354, 368 (S.D.N.Y. 2015) (emphasis added). As such, "the phrase services, programs, or activities has been interpreted to be 'a catch-all phrase that prohibits all discrimination by a public entity.'" *Noel v. N.Y.C. Taxi & Limousine Comm'n*, 687 F.3d 63, 68 (2d Cir. 2012) (quoting *Innovative Health Sys. v. City of White Plains*, 117 F.3d 37, 45 (2d Cir. 1997)); *see also Seremeth v. Bd. of Cty. Comm'rs Frederick Cty.*, 673 F.3d 333, 338 (4th Cir. 2012) (reaching the same conclusion while noting that the Department of Justice's regulations confirm that Title II is meant to apply to anything a public entity does). Safe housing in conditions of confinement that are not ruinous to the mental health of mentally disabled prisoners would seem to be among the most fundamental "services" that a prison provides to prisoners.

This view also comports with a broad reading of the ADA consistent with its status as a comprehensive remedial statute, which courts around the country have insisted upon when interpreting the scope and application of the ADA. *See, e.g., Hason v. Medical Bd.*, 279 F.3d 1167, 1172 (9th Cir. 2002) (holding that a narrow construction of the phrase "services, programs,

---

[1] Moreover, courts have accepted that fetal alcohol syndrome (one of the many mental disabilities that Mr. Tabler suffers) can be a qualifying disability under the ADA. *See, e.g., Sims v. Najera*, No. 1:12-cv-00466- AWI- JLT, 2012 U.S. Dist. LEXIS 123098, at *5-7 (E.D. Cal. Aug. 28, 2012) ("[h]ere, Plaintiff's allegation that he suffered from Fetal Alcohol Syndrome is sufficient to demonstrate that he is an individual with a disability."); *see also Lester v. M&M Knopf Auto Parts*, No. 04-CV-850S, 2006 U.S. Dist. LEXIS 70371, at *32-34 (W.D.N.Y. Sep. 28, 2006).

or activities" ran contrary to "the remedial goals underlying the ADA."); *see also Mary Jo C. v. N.Y. State & Local Ret. Sys.*, 707 F.3d 144, 160 (2d Cir. 2013); *Steger v. Franco, Inc.*, 228 F.3d 889, 894 (8th Cir. 2000); *Arnold v. UPS*, 136 F.3d 854, 861 (1st Cir. 1998).

Lastly, the question of whether Defendants refused to provide Mr. Tabler a reasonable accommodation is a question of fact that is to be decided by the factfinder. *See, e.g., EEOC v. Universal Mfg. Corp.*, 914 F.2d 71 (5th Cir. 1990). Mr. Tabler has plausibly alleged a reasonable accommodation that Defendant has refused—transfer out of Death Watch and back to death row. *See* Complaint, ¶ 86. "[T]he Fifth Circuit has held that a defendant's failure to make the reasonable modifications necessary to adjust for the unique needs of disabled persons can constitute intentional discrimination under the ADA and the RA." *Hacker v. Cain*, No. 3:14-00063-JWD-EWD, 2016 U.S. Dist. LEXIS 73014, at *40 (M.D. La. June 6, 2016) (citing *Melton v. Dall. Area Rapid Transit*, 391 F.3d 669, 672 (5th Cir. 2004) and *Garrett v. Thaler*, 560 F. App'x 375, 382 (5th Cir. 2014)). That said, as in all such disability discrimination cases, this question is "highly fact-specific and varies depending on the circumstances of each case, including the exigent circumstances presented by criminal activity and safety concerns." *Bahl v. Cty. Of Ramsey*, 695 F.3d 778, 784-85 (8th Cir. 2012) (citing *Bircoll v. Miami-Dade County*, 480 F.3d 1072, 1086 (11th Cir. 2007)).

Because Mr. Tabler has plausibly alleged Defendant's violation of his rights under Title II of the ADA, this Court must consider whether Defendant's conduct violates the Fourteenth Amendment. *See United States v. Georgia*, 546 U.S. 151, 159 (2006). If Defendant's misconduct also violates the Fourteenth Amendment, then Defendant is not entitled to sovereign immunity because Title II has validly abrogated such immunity under the facts of this case. *Id.* As explained above, Defendant's conduct has violated and continues to violate multiple protections afforded to Mr. Tabler by the Fourteenth Amendment. Moreover, "Congress' power 'to enforce' the [Fourteenth] Amendment includes the authority both to remedy and to deter violation of rights guaranteed thereunder by prohibiting a somewhat broader swath of conduct, including that which is not itself forbidden by the Amendment's text." *Arce v. Louisiana*, 306 F. Supp. 3d 897, 909 n.36 (E.D. La. 2017) (quoting *Bd. of Trustees of the Univ. of Ala. v. Garrett*, 531 U.S. 356, 365, 121 S. Ct. 955, 148 L. Ed. 2d 866 (2001)). "In other words, Congress may enact so-called prophylactic legislation that proscribes facially constitutional conduct, in order to prevent and deter unconstitutional conduct." *Nevada Dep't of Human Res. v. Hibbs*, 538 U.S. 721, 727-28, 123 S. Ct. 1972, 155 L. Ed. 2d 953 (2003). Plaintiff has plausibly alleged that Defendant's conduct violates both the ADA and the Fourteenth Amendment; therefore, Defendant is not entitled to sovereign immunity, and Plaintiff's ADA claim should not be dismissed.

In the alternative, if this Court were to conclude that Plaintiff has not plausibly alleged a violation of his rights under the ADA, he should be allowed a chance to amend his complaint to remedy any deficiencies. In a similar disability discrimination case, a district court in this circuit explained the necessity of amendment and allowed plaintiff to amend to cure deficiencies in her pleading. *See Wade*, 2017 U.S. Dist. LEXIS 216522, at *24-26. In *Wade*, the court explained:

> The court should freely give leave [to amend the pleadings] when justice so requires. FED. R. CIV. P. 15(a)(2). A decision on whether to permit amendment "is entrusted to the sound discretion of the district court." *Wimm v. Jack Eckerd Corp.*, 3 F.3d 137, 139 (5th Cir. 1993). Nevertheless, the Fifth Circuit has commented that the term "discretion" "may be misleading because FED. R. CIV. P. 15(a) evinces a bias in favor of granting leave to amend." *Mayeaux v. Louisiana Health Serv. & Indemn. Co.*, 376 F.3d 420, 425 (5th Cir. 2004)(citation omitted). "[A]bsent a 'substantial reason' such as undue delay, bad faith, dilatory motive, repeated failures to cure deficiencies, or undue prejudice to the opposing party, 'the discretion of the district court is not broad enough to permit denial.'" *Id.* (citation omitted).
>
> If a plaintiff's complaint fails to state a claim, the court should generally give her at least one chance to amend it under Rule 15(a), before dismissing the action with prejudice. *Great Plains Trust Co v. Morgan Stanley Dean Witter & Co.*, 313 F.3d 305, 329 (5th Cir. 2002)("District courts often afford plaintiffs at least one opportunity to cure pleading deficiencies before dismissing a case, unless it is

clear that the defects are incurable or the plaintiffs advise the court that they are unwilling or unable to amend in a manner that will avoid dismissal."); *United States ex rel. Adrian v. Regents of the Univ. of Cal.*, 363 F.3d 398, 403 (5th Cir. 2004)("Leave to amend should be freely given, and outright refusal to grant leave to amend without a justification . . . is considered an abuse of discretion.").

Wade, 2017 U.S. Dist. LEXIS 216522, at *24-26; *see also Hale*, 642 F.3d at 503 (remanding to allow plaintiff "opportunity to amend his Title II claim after being alerted to its deficiencies.").

For the reasons stated above, Plaintiff's ADA disability discrimination claim should be allowed to proceed, or he should be allowed to amend after being alerted to any deficiencies.

E. Plaintiff's claims are not barred by any statute of limitations.

Finally, Mr. Tabler's claims are not barred by any statute of limitations. Defendant asserts that Mr. Tabler's claims are barred by that statute of limitations for § 1983 claims. *See Def's Mot.* at 26-28. "This argument mischaracterizes the nature of harm that Plaintiff allegedly suffered. Plaintiff has pled a continuing injury. In a continuing injury case, the wrongful conduct continues to create an additional injury to the Plaintiff until the conduct stops." *Foddrill v. McManus*, Civil Action No. SA-13-CV-00051-XR, 2013 U.S. Dist. LEXIS 125837, at *7-9 (W.D. Tex. Sep. 4, 2013). As the Fifth Circuit has made clear, "[w]hen a tort involves continuing injury, the cause of action accrues, and the limitation period begins to run, at the time the tortious conduct ceases." *Donaldson v. O'Connor*, 493 F.2d 507, 529 (5th Cir. 1974). "In Texas, a continuing tort occurs where 'the wrongful conduct continues to effect additional injury to the plaintiff until that conduct stops.'" *Whitaker v. Collier*, 862 F.3d 490, 496 (5th Cir. 2017).

Mr. Tabler is not challenging his initial placement in the Death Watch section. He is also not challenging any other discrete-in-time decision by Defendant, especially considering he has not been provided process due to him to challenge his indefinite housing. Instead, he is challenging his continued housing in the Death Watch section, without due process and without reasonable accommodation to his known and obvious mental disabilities. As the various above discussions should make clear, he has plausibly alleged that every day he is kept in the Death Watch section is a new, compounding injury. His suit is similar to other challenges to indefinite solitary confinement that have involved long periods of time between the beginning of such restrictive confinement and the filing of suit. *See, e.g., Wilkerson*, 774 F.3d at 855-56 (addressing decades-long solitary confinement and collecting cases of similar years-long, indefinite confinements). The injuries that Mr. Tabler has suffered and continues to suffer can only be remedied by Defendant Davis ordering that he be moved out of Death Watch and back to death row. Therefore, Mr. Tabler's claims seeking only that prospective relief are not barred by the statute of limitations.

V. Conclusion

For the reasons stated above, Plaintiff respectfully requests that the court deny Defendant's motion to dismiss and allow his claims to proceed to discovery.

Respectfully submitted this 24th day of June 2020.

Killmer, Lane & Newman, LLP

/s/ David A. Lane
David A. Lane
Reid Allison
Killmer, Lane & Newman, LLP
1543 Champa Street, Suite 400
Denver, Colorado 80202
(303) 571-1000, Fax: (303) 571-1001
dlane@kln-law.com
rallison@kln-law.com

Richard Burr
Burr and Welch, PC
PO Box 525
Leggett, Texas 77350
(713) 628-3391
(713) 893-2500 fax
dick.burrandwelch@gmail.com

Attorneys for Plaintiff

CERTIFICATE OF SERVICE

I certify that on this 24th day of June 2020, I filed the foregoing via CM/ECF which will generate a notice and service to all counsel of record.

/s/ David A. Lane
David A. Lane
KILLMER LANE & NEWMAN, LLP

IN THE UNITED STATES DISTRICT COURT

FOR THE EASTERN DISTRICT OF TEXAS

LUFKIN DIVISION

RICHARD TABLER	§	
VS.	§	CIVIL ACTION NO. 9:20cv49
LORIE DAVIS	§	

ORDER

The defendant previously filed a motion to dismiss (doc. no. 9). The defendant has now filed a motion (doc. no. 12) seeking an extension of time to file a reply to the response.

After due consideration, it is

ORDERED that the motion is **GRANTED**. The defendant is granted an extension of time, December 30, 2020, to file a reply. Pending the filing of a reply, the motion to dismiss is **DENIED** for statistical purposes only.

Plaintiff previously filed a motion (doc. no. 10) seeking an extension of time to file a response. As a response was subsequently filed, this motion is **DENIED** as moot.

SIGNED this the 12th day of January, 2021.

KEITH F. GIBLIN
UNITED STATES MAGISTRATE JUDGE

IN THE UNITED STATES DISTRICT COURT
FOR THE EASTERN DISTRICT OF TEXAS
LUFKIN DIVISION

RICHARD TABLER, *Plaintiff*,	§ § §	
v.	§ § §	CIVIL ACTION NO. 9:20-cv-00049
LORIE DAVIS, *Defendants*.	§ § §	

DEFENDANT LORIE DAVIS'S RESPONSE
TO THE COURT'S ORDER OF JAN. 12, 2021

Defendant Lorie Davis, Director of the Texas Department of Criminal Justice—Correctional Institutions Division (TDCJ-CID), as sued in her official capacity, files this response to the Court's Order of January 12, 2021. ECF No. 13.

In his Original Complaint, Plaintiff Richard Tabler sues Lorie Davis, Director of TDCJ-CID, in her official capacity for cruel and unusual punishment in violation of the Eighth Amendment, denial of due process, under 42 U.S.C. § 1983, and for violation of his rights under the Americans with Disabilities Act ("ADA").[1] ECF No. 1. Tabler seeks injunctive relief in the form of a housing reassignment from "Death Watch" to death row. *Id.* at 14.

On May 27, 2020, Defendant Davis filed a motion to dismiss pursuant to Fed. R. Civ. P. 12(b)(1) and 12(b)(6). ECF No. 9. After a short extension, Plaintiff Tabler filed a response on June 24, 2020. ECF No. 11. Defendant Davis then filed a motion for extension of time to reply to Plaintiff Tabler's response, making the reply due July 15, 2020. ECF No. 12. On January 12, 2021, the Court

---

[1] Lorie Davis has retired from TDCJ. Bobby Lumpkin is the new Director of TDCJ's Institutional Division. A motion to substitute will be filed shortly.

granted Defendant's extension, ordering the reply due by December 30, 2020. ECF No. 13. Upon further consideration, Defendant informs this Court she will not be filing a reply brief.

Respectfully submitted,

KEN PAXTON
Attorney General of Texas

BRENT WEBSTER
First Assistant Attorney General

GRANT DORFMAN
Deputy First Assistant Attorney General

SHAWN E. COWLES
Deputy Attorney General for Civil Litigation

SHANNA E. MOLINARE
Division Chief, Law Enforcement Defense Division

/s/ Briana M. Webb
BRIANA M. WEBB
Assistant Attorney General
Texas State Bar No. 24077883
Briana.Webb@oag.texas.gov

Law Enforcement Defense Division
Office of the Attorney General
P. O. Box 12548, Capitol Station
Austin, Texas 78711
Office (512) 463-2080 / Fax (512) 370-9814

Attorneys for Defendant Davis

Certificate of Service

I, Briana M. Webb, Assistant Attorney General of Texas, do hereby certify that a true and correct copy of the above and foregoing has been served via ECF/PACER to all counsel of record on January 14, 2021.

/s/ Briana M. Webb
BRIANA M. WEBB
Assistant Attorney General

IN THE UNITED STATES DISTRICT COURT
FOR THE EASTERN DISTRICT OF TEXAS
LUFKIN DIVISION

RICHARD TABLER, *Plaintiff,*	§ § §	
v.	§ §	CIVIL ACTION NO. 9:20-cv-00049
LORIE DAVIS, *Defendants.*	§ § §	

DEFENDANT LORIE DAVIS'S MOTION TO SUBSTITUTE

Defendant Lorie Davis, in her official capacity as the Director of the Correctional Institutions Division of the Texas Department of Criminal Justice, submits this motion to substitute the parties pursuant to FED. R. CIV. P 25(d)(1).

Lorie Davis was named as a Defendant in above-styled and numbered cause in her official capacity only. Lorie Davis has now retired from State service. Effective, August 10, 2020, Bobby Lumpkin became the new Director of the Correctional Institutions Division of the Texas Department of Criminal Justice.

Bobby Lumpkin, accordingly, must be substituted for Lorie Davis, in his official capacity only.

Defendant Lorie Davis respectfully requests that this Court recognize the substitution of party adding Bobby Lumpkin as Defendant and removing Lorie Davis.

Respectfully submitted,

KEN PAXTON
Attorney General of Texas

BRENT WEBSTER
First Assistant Attorney General

GRANT DORFMAN
Deputy First Assistant Attorney General

SHAWN E. COWLES
Deputy Attorney General for Civil Litigation

SHANNA E. MOLINARE
Division Chief, Law Enforcement Defense Division

/s/ Briana M. Webb
BRIANA M. WEBB
Assistant Attorney General
Texas State Bar No. 24077883
Briana.Webb@oag.texas.gov

Law Enforcement Defense Division
Office of the Attorney General
P. O. Box 12548, Capitol Station
Austin, Texas 78711
Office (512) 463-2080 / Fax (512) 370-9814

Attorneys for Defendant Lumpkin

Certificate of Service

I, Briana M. Webb, Assistant Attorney General of Texas, do hereby certify that a true and correct copy of the above and foregoing has been served via ECF/PACER to all counsel of record on January 21, 2021.

/s/ Briana M. Webb
BRIANA M. WEBB
Assistant Attorney General

www.ingramcontent.com/pod-product-compliance
Lightning Source LLC
Chambersburg PA
CBHW071958070526
44583CB00015B/1244